Creative Destruction?

Creative Destruction?

Economic Crises and Democracy in Latin America

FRANCISCO E. GONZÁLEZ

The Johns Hopkins University Press
Baltimore

© 2012 The Johns Hopkins University Press
All rights reserved. Published 2012
Printed in the United States of America on acid-free paper
2 4 6 8 9 7 5 3 1

The Johns Hopkins University Press
2715 North Charles Street
Baltimore, Maryland 21218-4363
www.press.jhu.edu

Library of Congress Cataloging-in-Publication Data
González González, Francisco Enrique, 1970–
Creative destruction? : economic crises and democracy in Latin
America / Francisco E. Gonzalez.
p. cm.
Includes bibliographical references and index.
ISBN-13: 978-1-4214-0542-1 (pbk. : alk. paper)
ISBN-13: 978-1-4214-0603-9 (electronic)
ISBN-10: 1-4214-0542-3 (pbk. : alk. paper)
ISBN-10: 1-4214-0603-9 (electronic)
1. Financial crises—Latin America—History.   2. Democracy—Latin
America.   3. Latin America—Economic conditions.
4. Latin America—Politics and government.   I. Title.
HB3755.5.G66 2012
330.98—dc23   2011042886

A catalog record for this book is available from the British Library.

Special discounts are available for bulk purchases of this book. For more
information, please contact Special Sales at 410-516-6936 or specialsales@
press.jhu.edu.

The Johns Hopkins University Press uses environmentally friendly book
materials, including recycled text paper that is composed of at least
30 percent post-consumer waste, whenever possible.

To the merry-go-round of the generations and the harsh economic crises:
my grandparents, Matilde and Francisco, María Elena and Rafael,
endured the Great Depression as young women and men;
my parents, Laura and Francisco, worked for vulnerable
groups during the 1982 debacle and lost decade;
my wife, Amy, and I worked as a team during
the Great Recession;
our sons, Francisco and Tomás,
never give up.

Contents

Acknowledgments

I have incurred many debts and am grateful to many individuals and institutions for their support in helping me bring this work to completion. Heartfelt thanks for a good everyday working spirit to Riordan Roett and my other colleagues in the Latin American Studies Program (LASP)—Guadalupe Paz, Anne McKenzie, and Jennifer Zurek—at the Johns Hopkins University School of Advanced International Studies (SAIS) in Washington, DC. Likewise, I thank SAIS for the summer funds that allowed me to go back to the University of Oxford in 2008 and 2009 to explore and develop the material on the Great Depression, and for the sabbatical semester that allowed me to finish writing and correcting earlier versions of the manuscript. I owe special thanks to my students and research assistants: Todd Martinez, for his motivation and commitment to the end of the project; Antonio Martinez, for his motivation and availability; and Alfredo Zarate, for his participation in part of this process.

I am grateful to Laurence Whitehead for inviting me back to Nuffield College, Oxford, in 2008 and 2009, and for early conversations regarding the nature of shocks and their political implications. Thanks to Gail Martin and the rest of the staff at the Nuffield Library. I am also grateful to the Latin American Center (LAC) and St. Antony's College, Oxford, for allowing me to read and borrow material. Thanks to Elvira Ryan and the rest of the LAC staff, in particular to Alan Knight for the conversations over lunch that helped inform my early thinking. I am grateful to the Roger Thayer Stone Center for Latin American Studies at Tulane University for a kind invitation during the fall 2008 semester to present some of the work's early material. In particular, I thank Ludovico Feoli for his reminder to reread Mark Blyth's work, which is incorporated into my analysis. Thanks are also due to chairs Jonathan Hartlyn of the University of North Carolina at Chapel Hill and Cynthia McClintock of George Washington University, as well as the rest of the participants in a panel during the American Political Science Association meeting in Washington, DC, in

2010. This exercise produced excellent feedback. I got similarly good feedback from my colleagues at SAIS during a fall 2010 faculty research lunch seminar. I am particularly indebted to Mitchell Orenstein, who kindly read several versions of the manuscript and took me to task repeatedly regarding the sinews of the comparative analysis, the argument, and its implications. My friend Floris van Hövell kindly gave me access to many scholarly and journalistic papers surrounding Argentina's 2001–2 meltdown. Other Southern Cone experts, such as Juan Cristóbal Bonnefoy, Kevin Casas Zamora, and Peter De Shazo, read the entire manuscript, and Bill Booth and Mariano Turzi read the first part. They all made excellent suggestions and corrections that enhanced the quality of the text. Remaining mistakes are my sole responsibility. I want to express a special thank-you to the late Henry Tom, who took this project on board at the Johns Hopkins University Press, and to Suzanne Flinchbaugh for taking the project in the middle of the process, supporting it, and helping to steer it toward completion. A thank-you also to Kathleen Capels for her superb copyediting.

I cannot thank my family enough for their unconditional support and solidarity in helping me carry out this project. Jackie and Theo Birks, and Andy, Karen, and Katie Berrington looked after all of us, and particularly our then toddler Francisco, so my wife and I could do research and write while in Oxford in 2008 and 2009. My mother, Laura Ileana, spent several long visits looking after our household in Bethesda and caring for both Francisco and Tomás so that we could focus on work and I could get on with the manuscript. Without her loving care and support, this manuscript would not have been written on time. My father, Francisco, and his dreams of a capitalism animated by social justice kept me motivated. The love and support of my wife, Amy, keep me going, and our conversations about causality, risk, and the logic of comparative inquiry keep me on my toes.

Creative Destruction?

Institutions, Interests, and Ideas in Explaining Regime Change

The "creative destruction"[1] brought about by financial shocks and economic crises, although a means through which capitalism reinvigorates itself periodically, is both unsettling and challenging politically.[2] This is true regardless of the type of political regime in place when a country finds itself in the throes of an economic meltdown. Think of fragile parliamentary democracy and its demise in Italy, Portugal, Germany, and Spain in the interwar years of the twentieth century; authoritarianism in military-ruled countries, such as those in South America after the 1982 economic bust or in Suharto's Indonesia after the Asian financial collapse of 1997; and totalitarianism in Central and Eastern European countries and in the Soviet Union in the run up to its demise in 1989–91. In short, economic crises contributed to the fall of all types of political regimes around the world throughout the twentieth century.[3]

Concern and interest in "politics in hard times" returned with a vengeance after the 2008–9 global financial meltdowns and their aftermath,[4] the Great Recession, which took its name from having the Great Depression of the 1930s as its main point of reference in scholarly, policy, business, and media circles. This volume is part of that revival of interest in the political consequences of major international economic crises. I start with an in-depth comparative historical analysis of the political consequences of the Great Depression, and then use this as the baseline for further comparative historical analyses of the political consequences of major subsequent international financial shocks and crises: the post-1982 debt crisis, the emerging markets crises of the late 1990s and early 2000s, and the main political and economic events since the 2008–9 global busts.

Latin America is the area of the world that informs my inductive reasoning and therefore provides the evidence for my generalizations. Choosing this as the region in which to study the impacts of economic crises on political regimes makes sense for several reasons. First, Latin America suffered the greatest number of political regime transitions (from democratic to non-democratic and vice versa) in the second half of the twentieth century.[5] Second, it is a region known for the recurrence of international financial shocks and economic crises ever since its incorporation into the nascent modern capitalist system in the sixteenth century.[6] Third, within the developing world, Latin America is where governments throughout the twentieth century have experimented the most with different types of economic theories and economic policymaking—from inward-looking corporatism and varieties of populisms in the 1920s and 1930s to the aggressive promotion of import-substitution industrialization between the 1940s and the 1970s; and from the radical embrace of market liberalization, or neoliberalism, in the 1980s and 1990s to the backlash against what is known as the Washington consensus and the return of state-led development in some countries in this region in the 2000s.[7] These three reasons show why Latin America is fertile ground to study the political impacts that the greatest economic shocks and crises since the Great Depression had on their regimes.

For reasons spelled out in chapter 1 (early democratization and early socio-economic modernization, given the Latin American regional context), in parts I and II of the book I focus on the Southern Cone countries of Argentina, Chile, and Uruguay. In the final chapter, the general conclusion, I then extend my range of inquiry across the region and cross-regionally as I draw out the general implications and limitations of my explanatory framework. First, I posit that democracy's chances of survival during harsh economic crises have increased substantially, particularly since the end of the Cold War. I subsequently contrast this general proposition with the contemporary politics of other major Latin American nations—Brazil, Mexico, and the countries of the Andean region (Bolivia, Colombia, Ecuador, Peru and Venezuela)—and two other emerging market regions of the world, East Asia and Central and Eastern Europe.

In addition to historical and analytical justifications, this book also highlights a normative concern. Given their traditionally polarized, conflict-prone, and at times brutally violent politics, it remains a surprising and desirable state of affairs that most Latin American countries have been and remain under electoral democratic regimes since the start of the third wave of democratization, which took off in the region in the late 1970s. Authoritarian regressions have almost dried up since then (although there is no historical law banning military regime coups, as the case of Honduras in the summer of 2009 reminded us), and the end result has been that never before have so many countries in Latin America been under electoral democratic rule for so many uninterrupted years. It would be reprehensible and dangerous if this general takeoff of democracy in Latin America were to be punctured by authoritarian solutions that, if established successfully in one or two nations, could then be used as examples for anti-democratic forces in neighboring countries to install authoritarian rule, too.

Although quite unlikely, it is not inconceivable that such a scenario could materialize, because it has happened twice since the Great Depression. Adam Przeworski and colleagues have identified Latin America as the only region in the world where it is appropriate to speak of three waves of democratization (including their two respective counterwaves of dictatorships) in the twentieth century, because it is the only region where the change in the distribution of democracies and dictatorships over time resembles the strong ebbs and flows of waves.[8] In addition, leading scholars of Latin American politics have emphasized the paradox of the persistence of electoral democracy since the late 1970s in an area with comparatively high levels of socioeconomic inequality, social exclusion, ethnic discrimination, violence, organized crime, and criminality on top of recurrent economic shocks and crises.[9] Given such inauspicious underlying conditions, it is not surprising to have seen renewed interest and concern about democracy's capacity to withstand politics in hard times.

REASON FOR OPTIMISM: STRUCTURAL CHANGES AND DEMOCRATIC REGIME SURVIVAL

The simplest explanation for why political regimes throughout Latin America at the end of the 2000s have not faced the type of escalating and spreading social and political turmoil triggered by the harsh financial shocks and economic crises that toppled their forebears in the early 1930s is, as analysts have succinctly put it, "Crisis, what crisis?" In sharp contrast to the Great Depression, the Great Recession only created a blip in the growth trajectories of many emerging markets, including several Latin American ones that are expected, in the medium term, to continue growing above the average of the advanced economies of Organisation for Economic Co-operation and Development (OECD) nations.

This study argues instead that longer-term structural changes during the second half of the twentieth century contributed to a growing (though by no means general or systemic) bias in favor of either democratic regime transitions or the survival of democratic regimes during harsh financial shocks and economic crises. Thus it is not only the absence of painful economic crises in most Latin American countries in the late 2000s that explains the apparent resilience and continued viability of electoral democracy in the region, but also the structural changes that, since the 1980s, have allowed democratic regimes to have a greater likelihood of survival in the midst of such grim crises.

ANALYTICAL PERSPECTIVE AND ARGUMENT

To identify and trace these structural changes, I follow Robert A. Dahl's now classic analytical perspective, which contemporary political economists like Daron Acemoglu and James Robinson have also used. They consider the outcome of struggles over the establishment and survival/demise of political regimes (non-democratic or democratic governments) to be a function of the changing relative costs for contending political and economic forces.[10] I follow this general point of view and argue that in both international and domestic politics, the chances for the survival or installation of democratic regimes during harsh economic crises has increased in Latin America since the 1980s, because the relative costs of organizing to exercise pressures against democracy have risen, compared with the costs of organizing to defend or promote democracy, which have fallen. Specifically, I propose that this change in the relative costs for supporting or attacking democracy has been due to structural transformations that took place in what I refer to as basic international and domestic institutions, interests, and ideas since the Great Depression years.

RESEARCH METHODS:
COMPARATIVE HISTORICAL ANALYSES

In academic parlance, the independent variable for this study is economic crises, and the dependent variable is political regime change (from non-democratic to democratic political regimes and vice versa). The time period starts with the Great Depression and includes the subsequent major international financial booms and busts, as well as the economic crises that they led to, namely, (1) the late 1920s–early 1930s, (2) the late 1970s–early 1980s, (3) the late 1990s–early 2000s, and (4) the early 2000s–late 2000s. The independent and dependent variables are connected by the changing international and domestic conditions that financial shocks and economic crises generated in the societies under consideration. Scholars can choose from a variety of research methods to try to make sense of such fluctuating conditions and their impact on political regimes. Some, like Przeworski and colleagues, have used statistical analyses to assess the effect on democracy of as many social, economic, political, and cultural variables as possible, in as many countries as possible.[11] Others, like Acemoglu and Robinson, have used game theoretic models to assess general, formal conditions under which democracy is more likely to be either installed and developed or unseated and replaced by non-democratic regime alternatives.[12] Much has been learned from these works, and their breadth and scope remains unparalleled.

The aim of this book is narrower, namely, to elucidate the chances for democracy during harsh economic crises by observing a small number of cases across time in greater detail than these other authors devote to any of their examples. Situated between the deductive logic of the game theorists and the inductive logic of the statisticians, the approach I employ is widely used in mainstream Anglo-American political science and is known as comparative historical analysis.[13] This research method sacrifices the level of generalization that explanations based on game theory or statistical analysis can aspire to, but it gains in its capacity to specify and then follow complex events in detail through process tracing, a tool of qualitative analysis whose aim is to "identify the intervening causal process—the causal chain and causal mechanism—between an independent variable or variables and the outcome of the dependent variable."[14]

Process tracing focuses on actors and their decisions. It compares different sequences of events that share a trigger and then traces how these events unfold toward an outcome. The common trigger in this work is the set of international financial shocks that led to harsh economic crises, and the outcome is political regime change—or the lack thereof. Tracing different sequences of events through the same set of criteria (see below for the criteria I use, which are based on an analysis of institutions, interests, and ideas) and finding basic similarities and differences in how processes unfolded and what outcomes they produced can, in turn, help to generalize and underscore likely sources of causality for past events. Such midrange generalizations and their limits, established by the real past events of the small number of case studies analyzed in depth—rather than by mathematical deduction (as in game theory) or snapshots of correlated numbers (as in statistical analysis)—are the aim and the principal contribution of this volume. I make sense of these past events through the wealth of secondary sources that scholars have produced in the fields of comparative politics, international relations, and political and economic history in Latin America, the United States, and Great Britain.

If process tracing observes individual actors and their decisions, what reasonable assumptions can be made about their expectations and how they try to anticipate events to further their interests? Following Dietrich Rueschemeyer, Evelyne Huber Stephens, and John D. Stephens, I adopt "a political economy perspective that focuses on actors—individual as well as collective actors—whose power is grounded in control of economic and organizational resources and/or of coercive force and who vie with each other for scarce resources in the pursuit of conflicting goals."[15] Such systematic observations of actors and their decisions can be done by focusing on one or several slices of a given social process. I carry out process tracing based on the three pillars of mainstream Anglo-American comparative politics: institutions, interests, and ideas.[16] In my analytical framework, institutions have two components. I follow Douglass North in defining institutions-as-rules as the basic laws that underpin a political regime and, therefore, as the rules of the game that the incumbents and the opposition might fight over during major financial shocks and economic crises. Institutions-as-organizations are the vehicles for collective action that individuals join in pursuit of common aims.[17] Interests and ideas, in turn, are the main shapers of individuals' decisions to join (or refrain from joining) and then act through groups whose common goal is either to defend and preserve a standing political regime, or to attack and try to replace it with another one, in the context of a deep economic crisis. In short, interests and ideas establish the motivational bases for individuals to join institutions-as-organizations that confront one another over the conservation or replacement of a collection of institutions-as-rules that make up a given political regime during harsh economic crises.

Table I.1 presents a summary of my analysis, which highlights the key structural changes identified by my exercise in process tracing—changes that have led to a greater likelihood of democratic regime survival or (re)instatement during harsh economic shocks/crises since the 1980s (as compared with the 1930s) in Latin America generally, and in the three Southern Cone countries specifically.

The first type of mechanism I examine is institutions. In the international sphere, the establishment and growth of the United Nations (UN) and Bretton Woods (International Monetary Fund [IMF] and World Bank [WB] institutions) systems—created in 1945–46—have tended to move in the direction of rewarding and promoting electoral democracy while, at the same time, sanc-

TABLE I.1
*Structural changes between the Great Depression (1930s)
and the Great Recession (2008–9)*

Type of mechanism/ Spheres	Main changes	When?
Institutions		
International	UN / Bretton Woods systems	Particularly since the end of the Cold War
Domestic	Fall of military-as-government option	In the course of the 1980s
Interests		
International	Illiquid to liquid wealth; growing trade	Since the mid-1960s; post-1945
Domestic	Slower move from illiquid to liquid wealth; trade opening	Since the mid-1970s; 1980s–1990s
Ideas		
International	Political: tripolar to bipolar to unipolar	1930s–1945; Cold War; since 1990
	Economic: from pro-cyclical to Keynesian + a continued conflict between advocates of a state-led versus a market-led economy	Since the early 1930s
Domestic	Political: tripolar to bipolar to unipolar + a variable incidence of populism	1930s–1945; Cold War; since the 1980s
	Economic: from pro-cyclical to Keynesian back-and-forth synergies with populist leaders	Since the early 1930s

tioning and punishing anti-democratic forces around the world, particularly since the end of the Cold War (1989–91). Such a move has not been systematic, and its implementation has been patchy, yielding great variations in its effectiveness and usually quite limited success on the ground. Still, the point here is the existence and application of such an internationally sanctioned process, one that did not exist during the Great Depression years.

Moreover, the internationalization of rules and organizations—a process that the world has experienced since the end of the Second World War—has not been mechanical and unidirectional. Evidence from my comparative historical analysis shows that actions by different international organizations are pulled in different directions, weakening the net potential result they could produce regarding the survival or breakdown of given political regimes. For example, while UN bodies such as the General Assembly protested, condemned, and called for sanctions against the military repression unleashed in Chile by the regime led by General Augusto Pinochet during the 1970s and 1980s, the Chilean Finance Minister was able to negotiate credit lines and

guarantees with the IMF after the 1981–83 implosion of the country's economy, which gave the regime the time and the wherewithal to strengthen its response to the crisis. The resultant incongruence was that, while the Chilean
authoritarian regime was condemned and sanctioned in some forums (the UN
system and the myriad nongovernmental organizations that advocate for
human rights), at the same time it received credit lines and guarantees (from
the IMF and other multilateral international financial institutions) that allowed it to surmount the country's short-term financial/economic crisis.

Looking at institutions in the domestic sphere, however, the military in all
three of the Southern Cone countries lost its capacity to be a decisive factor in
controlling the fate of political regimes during the course of the 1980s. This was
a major structural change, because up until then the military had been a deter-
minative force in the breakdown of democratic regimes, not only in my subset
of countries, but more generally in most countries in Latin America. Again, this
change was not mechanical or unidirectional, and the role of the armed forces
in each of the countries considered in depth has had important variations, but
the main point here is the military's greatly diminished capacity to impose itself through political regime change since the 1980s. This is an observation
that applies particularly strongly to the Southern Cone countries (excluding
Paraguay), where urban-based modern societies with relatively high per capita
income have swung decidedly in favor of civilian supremacy over the military,
given their abhorrent experience with 1970s–1980s military rule. In the conclusion, I flesh out the extent to which this also applies in other Latin American
countries and beyond.

The second type of mechanism I study is individuals' material interests. Following political economists like Carles Boix or Acemoglu and Robinson, I argue
that the main structural changes in the sphere of interests involve wealth and
trade. There has been a change in wealth, going from a predominance of land-
based, illiquid assets in the 1930s to financial-based, liquid, and therefore highly
movable ones since the 1980s. This structural alteration has meant that given a
relatively easy exit option, foreign and domestic capitalists have felt less threatened by potential expropriation or higher taxation since the 1980s and, therefore, have been less likely to promote or support non-democratic regime alternatives, as was clearly the case during the Great Depression years.

As for trade, there is great difference between the wholesale move toward
protectionism and inward-looking development that happened during the
Great Depression years, and the global move toward trade liberalization that
gathered momentum during the closing round of the multilateral General

Agreement on Tariffs and Trade (GATT) in the 1980s, which culminated in the establishment of the World Trade Organization (WTO) in 1994. This change has meant that major financial shocks and economic crises since the 1980s have happened with an opening and growing world trade system in the background and, therefore, with more international sources for economic recovery than in the 1930s. Of course, the opening up and expansion of international trade cannot be assumed to continue indefinitely, and an increasing number of voices since the 2008–9 global busts have joined the chorus warning about the perils of beggar-thy-neighbor policies through currency wars or full-blown trade wars. These warnings have to be taken seriously, although the international economy has continued to blossom. This is particularly the case if we contrast the 1980s–2000s with the trade-destroying, market-shrinking protectionism of the 1930s.

The third type of mechanism included in my analysis is ideas—both political ideologies and economic ideas. In the realm of political ideologies, there has been a transformation in international ideological conflicts (and their domestic impersonations), shifting from a trilateral conflict between the end of the First World War and the end of the Second World War (the uncompromising conflict that pitted liberal democracy, communism, and fascism against each other); to the bipolar conflict between the United States and the Soviet Union during the Cold War years (the late 1940s–1989–91); and, since then, to the unipolar moment of US global hegemony, which has been accompanied by the growing economic and geopolitical clout of major developing countries, such as China, India, and Brazil. The likelihood of democratic survival during a sharp economic crisis was lowest in the interwar years of irreconcilable three-way ideological conflict.

In addition to the competition and antagonism among the main international political ideologies since the 1920s, populism—in its recurrent ignition or its absence—is central to crisis contexts. Though it is not a specific political ideology or a defined set of economic ideas and economic policy, I treat populism in the ideas section, following those scholars who have noted the formative role the development of mass communications since the 1920s has played in forging the personal relationship that has allowed would-be populist leaders to connect successfully time and again with the masses, not only in Latin America, but also in Europe and the United States.[18] The recurrence of populism (from precursors in the 1910s to classic populists in the 1930s, and from post–Second World War populist experiments in the 1940s–1970s to the neoliberal populists of the 1990s and the return of both left- and right-wing populism in the 2000s) and its defiance of established institutions, interests, and ideologies makes it a relevant factor in my analysis.[19]

In the realm of economic ideas and economic policymaking, I examine the structural change represented by the international and domestic institutionalization of countercyclical economic policy. Although the world's leading economies implemented a disastrous procyclical response to deflation after the 1929 US market bust, it was not until after the 1931 global banking crisis that governments were forced to adopt countercyclical fiscal and monetary policies, following John Maynard Keynes's prescriptions. Another point is that inasmuch as the incumbents have been able to benefit from countercyclical injections of credit and guarantees through the IMF without it mattering who was in power (as long as a country was a member and paid its contributions), both democratic and non-democratic regimes have reaped advantages from internationally provided countercyclical macroeconomic policy since the creation of the Bretton Woods institutions.

INEXORABLE MARCH OF PROGRESS?

In addition to identifying a greater likelihood of democratic regime survival in Latin America since the 1980s, the comparative historical evidence presented in this work helps to qualify the thrust of this general argument. Even though the structural changes emphasized in table I.1 can be regarded as evidence of general progress, or at least of a Western version of progress (what British historians call the Whig interpretation of history—"the past as an inevitable progression towards ever greater liberty and enlightenment, culminating in modern forms of liberal democracy"[20]), there are substantial empirical variations that weigh against a linear, mechanical reading. Two types militate against the idea of an inexorable march of progress. The first involves expected change over time. Although one might assume that, in general, democracy should have collapsed or failed to be instated in the 1930s, while it should survive or be reinstated since the 1980s, the three Southern Cone countries provide contrasting evidence. The outcomes in Argentina's and Uruguay's political regimes did conform to the general argument—and perhaps encourage a qualified but optimistic view about better chances for democracy in the present or recent past than in the first two-thirds of the twentieth century—but the situation in Chile did not. The Chilean case was an outlier both in the 1930s and in the 1980s. During the early Great Depression years, Chile was the only country in Latin America that shed authoritarian rule and reinstated a democratic regime (in 1932). In contrast, in the debt crisis years of the 1980s, the regime led by General Pino-chet did not give in to popular domestic and international pressures; a forced return to democracy did not occur until 1990, which even then was tightly reg-ulated by constitutional rules and a calendar created by the military and its al-lies. The case of Chile highlights the fact that, in spite of adverse conditions, democracy was not impossible in the early 1930s, but neither was it a foregone conclusion during the 1980s.

Another kind of variation also helps qualify a uniformly optimistic reading of history. This second type refers to the persistence of significant differences in the way governments have dealt with harsh economic shocks and crises in the recent past. The general argument in this book should lead one to expect elec-toral democracies to survive the heavy pressures imposed during episodes of economic collapse since the 1980s (a condition in fact met by our three coun-tries, as well as by most other large countries in Latin America), but some na-tions have done so in a less predictable and more disorderly fashion than others. A comparative analysis of the Southern Cone countries again demon-strates substantial empirical variations in how their governments have coped with these difficulties. Since the return of democracy in 1983, two Argentine presidents have resigned before completing their constitutionally mandated terms in office. The background to both Alfonsín's and de la Rúa's interrupted presidencies in 1989 and 2001, respectively, was the heightened social and politi-cal conflicts in the streets of the country's major cities as a consequence of sig-nificant financial shocks and economic crises. In contrast, despite confronting their own economic shocks and crises since their return to democracy, Chile and Uruguay have been characterized by the stability and endurance of their governments.

In short, despite democratic regime survival across the board, substantial variations persist, even in a small subset of countries like the three Southern Cone ones, in terms of governability and the fate of democratically elected gov-ernments in periods of severe financial shocks and economic crises. Therefore, despite an apparently solid return of democracy as a form of rule, the process of government during politics in hard times has remained more uncertain and conflict ridden in Argentina than in Chile or Uruguay. These caveats and varia-tions support the view that despite the structural changes summarized in table I.1, which have raised the odds for democratic regimes to survive during hard times, it would be erroneous to conclude that we have arrived at a destination like the "End of History," where liberal democracy rules unchallenged.

STRUCTURAL OVERVIEW

Chapter 1 presents the scholarly debate about the political consequences of economic shocks and crises, develops an innovative analytical framework for the comparative historical study of this problem, and highlights the contributions of this book to the debate.

Part I (chapters 2–5) analyzes the Southern Cone countries during the Great Depression and constitutes the baseline for comparing subsequent economic shocks/crises and their political consequences. Chapter 2 presents a synopsis of how the Great Depression happened and how it affected both Latin America generally and the Southern Cone nations specifically. Chapter 3 offers an analysis of their institutions, chapter 4 of their interests, and chapter 5 of their ideas.

Part II (chapters 6–9) studies the political consequences of economic shocks since the Great Depression and, in particular, focuses on the two worst subsequent ones since the end of the Second World War in Latin America: (1) the 1980s debt crisis, and (2) the emerging markets crises that started in Southeast Asia in 1997, spread to Russia and Brazil in 1998, and subsequently led to the implosion of Argentina's economy in 2001–2 and the largest sovereign default in history (95 billion USD). Chapter 6 presents an overview of the two shocks discussed in this part of the book. The next three analytical chapters follow the same structure as in part I, each dealing with one of the pillars of comparative politics: chapter 7 observes institutions, chapter 8 looks at interests, and chapter 9 focuses on ideas.

The first section in each of chapters 7, 8, and 9 observes the early 1980s and the debt crisis in Chile. The outcome of the baseline (the Great Depression) was that the existing political regimes in the three Southern cone countries broke down. Argentina and Uruguay experienced the collapse of democratic governments, while in Chile the authoritarian government foundered. In contrast, Chile's military regime survived the economic earthquake of the early 1980s and did not retreat until 1990—doing so, moreover, on its own terms. This is in marked contrast to the baseline Chilean case, where General Ibáñez's authoritarian regime was brought down by working- and middle-class protests in 1931. Between then and late 1932, Chile experienced great social and political unrest, including a military takeover that created a short-lived Socialist Republic, which was then brought down by a countercoup of conservative and moderate generals. They, in turn, restored power to civilians, and the constitutional process was finally reinstated after Arturo Alessandri won the presidential elections in late 1932. Therefore, the question in the first section of these three chapters is, Why were the transitions to democracy in 1929–32 and 1982–90 in Chile so different?

The second section in chapters 7, 8, and 9 observes the emerging markets crises of the late 1990s and early 2000s and their effects in Argentina and Uruguay. In light of the baseline cases, where democratic regimes broke down in these two countries in 1930 and 1933, respectively, the question in the second section of these chapters is, Why did democracy survive after the 2001–2 economic earthquakes in both countries, given its collapse in the 1930s? (See table 1.1 for the logic behind the selection of the historical cases for comparison in both parts of chapters 7, 8, and 9.)

In the conclusion, I present the scholarly and policy implications of my analysis of the Southern Cone countries. I also apply the comparative historical lessons of parts I and II to examine their significance for Latin America more generally—including not only the Southern Cone countries, but also Brazil, Mexico, and the Andean nations (Bolivia, Colombia, Ecuador, Peru, and Venezuela). Lastly, I make some cross-regional observations, particularly in the emerging market areas of East Asia and Central and Eastern Europe. The aim of this last exercise is to identify limits to the applicability of my analytical framework—to look at how well it does or does not travel across regional contexts—which can lead, in turn, to relevant questions for further research.

Financial Shocks, Economic Crises, and Democracy

Theory and Practice

Financial shocks and economic crises can be studied from different scholarly perspectives and the choice of methodology helps to define the types of questions and the level of detail contained in any analysis. I deploy a comparative historical analysis based on middle-range generalizations, which are anchored in a small *n* comparison.[1] Comparative historical analysis is prevalent in mainstream Anglo-American political science in the subfields of comparative politics, political economy, and comparative democratization.[2] As a practitioner of this methodology observes, the comparative historical research tradition can be useful in studying contemporary politicoeconomic events, because placing them in historical perspective "helps us see what is unique and what is not about the current [events]. . . . The exclusive focus on the contemporary period . . . makes it difficult to isolate the influence of any [factor]. . . . Incorporating earlier periods into the analysis makes it possible to control for some of these factors and expands the number of observations that can be used to identify cross-national and cross-temporal patterns and trajectories."[3]

Analyzing and comparing past instances of economic shocks/crises and the pressures that they generated in favor of *and* against democracy in specific countries, while not allowing one to make specific predictions about the future, nonetheless can help to establish a range of likely outcomes in the light of past experience. The aim of such an analysis is to identify the international and domestic institutional, interests-based, and ideas-based mechanisms whose transformation, in turn, changed the relative costs for pro- and anti-democratic organization and action, and (according to my argument) have helped democratic regimes be more resilient during the harsh economic shocks and crises in Latin America since the 1980s.

WHY THE SOUTHERN CONE COUNTRIES?

Political and economic factors justify the choice of Argentina, Chile, and Uruguay as in-depth case studies to analyze economic crises and democracy in Latin America since the Great Depression.

Politics

On the politics side, scholars who have developed political regime typologies to follow countries' regime change trajectories throughout the twentieth century agree that these three countries were the first in Latin America to establish democracies.[4] All the authors concur that the earliest full democracies were installed in Argentina and in Uruguay, because they were the first two countries to introduce full male suffrage and the secret ballot (in 1912 in Argentina and 1917 in Uruguay).[5] It is important to note that by full electoral democracy these authors mean what the term democracy used to stand for at the turn of the twentieth century, that is, male suffrage rather than universal suffrage (the inclusion of women and all individuals over a minimum age).

Although the same authors disagree about the *extent* of democracy in Chile, they all agree that, along with Argentina and Uruguay, it had the earliest *experience* with electoral democracy in the region. Thus Ruth Berins Collier traces elite-driven democratization in Chile to the years 1874–91, while Boix places the establishment and first practice of democracy in Chile in the years 1909–24.[6] More specifically, Rueschemeyer and colleagues state that Chile had a constitutional oligarchic regime before 1920, a restricted democracy in 1920–24, authoritarian regimes of different ideological stripes in 1924–32, and a second restricted democracy between 1932 and 1970.[7] Peter H. Smith considers Chile to have been under oligarchic rule between 1900 and 1924, under authoritarian rule in 1924–32, and under democracy in 1932–73.[8] Peter De Shazo highlights 1891–1924 as a period of oligarchic rule under the Parliamentary Republic, emphasizing that Arturo Alessandri's first presidency was in keeping with the status quo, because he "talked a good game with the working classes but ended up being very similar (during the early 1920s) as his predecessors."[9]

Scholars disagree fundamentally about when democracy was born in Chile because, even though the secret ballot was introduced there earlier (in 1890) than in Argentina or Uruguay, suffrage eligibility was restricted by literacy requirements until 1970. It is in light of this evidence that authors like Rueschemeyer and colleagues, following earlier scholars (such as Göran Therborn), argue that Chile remained a restricted democracy until 1970.[10] Suffrage restrictions, which provide the rationale for the political category known as restricted democracy (as opposed to full electoral democracy), were based on socioeconomic criteria such as literacy, ethnicity, the ownership of assets or the possession of a certain level of income, or special fiscal contributions (such as poll taxes). Such restrictions were not a practice confined solely to Chile, however; they were also used in Western European countries, in the United States, and in other Latin American countries that have held elections since the nineteenth century.

For the purpose of my comparative analysis, the issue I emphasize is that even if we make restricted rather than full electoral democracy the yardstick for inclusion in this study, Argentina, Uruguay, and Chile are the earliest democracies in scholars' classifications. Argentina did not experience restricted democracy early on, but rather transitioned from a constitutional oligarchic regime before 1912 to a full democracy thereafter, until the 1930 military coup. Uruguay was a restricted democracy between 1903 and 1918, and thereafter a full democracy until the 1933 *autogolpe* by President Gabriel Terra. Chile was governed by constitutional oligarchic rule before 1920, restricted democracy between 1920 and 1924, a succession of democratic/authoritarian regimes from 1924 to 1932, and the subsequent reestablishment of a restricted democracy in 1932–33.[11]

The main point for the present analysis is that these three countries had experience with full or restricted electoral democracy *before* the Great Depression. In contrast, the rest of the Latin America nations first saw restricted or full democratic governance in the aftermath of the Great Depression. The countries scholars think were closest in time to when Argentina, Uruguay, and Chile first established electoral democracy were Peru (1934–48) and Colombia (1936–53), with Brazil (1945–64) a distant third.[12] The rest of the Latin American nations did not democratize (in a restricted or full sense) until after the Second World War. Given the comparative historical perspective of this work, choosing the countries in the region that adopted electoral democracy earliest makes sense; this maximizes the observations that can be used to search for similarities and differences, while still maintaining a small and manageable number of countries as its base. Also, for an analysis of pressures for and against democracy during the Great Depression, it's more logical to study how these unfolded in countries where a real sense of the practice of electoral democracy—and therefore of the potential costs and benefits of pre-serving or destroying it—already existed.

Economics

In the sphere of economics and socioeconomic development, the Southern Cone countries were also regional forerunners in Latin America in the early twentieth century. This is another criterion that justifies studying them together. As Victor Bulmer-Thomas observes, in the 1920s "Argentina, the richest republic [in Latin America], was still in a class of its own in terms of industrial advance, with manufacturing accounting for nearly 20 percent of GDP [gross domestic product]. . . . The second rank of countries included Chile and Uruguay, with a share of manufacturing in GDP between 12 and 16 percent."[13] The rest of the countries in the region lagged behind these three nations in terms of per capita income and industrialization. These measures are important because, as Rueschemeyer and colleagues point out, they are good proxies for "the organization of effective mass pressure [without which] democracy [or democratization pressures] were unlikely to emerge" in early twentieth-century Latin America.[14]

From an economic history perspective, Kevin O'Rourke and Jeffrey Williamson also refer to Argentina, Chile, and Uruguay as Latin exceptions, thanks to a high level of growth that brought them closer to US and Western European economies in the 1870s to 1914 (a distinctive period known to economic historians as the first globalization).[15] Even though all Latin American nations were low-wage economies compared with most of Western Europe and the United States, the "low-wage but resource-abundant Southern Cone was catching up to high-wage and industrial Britain."[16] Rosemary Thorp confirms that sustained high economic growth during the last third of the nineteenth and the first third of the twentieth centuries led to a comparatively early socioeconomic modernization in the Southern Cone countries (given the broader Latin American context). Like Rueschemeyer and colleagues, Thorp goes on to emphasize that this process led to the "growing middle and working classes [being involved in and shaping] political trends."[17]

Considering these three Southern Cone nations to be similar in terms of their relative economic development in the first third of the twentieth century should not lead one to underestimate their differences, such as the significantly lower real wages in Chile compared with Argentina and Uruguay. The cost of living for the Chilean working classes was considerably greater than in the Río de la Plata countries, due to higher inflation and unemployment, one among several reasons why Chile did not experience the substantial rates of European working-class immigration that Argentina and Uruguay did during the first third of the twentieth century. The Chilean economy was also more exposed to international economic booms and busts, given its dependence on mining (particularly nitrates), than the foodstuffs-exporting economies of the Río de la Plata nations. Thus the former's 1907 mining crisis—combined with a harsh financial shock in Wall Street, the outbreak of the First World War, and the postwar economic downturn in 1919–21—led to greater unemployment, a higher cost of living, and more social unrest in Chile than in Argentina or Uruguay.[18] Still, in relative terms the three southernmost Latin American countries registered the highest levels of industrial advance and manufacturing, which is an important historical proxy for the creation and development of democratization pressures from below.

Because the aim of this book is ultimately not only a comparative historical analysis but also a means to use this analysis to shed light on post-2008 events—and given that by the early twenty-first century most countries in Latin America have growing middle and working classes that participate in electoral democracy—closely examining countries where such involvement came earliest in the region, in order to reflect on the contemporary scene, provides more historical evidence against which present and future conditions can be compared. Likewise, looking at different economic shocks and crises in the same group of countries makes sense, because it allows me to control for many context-specific variables, which in turn raises the likelihood that the similarities and differences that my analysis uncovers are not just due to chance. In short, the Southern Cone countries' comparatively early socioeconomic modernization and democratization in Latin America are the criteria used to select the cases for this study of economic shocks/crises and their effect on democracy.

WHICH SHOCKS AND CRISES SHOULD BE COMPARED?

My three-country comparison of Argentina, Chile, and Uruguay during the Great Depression is the equivalent of a cross-sectional analysis, in the sense that the same variables are used to assess the state of politics and the economy in different countries within the same period of time. Comparing the results of this qualitative analysis with the impacts of the major subsequent financial shocks and economic crises in the Southern Cone countries (the 1982 external debt crisis, the late 1990s–early 2000s emerging markets crises, and the Great Recession since 2008) then becomes the equivalent of a longitudinal analysis, in the sense that observations about the same countries are compared at different points in time. Table 1.1 summarizes such observations, listing the type of political regime in the run up to and the triggering of the major financial shocks and economic crises that I analyze alongside the fate of that regime (survival or breakdown).

The main criterion for selecting which cases to compare across time is having the same type of political regime in place in the run up to and the start of at least two of the major financial shocks and economic crises considered in this work. The italicized entries in table 1.1 show such pairings by country. For example, Chile had a dictatorship both at the beginning of the financial shocks that morphed into the Great Depression and at the start of the 1982 external debt crisis. Argentina and Uruguay, however, had democratic regimes both at the onset of the financial shocks that led to the Great Depression and at the beginning of the emerging markets crises that hit both countries in 2001–2. Thus a similar political regime at otherwise different times and during different economic crises provides the qualitative controls that help to structure the three paired comparisons contained in part II of this book.

The first set of paired comparison I address is Chile in the early 1930s versus the same country in the early 1980s. The outcome of the baseline case (the Great Depression) was the breakdown of the dictatorship led by General Ibáñez in July 1931. In contrast, the Chilean military regime led by General Pinochet survived the economic earthquake of the early 1980s; it was not until

TABLE 1.1
Selection and pairing of cases for historical comparison

Countries	Years			
	Late 1920s–early 1930s	Late 1970s–early 1980s	Late 1990s–early 2000s	After the 2008 global shock
Chile	*Dictatorship/ breakdown*	*Dictatorship/ survival*	Democracy/ survival	Democracy/ survival?
Argentina	*Democracy/ breakdown*	Dictatorship/ breakdown	*Democracy/ survival*	Democracy/ survival?
Uruguay	*Democracy/ breakdown*	Dictatorship/ breakdown	*Democracy/ survival*	Democracy/ survival?

1990 that it retreated, and then on its own terms. Therefore, the question for this paired comparison is, Why did the military regime under General Pinochet not fold, as did the regime under General Ibáñez? The first sections of chapters 7–9 are devoted to the Chilean situation.

The other two paired comparisons in part II are (1) Argentina in the early 1930s versus the same country in the early 2000s, and (2) Uruguay during those same two periods. The outcome of the baseline case here was a breakdown of democracy, which happened in Argentina in September 1930 and in Uruguay in March 1933. In contrast, democratic regimes in these two countries in the early 2000s—although rocked and destabilized (particularly in Argentina), given both countries' financial and economic implosions—nonetheless survived. Therefore the question for these paired comparisons is, Why did democracy survive the 2001–3 financial and economic earthquakes, given its collapse in 1930 and 1933? The second sections of chapters 7–9 expound on the Argentine and Uruguayan comparisons.

SHOCKS AND CRISES

After the global financial bust triggered when the Lehman Brothers investment bank declared bankruptcy on September 15, 2008, it became fashionable (yet again) to speak of shocks and crunches, crises, recessions, and depressions. Thus far I've used the terms shocks and crises interchangeably, but they have to be differentiated.

Shocks

Generically, a shock is a violent impact. The concept is used in several disciplines, including physics, seismology, psychology, medicine, and economics. Economic shocks are unexpected and unpredictable events that impact national economies (either negatively or positively), even though they originate outside of them; in academic parlance, they are exogenous.[19] Shocks are intense and short term. Many different phenomena—some natural (like hurricanes or earthquakes) and some social (such as the start or end of a war, the decision by an international cartel to fix the price of a commodity like oil, or herd behavior in financial markets after unexpected bad news)—can trigger economic shocks.[20]

Because many different causes can initiate them, the term economic shocks remains a general category. In this book, whenever I refer to economic shocks I mean the major international financial booms and busts since the late 1920s:

- the Great Depression (late 1920s to early 1930s)
- the external debt crisis (late 1970s to early 1980s)
- the emerging markets crisis (late 1990s to early 2000s)
- events since the 2008–9 global financial and economic implosion

It is part of the nature of modern finance to be subjected to recurrent shocks. This is due to the myriad unpredictable factors that influence buyers' and sellers' short-term decisions. As a consequence, markets obey the laws of complex systems (to use the words of mathematicians). In complex systems, mild upward or downward corrections can be amplified into catastrophic changes that cannot be anticipated, because they follow chaotic (unpredictable) trajectories. Applied to today's global markets, this means that credit expansions and contractions periodically lead to financial and economic booms and busts, some of which can end up having cataclysmic effects wherever extreme ebbs and flows of money and credit occur in the short term.

The not-insignificant occurrence of black swans (rare events) that the efficient market hypothesis cannot account for led economists and mathematicians like Hyman Minsky and Benoit Mandelbrot to rethink these developments and argue that what they call the misbehavior of markets is systemic and recurrent, rather than being incidental, infrequent events.[21] Time and again, financial shocks—sudden, serious interruptions in the credit channel— have choked the reproduction and growth of economic activity. An economic slowdown or decline leads to falling prices, and this is usually how a given initial financial shock propagates and produces a full-blown economic crisis, where the deterioration of financial intermediation hits the real economy, affecting employment, output, and consumption.

Charles Kindleberger has signaled another aspect of financial shocks that is important to keep in mind: their two-way dynamics. First, a credit bubble needs to inflate. The *causa remota* of a financial shock is therefore a given process involving the expansion of credit and subsequent speculation by investors. The bubble-pricking trigger that produces an initial selloff, which then gathers momentum as investors move their funds out of risky assets and race for liquidity, ends up in a severe credit contraction; this is the *causa proxima* of a financial collapse.[22] I identify both types of causes for each of the four major international financial shocks discussed here.

Crises

Economic crises exhibit differences in their intensity and duration, but their primary characteristic is the continued deterioration of the main macro-economic variables for a country or group of countries. Economists only started distinguishing bad crises (recessions) from very bad ones (depressions) after the Great Depression. Although there is still disagreement about the definition of these concepts, a recent analysis concludes that two criteria are usually invoked to separate a depression from a recession: "a decline in real GDP that exceeds 10%, or one that lasts more than three years."[23] The same analysis adds that a third feature, the monetary cause of the economic downturn, can also be useful to distinguish recessions from depressions: "a standard recession usually follows a period of tight monetary policy, but a depression is the result of a bursting asset and credit bubble, a contraction in credit, and a decline in the general price level."[24] Therefore, recessions are more likely to respond to loosening a monetary policy, while depressions, once interest rates are zero or very close to zero, require expansionary fiscal policy and, in some cases (like the post-2008 global financial and economic bust), nonconventional monetary policy, such as quantitative easing (central banks printing money to finance the purchase of government bonds, which stimulates public spending and props up demand).

When fiscal policy comes into play as a crisis management tool of economic policy, the main concern for neoclassical economists is that pumping up demand through public spending can lead to inflation and, in the worst case, to stagflation, a situation in which both prices and unemployment increase. Keynesian economists, however, fear that once monetary policy has lost traction—when interest rates are close to or at zero—the economic risk is that in the absence of a reflationary strategy, it will descend into deflation. Deflation is a self-reinforcing spiral of falling prices in which consumers forgo spending decisions in the expectation of lower future prices. Likewise, suppliers forgo production decisions in light of falling prices in the future. The end result is that the real value of debts increases over time—the dreaded debt deflation, which was behind the Great Depression.

The long-running debate between fiscal doves and hawks was reignited with a fury by the 2008–9 global busts and the response of governments around the world in the direction of massive and concerted monetary and fiscal expansion. The question became, When should these fiscal and monetary stimuli be withdrawn?[25] The Great Recession also forced the redrawing of battle lines at the level of ideas and paradigms, with economics scholars on both sides of the fence putting up spirited defenses of their ideas. The debate will no doubt influence the future of the discipline and its policy prescriptions, just as the maelstrom of the Great Depression did.[26]

Origins: External or Internal?

In addition to distinguishing shocks from crises and, within crises, recessions from depressions, it is also important to specify whether their origin is external or internal. In the three Southern Cone countries, external shocks and crises can be considered to be those that started in the advanced capitalist countries (the Great Depression and the 2008–9 global implosions both began in the United States and Western Europe), while internal crises can be thought of as those that first arose domestically or had a significant domestic component. The external debt crisis of the early 1980s and the emerging markets crises of the late 1990s and early 2000s had significant domestic factors behind them, although in both cases it was foreign credit—its cheap availability, followed by sudden stops and panics—that allowed a boom followed by busts to happen in the first place. Distinguishing primarily external from primarily internal shocks and crises is analytically useful, because it helps to emphasize the different economic policy responses required to tackle each type effectively.

Given external shocks such as the Great Depression and the Great Recession (since 2008–9), the principal danger is debt deflation. Indeed, the mass liquidation of assets that occurred in the early 1930s was due to the absence of an internationally coordinated reflationary policy. The unprecedented fiscal and monetary stimulus that governments around the world adopted after the 2008 global financial implosion—through the Group of 20 (G-20) as the international forum for crisis management coordination—was almost a kneejerk reaction against precisely those fiscal and monetary policy mistakes made in the advanced capitalist economies in 1929–31.

In contrast, the most significant danger after internal crises such as the 1982 Latin American debt bust and the late 1990s–early 2000s emerging markets crises was the potential for the onset and spiraling of inflation. The problem for emerging market countries (those in Latin America, East Asia, and Eastern Europe) was their growing reliance on foreign capital, since they could not control its price and availability. Such dependence on capital inflows and a lack of control over their pace and rhythm have exposed both advanced and emerging market countries alike to sudden, massive financial outflows following periods of substantial credit expansion and the unsustainable growth of lever-age.[27] Time and again, such outflows have forced disorderly exchange rate de-valuations, which in turn have led to higher prices (from consumer basics to the value of debts, particularly when loans had been made in foreign currencies), the corollary of which has been greater debt burdens in real terms (and an in-creased likelihood of bankruptcy), and—more generally—the danger of grow-ing inflation that could only be brought under control by tightening monetary and fiscal policy, reinforcing the economic downside.

Throughout this work I sometimes refer to financial shocks and economic crises and, at other times, for brevity's sake, only to economic crises. Whenever it is relevant to my analysis I separate recessions from depressions; otherwise I use the generic term crises. I also distinguish between externally and inter-nally led crises, particularly with regard to the dissimilarity of their economic policy implications and the varying political challenges that such differences have entailed. I relate economic shocks and crises to democratic transitions and breakdowns, and then analyze their connections from a political economy perspective by focusing on the strategic interaction of actors.

LITERATURE REVIEW AND THIS
VOLUME'S CONTRIBUTIONS

The Anglo-American scholarly literature on transitions to and breakdowns of democracy that took off in the 1970s and dominated the field in the 1980s and 1990s identified economic shocks and crises as being among the impor-tant factors that have contributed to the toppling of political regimes, demo-cratic or otherwise.[28] Yet this school of literature also called for analysts to be mindful about what it referred to as the relative autonomy of the political, meaning that coups d'état, revolutions, aborted coups, and counterrevolu-tions could not be inferred just by observing changes or continuities in big so-cioeconomic structures and processes or short-term economic junctures, as both Marxist and structural-functionalist social scientists had tried to do in the 1950s and 1960s.

This was a salutary change of perspective that allowed scholars to rebal-ance the components in their arguments so that, in addition to fundamental structural elements, they could also pay attention to agency factors, such as the strategic interaction of leading actors (civilian and military, domestic and international, economic, political, and social) in the battle over the definition of present and future political institutions.[29] After all, it is some individuals imposing their will over others that destroys/creates political regimes. I follow the actor-centered perspective of this literature in analyzing the political consequences of economic shocks and crises.

A relevant feature in this book—one that the 1970s–1990s literature did not explore in the depth and detail that scholars writing in the 2000s have done, relates to the work of political economists who have studied the microfoundations underlying political regime dynamics. These scholars have reemphasized the material bases of actors—be they risk-averse elites or enraged revolutionary masses—when it comes to what kinds of things individuals are willing to do to ensure that the rules of the game (the type of political regime that competing politicoeconomic actors are struggling for) favor their access to control of the decision-making process through which resources and opportunities will be allocated in future. Boix has observed that "redistributive struggles are at the heart of the choice of political regimes."[30] Likewise, Acemoglu and Robinson note that "distributional conflict lie at the heart of politics" and that preferences over democratic and non-democratic regimes are a function of answers to the question, Will a given political regime produce more pro-majority or pro-elite policies?[31]

Although they reiterate the material bases of politics, these authors do not want to go back to old structural-functionalist tautologies. On the contrary, their perspective is that of game theorists, who formally model the strategic interaction of rational actors, which means that they are interested first and foremost in specifying (formally and *ex ante*) ways in which rational individuals try to maximize their material self-interest (by crafting political institutions that will further such interests) when they interact strategically with others. I do not adopt the formal methodology of game theory, but I nonetheless share with these authors a political economy perspective that, as Rueschemeyer and colleagues remind us, informs most of the comparative historical studies about democratization "from Max Weber to Guillermo O'Donnell."[32]

The influential political economy explanations put forward by game theorists like Boix and Acemoglu and Robinson focus on two of the three analytical pillars highlighted in mainstream Anglo-American literatures in comparative politics and political economy: institutions, interests, and ideas.[33] The pillars these authors have incorporated are interests (the prospect of economic gains and losses) and institutions (the rules of the game embodied in alternative types of political regimes), which are the factors that are traditionally used in formal modeling.

I add two novel features in my analysis. First, in addition to institutions and interests, I also consider the third pillar of comparative politics, the role of ideas—economic (ideas about how economies operate and should be managed) as well as political ones (ideologies such as liberalism, fascism, communism, and left- and right-wing nationalism)—in the creation of pressures for and against democracy. Second, I use the contents and interactions of domestic and international spheres to explain the changing relative costs for pro- and anti-democratic action that these countries experienced in the context of deep economic crises.

CONCEPTUAL FRAMEWORK
Initial Conditions: Political Regime Type

The first question to ask in understanding the relative costs that pro- and anti-democracy forces face in organizing and exercising pressures in favor of and against democracy is, What types of political regimes were in place for each of the Southern Cone case studies when economic shocks struck and a crisis started unfolding? When the answer is that the regime was democratic, then the general challenge for democracy and its supporters was to confront and manage the crisis without breaking down (democrats playing defense, so to speak), while those who opposed democracy exploited the opportunity to try to substitute a non-democratic alternative for the democratic regime (anti-democrats playing offense).

If the answer is that the regime was non-democratic, then it is the officials and supporters of this type of regime who had to carry out crisis management (anti-democrats playing defense) while the supporters of democracy could try to bring the regime down (democrats playing offense) and install or reinstall democracy. This is also true for supporters of other types of non-democratic rule (i.e., not that of the incumbents). For example, in the 1930s the communists' strategy was to form an alliance with bourgeois democrats to combat fascism and bring down right-wing dictatorships, but once this was achieved they continued to push for the dictatorship of the proletariat, thus continuing to engage in and promote anti-democracy activities. The first step is therefore to establish which groups—in particular, which alliances of groups—defend a given status quo (the political regime in place) and which ones want to change it (in a democratic or non-democratic direction), before moving on to distinguish domestic and international sources of pressures for and against democracy and track their interactions.

International and Domestic Pressures

By definition, international economic shocks and crises affect both foreign and domestic groups. Short of a successful foreign invasion and occupation, during which the occupiers impose a new political regime on the conquered (like the Allies did in Germany and Japan after the Second World War), international factors and resources have a more indirect influence than domestic ones on the fate of national political regimes. Generally, even when powerful foreign actors channel money, weapons, and propaganda to try to overturn a given political regime, it is domestic forces who by and large do the fighting, some rising and others falling. This does not mean that international factors are less important than domestic ones. Historically, foreign support for one or the other side in a quarrel over a political regime has repeatedly tipped the balance. Rather, the point here is that international resources are *mediated* by contending domestic forces.

To put the changing interactions of the international/domestic spheres in historical perspective, we have to remember the wide-ranging process of technological and economic internationalization, or globalization, of human activity that took root and gathered strength during the second half of the twentieth century, particularly in the aftermath of the Cold War. Contemporary political economists acknowledge that some of the economic effects that globalization can produce (not that it produces them automatically)—such as an increase in trade and economic growth—can have a strong impact on the calculations that elites and popular classes make regarding the rules of the game (democratic or non-democratic political regime alternatives) under which they live.

Two such features have been particularly influential. First, the explosive growth of financial capitalism (a switch from more specific, relatively fixed assets to more liquid, movable ones—say from land to finance) has raised the mobility of wealth. This means that the owners of capital have increasingly enjoyed ways to cheaply and immediately move (exit) some or most of their assets out of a given country. Globalization, in the words of Acemoglu and Robinson, makes it "more difficult to tax elites and reduces the extent to which democracy can pursue populist and highly majoritarian policies. International financial integration, therefore, makes the elites feel more secure about democratic politics and discourages them from using repression to prevent a transition from non-democracy to democracy."[34] Second, greater growth and expanding international trade, if accompanied by social mobility and falling socioeconomic inequality, conditions not sufficient in and of themselves to ensure the birth or survival of a democracy, can raise the benefits of democratic rule for the have-nots and reduce the costs for the haves. Inasmuch as growth and trade raise the real income of the poor, the rich can expect less demand for radical redistribution, which in turn can make democracy a regime option that garners support from both above and below.[35]

I incorporate the economics-based perspective that these authors have used to assess the impact of globalization on democracy, but I also complement it by including more political considerations in my analyses, which I disaggregate into institutional, interests-based, and ideas-based mechanisms. The international sphere was transformed after the Second World War and the subsequent creation of the UN and Bretton Woods systems. Since then, international factors have had a growing influence in domestic spheres (in the economy and the politics of individual nation-states), though such growth has been neither linear nor unidirectional. For example, during the Cold War, the planet was divided into two irreconcilable camps, each led by a superpower. The end of the Cold War (1989–91) lifted these barriers, leading to a new world order (an age of globalization) in which there has been a significant expansion in the influence of international factors in individual countries' national and local affairs, as well as vice versa (local events are transmitted and watched globally in real time). If the 1989–91 events transformed geopolitics to make globalization possible, the information- and communications-based technological revolutions of the 1990s–2000s (the Internet, portable computing, and cellular telephony) were the catalysts of collective action from below. These have enhanced international-domestic interactions, which, in turn, have accelerated their reciprocal influences.

This process can be summarized visually (figure 1.1) as the growing overlap and influence of international and domestic factors. The circles on the left-hand box represent international and domestic spheres at time t1, which is the interwar years of the twentieth century (1920s–1930s). The circles on the right-hand box represent international and domestic spheres at time t2, which is the world order that emerged after the Second World War, in particular the globalization occurring since the end of the Cold War. Compared with the past (the circles at t1), the bigger circles at t2 show the growth of international and domestic economies and, more generally, of human exchange (not only commodities, goods, and services, but information). The substantial increase in the overlap of the international and domestic spheres at t2 compared with t1 represents the growth of reciprocal influence in the global and domestic spheres.

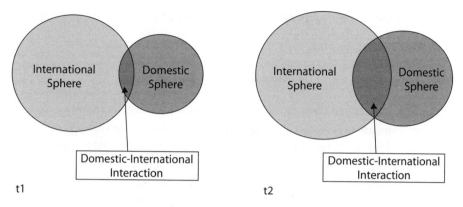

Figure 1.1. Growing reciprocal influence of international and domestic factors because of globalization

Two qualifications are in order to understand the implications of figure 1.1. First, this schematic view of global political and economic change differs according to the international hierarchy of power. It should be obvious that what happens in the domestic politicoeconomic sphere of the United States, a world superpower, is much more influential in the international sphere (in international organizations, the international economy, and global consumer culture) than whatever happens in the domestic sphere of poor or middle-income countries, such as those in Latin American and in other emerging market regions. Similarly, the influence that international factors can have on the domestic sphere of the United States is much more limited than the influence such foreign forces have in small and poor countries. Second, the growth of domestic-international economic and political overlap and interactions in the course of the second half of the twentieth century does not mean that, on its own, such growth could have led to the irreversible triumph of democracy over other forms of rule around the world. Pro-democracy regime alternatives have been nourished by the international architecture built after the Second World War and by the victory of the United States in the Cold War (among other factors), but we can also imagine how alternative possibilities, such as an Axis victory in 1945 or triumph by the USSR in 1989–91, would probably have weakened or restrained the democratic impulse, irrespective of satisfactory economic growth and the 1990s–2000s revolution in information and communications technologies.

In short, my framework emphasizes that international and domestic interactions have grown substantially in scope and intensity since the 1980s, and these reciprocal influences have raised the likelihood that a democratic regime can survive or be born in the face of deep economic crises.

Political Regime Dynamics

A more extensive and deeper interaction of international and domestic political economies has created challenges and opportunities for democracy and democratization. Here, I follow the perspective that Robert A. Dahl articulated and other authors continue to use, which sees the outcome of struggles over the establishment and survival/demise of political regimes as a function of the changing relative costs that contending forces face.[36] The drama of regime change is underlined by the irreconcilable conflict of interests that prevails between those who enjoy the power, wealth, and prestige of running a political regime (the incumbents) and those who do not possess these advantages but would like to (the opposition). Dahl and some contemporary political economists do not make explicit what I, along with Rueschemeyer and colleagues, emphasize: the importance of analyzing the domestic class coalitions as well as the transnational ones that both the incumbents and the opposition can activate to pursue a common objective (the preservation or change of a political regime).[37]

The incumbents (and their domestic and international allies) know that their relative position, influence, and interests will be negatively affected in proportion to the extent to which other groups have to be incorporated into the regime, since power, wealth, and prestige will have to be divided among a larger number of interests. At the extreme, if the opposition (and its domestic and international allies) is successful in bringing down a political regime and decides to exclude the ex-incumbents (and their allies) completely from the new regime— they might even send them to the guillotine—the voice, power, wealth, and influence of those who had been in office could be completely overturned and they could lose everything. It is therefore not difficult to understand why conflicts over the definition of political regimes—particularly during periods of harsh economic shocks and crises—can easily turn into life-or-death, all-or-nothing affairs.

The stakes for the incumbents, the opposition, and the allies of both vary greatly according to context-specific conditions but, following Dahl, it is reasonable to infer that "the greater the conflict between the government and its opponents, the more costly it is for each to tolerate the other."[38] The more the interests and/or ideas of one party are or become irreconcilable with those of the other party, the higher the stakes will be for the adversaries; in other words, one side will have more to lose, given the other's gains, and vice versa. I subscribe to this emphasis on the relative costs that the incumbents and the opposition face to organize and exercise pro- or anti-democratic action. A schematic way to observe the interaction of adversaries is by thinking in terms of pressures from above and from below.

Pressures from above can be seen as going back to Dahl's original insights regarding the costs of tolerating the opposition (and, therefore, the costs of having to suppress it). Elites can either use repression (which is costly) or compromise (extend concessions to those fighting for democracy). Those who organize to exercise pressures from below can opt for a wide variety of actions, from uncompromising revolution to absolute submission, with a range of options in between. Many factors help decide the strength of those exercising pressures from below and their ability to achieve common aims, but the most basic one is their capacity for sustained, effective, collective action. Boix states that "whenever the lower classes overcome their collective action problems and organize in political parties and trade unions [or work toward] the formation of guerrilla movements, the costs of repression become high."[39] Acemoglu and Robinson also argue that a "relatively effective threat of revolution from the citizens is important for democratization. When the citizens are not well organized, the system will not be challenged and transition to democracy will be delayed indefinitely. Similarly, when civil society is relatively developed and the majority is organized, repression may be more difficult. Therefore, some degree of development of civil society is also necessary for democratization."[40] Given the broad Latin American context, the Southern Cone countries of Argentina, Chile, and Uruguay are good case studies, because pressures from below in these nations were well organized since the turn of the twentieth century.

MY HYPOTHESIS

I argue that the structural changes in international and domestic institutions, interests, and ideas summarized in table 1.1 have raised the costs for anti-democratic organization and action while concomitantly lowering them for pro-democratic organization and action. Compared with the baseline analysis of the Southern Cone countries during the Great Depression years, such structural changes have raised the likelihood that democracy can prevail—either by surviving or by being (re)instated—during harsh economic shocks and crises.

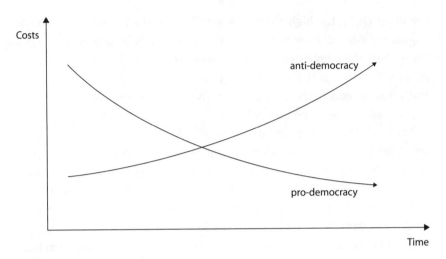

Figure 1.2. Tilting the balance in favor of democracy

Figure 1.2 represents an increase in the costs for the organization and exercise of anti-democracy action over time and an accompanying decrease in the costs for pro-democracy action. To put it in a historical context, this relative change in costs means that individuals who, for interests-based and/or ideological reasons, wanted to organize to undermine liberal democracy back in the 1920s–1930s faced lower costs to do so than individuals who wanted to defend and preserve it. In contrast, in the 1990s–2000s individuals who have tried to organize and exercise anti-democratic actions have faced higher relative costs than those who want to defend and preserve democracy.

My argument and its graphic representation in no way imply that all or even a majority of countries around the world will embrace democracy, or that democracy will not only be preserved but will also become the only game in (the global) town, with humanity arriving at the "End of History." Figure 1.2 first and foremost has the Western Hemisphere in mind, and it probably seems less useful to specialists focused on the Middle East or Africa, although the 2011 popular revolutions in North African and Middle Eastern countries should remind us that aspirations about government based on popular consent and accountability are universal rather than culture constrained.

Aside from its applicability in Latin America,[41] the change in costs for pro- and anti-democratic action in figure 1.2 also works for observers of countries in other emerging market economies of the world, such as East Asia and Central and Eastern Europe, where, since the end of the Cold War, dominant US and/or

European Union influences have also promoted liberal democratic rule in the political sphere and market-based exchange in the economic sphere. Despite myriad differences among the countries in these regions, the fact that a majority experienced dual transitions more or less synchronically in the 1980s and 1990s makes it plausible to compare them in terms of the political impact (regime-wise) of harsh economic shocks and crises.[42] The conclusion to this volume includes some cross-regional observations that help identify the extent of and certain limits to my analytical framework, as well as pose relevant questions for further research.

In Latin America, long-lived US hegemony in the Western Hemisphere means that American action—be it by high-level representatives of the United States in the UN and Bretton Woods' organizations; by top executives of American multinationals, banks, and other US private businesses with operations in periphery countries; and by senior officials and officers of US interests abroad (be they political and/or economic) in the Treasury Department, the State Department, and the Pentagon, along with the role of the US Congress in protecting US interests through legislation—remains a key force that should be prominently incorporated in any analysis aiming to observe and evaluate the changing relative costs for pro- and anti-democracy action in the Western Hemisphere, particularly in Latin America. Thus my analysis of international institutions, interests, and ideas is dominated (although not exclusively) by the actions, policies, and omissions of American politicians, government officials in both domestic and international agencies, private businessmen, growing civil society groups (some progressive, some conservative), and, sporadically, military officers and troops.

Still, for all the enhanced influence of international factors, particularly US-dominated ones, in the national economies and politics of the Latin American countries (or, for that matter, any country around the world) in the early twenty-first century, domestic institutions, interests, and ideas continue to dominate the way individuals interact on the ground (short of foreign invasion and occupation). Therefore, my analysis includes relevant factors from both the international and domestic components of these three basic mechanisms, exploring the ways in which they interact at given points in time and examining how such interactions have helped to set and change the relative costs for pro- and anti-democratic action—which, in turn helps to establish the likelihood that democracy can survive or be (re)instated in the aftermath of harsh economic shocks and crises.

INSTITUTIONS, INTERESTS, IDEAS,
AND CHANGING RELATIVE COSTS
Institutions

I follow Douglass C. North's distinction of rules and organizations in my study of institutions.[43] Specialists and the public alike tend to conflate the two concepts, for example by referring to the church and the armed forces as institutions. North reminds us that institutions-as-rules are the laws and regulations that determine how power is created, divided (or not), exercised, and transmitted. Institutions-as-organizations refer to the different groups that individuals form or join in pursuit of their interests. As North puts it, "separating the analysis of the underlying rules from the strategy of the players is a necessary prerequisite to building a theory of institutions."[44] North's conceptual distinction is central to my arguments, because it helps to specify the general chain of causation that I observe comparatively. While economic shocks and crises constitute the independent variable, and political regime change (institutions-as-rules) the dependent variable of my analysis, competing individuals operating through groups (institutions-as-organizations) are the intervening variable, that is, the link that connects instances of economic shocks/crises with either the preservation or the overthrow of a given political regime (and, in the latter case, the substitution of another type of government).

INTERNATIONAL FACTORS

International factors have a broader connotation in my analysis than in the economics-based considerations of Acemoglu and Robinson, since I incorporate rules and organizations as explicit elements in my framework. For international institutions-as-rules, I examine the relevant international laws, treaties, and regimes regulating the different transnational policy spheres, as well as the role of the United States in them. Regarding international institutions-as-organizations, my analysis includes two different groups:

1. Organizations that structure the international community of nations, and the role of the United States in them. These include the presence or absence at the multilateral level of the UN (1946) and the Bretton Woods systems (IMF, 1945; WB, 1946); and the presence or absence of the inter-American system and its three pillars at the regional level: the Rio Treaty (1947), the charter of the Organization of American States (OAS, 1948), and the charter of the Inter-American Development Bank (IADB, 1959).

2. Non-state actors, whose interests and power can vary widely. These range from multinational institutions like the Catholic Church and evangelical churches to environmental, human rights, and indigenous-support organizations (many of which are American, and their voices can be powerful in helping to set the agenda and actions of the US federal government and Congress). Other prominent non-state actors are international police and defense institutions, and clandestine groups (such as insurgencies and other guerrilla-type groups).

DOMESTIC FACTORS

The main domestic institutions-as-rules that my analysis includes are (1) the constitution or other fundamental laws and decrees that spell out the way power is exercised in any given country; and (2) the electoral laws, which translate votes into political representation and, therefore, into the main fault lines of negotiation over governance and resources. The primary domestic institutions-as-organizations I examine are (1) the armed forces, which are relevant due to their coercive capacity to participate decisively in the choice and imposition, if needs be, of a political regime; and (2) political parties and party systems, which are relevant because they are the vehicles through which power is contested and accessed in most modern political regimes.

In selecting which institutions (as rules and as organizations) to analyze, I have followed mainstream Anglo-American academic literature in Latin American politics. This has consistently identified the following as the main actors in the long-term drama of the democratization of the countries in this region: the various sides in the conflict over constitutional orders and political representation; the state and its main coercive arms (such as the military and police forces), and the different branches of government and main political parties that participate in the government in power and the opposition; and the social movements and pressure groups (for-profit and nonprofit groups) that operate within the law, as well as those operating outside it (guerrilla and other clandestine groups).[45]

The next two sections—interests and ideas—look at the two types of inputs that frame individuals' preferences, calculations, and behavior towards institutions-as-rules (to support or oppose a given political regime) and institutions-as-organizations (to join different groups and act through them—or not—to keep or change a political regime).

Interests

Like contemporary game theorists, I assume that material interests lie close to the heart of individuals' behavior, although (unlike these scholars) I also consider ideas, specifically, political ideologies and ideas about economics and economic policy. I do not elaborate on how interests and ideas interact and mix to create individual preferences to either support or overturn a political regime (or to do nothing and just stand on the sidelines). Instead, I continue to follow Dahl's general observation and explicitly incorporate interests and ideas into it. In other words, I posit that the greater the conflict between the interests and ideas of regime incumbents and regime opponents, the costlier it becomes to tolerate each other and, therefore, the greater the likelihood that conflict will escalate. This escalation, in turn, leads to the growth of a zero-sum mentality (what others gain, I lose, and vice versa), accompanied, unsurprisingly, by all-or-nothing behavior, where individuals end up trying to impose their irreconcilable preferences on one another.

FOREIGN INTERESTS

When observing foreign interests, I emphasize the interests of foreign private capitalists. This is a reductionist definition but one that is in accordance with my aim of identifying and systematically observing the behavior of key actors in the drama of political regime change. There can be no doubt that foreign capitalists were and have remained relevant players in the political economies of the Latin American countries since the region's independence from Spain two centuries ago. This general statement, however, has substantial intraregional variations. By and large, smaller countries in the Western Hemisphere have been and will remain more dependent on international markets and business than the biggest ones. My analysis looks at two aspects of foreign interests: (1) how liquid or fixed their assets are, and (2) how they are affected by trade laws and regulations.

First, I follow the works of Boix and of Acemoglu and Robinson, who classify actors according to the specificity of their assets. Boix creates a range that goes from very liquid and therefore very movable assets (e.g., knowledge and finance) at one end of the spectrum; to somewhat liquid assets (e.g., certain industrial ones) in the middle; to very illiquid and therefore fixed wealth (e.g., landowning, or control of raw materials like energy and mining) at the other end.[46] Similarly, Acemoglu and Robinson identify the equivalents as human capital, physical capital, and land. These authors also expect the owners of illiquid wealth to be the most adverse to democracy (their wealth is easiest to tax or confiscate because it is immobile); the owners of industrial wealth to be less adverse (they can move the liquid part of their wealth, or try to relocate a firm if it is threatened); and the owners of highly liquid assets (e.g., financial, service, and knowledge-based assets in general) to be the least adverse to democracy (most of their wealth is highly mobile and can therefore be removed if threatened).[47]

Following this classification, it is reasonable to think that foreign interests whose assets are mainly in liquid form would generally be less intensely concerned about a given regime's policies (or the potential policies of a would-be regime if a regime transition/breakdown seems close at hand) than interests whose assets are mainly in illiquid form. A clear example of this difference is the business of multinational banks versus the business of international energy and mining companies. There is no doubt that the former face important risks, such as the suspension of interest payments or, worse, borrower default; but the bulk of their potential future profits from such liquid economic activity comes from intangibles, such as borrowing short and lending long, fees from trades, advice on wealth management, and the management of initial public offerings and mergers and acquisitions.

Contrast these sources of profits with those of energy and mining companies, which instead rely on that most tangible of activities, the extraction and sale of materials from the earth. Access or denial of access to the land can mean all or nothing for these businesses. Examples from the actions of Anglo-American oil companies such as Standard Oil and Royal Dutch Shell in Argentina and Uruguay in the late 1920s and early 1930s (see chapter 4) illustrate such high stakes. Similarly, multinational agribusinesses and trading companies that own vast tracts of land overseas, and whose profits derive from the fruits of that earth, face similarly high stakes to their core business as energy and mining companies do. The classic example in twentieth-century Latin American history is the United Fruit Company and its operations in all the countries of Central America, plus Colombia and Ecuador.[48]

Second, I observe the extent to which foreign interests are affected by prevailing or changing trade rules and regulations, trade flows, and trade growth, particularly in the wake of harsh economic shocks and crises. Here, it is not enough simply to identify private interests. Governments are central to trade assessments, given that they set the rules (and changes to the rules) of the trading game. Therefore, aside from the most influential foreign private economic interests, I follow the governments of the three Southern Cone countries and those of their major trading partners (in the 1920s–1930s these would be Great Britain for Argentina and Uruguay, and the United States for Chile), also taking into account the domestic sources of organized support for free trade or protectionism.

Looking at the strategies that the foreign businesses of advanced capitalist countries have, the key issue for my analysis is the extent to which they can forge a communion of interests and a common strategy for action with the domestic elites and/or the governments of the less advanced countries where they operate (in this case the Southern Cone countries). Both foreign and domestic actors will try to protect their economic interests. Most of the time leading foreign and domestic economic interests overlap to varying degrees, but sometimes they can be one and the same, while in other instances they can be solely antagonistic. The main question is, To what extent can international interests and an influential section of domestic interests identify, pledge, and build mutual support for a given course of action (which, in the case of this volume, is either defending and preserving or plotting against and trying to change a political regime)?

DOMESTIC INTERESTS

In discussing the main domestic economic interests, I continue to follow Boix and Acemoglu and Robinson, who elaborate a classic tripartite schema that describes the main domestic actors and the cross-class coalitions that can be created to advance their preferences (i.e., the type of political regime they favor). Thus Boix identifies (1) the rich, (2) the middle classes, and (3) the poor; similarly, but using somewhat different language, Acemoglu and Robinson list (1) the elites, (2) the middle classes, and (3) citizens.[49]

First, domestic elites (like their foreign counterparts) have traditionally been opposed to democracy, inasmuch as such a system opens the door to pro-majority policies, such as progressive taxation and asset nationalization. Staying with the theories of Boix and Acemoglu and Robinson, we can assume that, just as with foreign interests, both the asset specificity (how liquid and mobile one's assets are, or not) of domestic actors and the given level of socioeconomic inequality prevalent in a given context help to determine how well the elites and the masses can tolerate each other. In general, the greater the percentage of their fixed wealth and the higher the levels of socioeconomic inequality—and Latin America is the most unequal region in the world—the more risk-averse the elites are and the more temptation there is for the masses to back a radical movement or government that supports substantial, short-term redistribution.

Second, the urban-based industrial working classes (and their allies among the middle classes) have been the actors from below that have been most effective at overcoming the problems of collective action and building a permanent resource base to promote democratization.[50] Thus I focus on the changing strength and independence of trade unions, and of the organized labor movement more generally, to assess the contribution of this sector to pressures for and against democracy. The other economically poor sector, the peasantry and other rural workers, have played a less clear-cut role in democratization than the urban industrial working classes. For the former, their pro- or anti-democratic stance and its strength have been a function of "their capacity for autonomous organization and their susceptibility to the influence of the dominant [land-owning] classes."[51] From millenarian movements to Maoist guerrillas, from Amerindian-based to multiethnic landless movements, and from libertarian gauchos to Christian Democrat rural trade unions, Latin America offers a great variety of rural-based pressures from below. Therefore, I also consider the changing strength and independence of these movements to assess this sector's contribution to pressures for and against democracy.

Third, the middle class (as a generalized set of distinctive income groups between the poor and the rich) is tricky. Some authors think that its contribution to democracy is proportional to its size. Thus societies with a large middle class or classes, by virtue of the fact that inequality in them will be lower than in societies with a smaller middle segment and a larger proportion of poor, tend to demand less radical redistributive policies that, in turn, lower the elites' opposition to democracy. In this view the size of the middle classes acts like "a *buffer* [authors' emphasis] in the conflict between the elites and the citizens."[52] In contrast, from a comparative historical perspective some authors consider the role of the middle class in the process of democratization to be ambiguous. According to this view, the middle classes pushed for their own inclusion and used alliances (if convenient) with the working classes to force democratization. If the middle classes have felt threatened by strong pressures from below, however, they have tended to support the installation of non-democratic regimes.[53] Rather than supporting one side of this debate or the other, I determine the middle classes' support for or opposition to democracy empirically rather than theoretically. There is no question that the middle classes are the linchpin between the elites and the poor. What remains unanswered—and can only be determined by observing specific politico-economic contexts—is when the middle classes follow the elites and when they ally with and mobilize the poor.

As with foreign interests, my analysis of domestic interests considers the extent to which these were affected by prevailing or changing trade rules and regulations, trade flows, and trade growth. Thus I examine the governments of the three Southern Cone countries and their interactions with the elites, the middle classes, and the popular classes in their societies during harsh economic shocks, looking in particular at the political influence of these groups' preferences for protectionism or free trade.

Ideas

I also want to be able, in a systematic way, to identify factors other than just material self-interest in individuals' and groups' decisions to fight for or against democracy at different points in time. Ideas are prominent among such factors, since the strategic interaction of contending domestic and international actors is also a function of their political and economic ideas. For this last analytical pillar, I assume that ideas are somewhat independent from narrow material interests in informing an individual's motivation to act. Otherwise, neither rabid socialists/communists from upper-class backgrounds nor equally rabid working-class or lower-middle-class supporters of conservative economic policy make sense. My thinking along these lines follows that of mainstream scholars who, like Judith Goldstein and Robert Keohane, have observed that "ideas as well as interests have causal weight in explanation of human action."[54]

From the perspective of this volume, the power of ideas stems from their capacity to draw up and cement collective allegiance to a politicoeconomic program by delineating road maps of political and public policy action (the means) that can deliver the social objectives (the ends) promoted and justified by such ideas. According to a leading scholar of ideas-based comparative political economy, Mark Blyth, there are at least two ways in which ideas can be seen as having independent effects. First, "ideas can be investigated as providing the necessary conditions for successful collective action among agents with an interest in restructuring distributional relationships." Second, "ideas can be seen as both facilitators of radical policy change and a prerequisite of it."[55]

These general statements are very much in line with my focus in this book, according to which economic shocks and crises raise the relative scarcity of resources and opportunities, forcing groups to engage in collective action to protect and (if possible) continue to advance their interests. One of the main ways in which such protection and advancement of interests has been pursued historically is by fighting to preserve or change political regimes as a prerequisite to implementing radical policy change (or retaining a status quo). The main lesson I draw from Blyth's line of inquiry is that it is not just the material interests that are in contention, but also the ideas prevailing at that point in time and the way political leaders use them, that help draw the battle lines of who fights whom, and for what reasons.

While Blyth's influential analysis concentrates on changes in economic policy ideas, which I follow as one line of inquiry, I add a second one, namely, changes in competing political ideologies since the Great Depression. Thus I distinguish between the words *ideas* (in the economic sphere) and *ideologies* (in the political one). The main difference between these two formulations is that while ideas in a technical field of knowledge such as economics lead to accumulation, revision, and learning—such as in the way economic policy paradigms grow, are modified, and challenged by new ideas—ideologies in the political sphere are public formulations by leaders, movements, and parties that are used to promote collective action to gain or retain power.[56]

As I do with institutions and interests, I examine both the international and the domestic spheres in my analysis of economic ideas and political ideologies. When looking at the ways in which they have changed since the Great Depression, the main issue is to establish how international and domestic ideas and ideologies interacted, and to consider the results of such interactions in terms of the relative costs for pro- and anti-democratic action.

INTERNATIONAL SPHERE

First, I emphasize dominant or hegemonic countries' changing foreign policies, given the extent to which their own political ideology has been challenged by competing ones in what they consider to be their immediate sphere of influence (the region of the world where they are undisputed dominant players). For Latin America, this means considering the United States and alterations in its foreign policy in the Western Hemisphere since the Great Depression years.

Second, when I observe and analyze the evolution of economic ideas and policy in the international sphere, I follow Blyth. From this perspective, explaining a fundamental change in economic ideas and economic policy helps to assess the impact of various economic policy styles of crisis management and the adjustment costs they impose on different organized groups during harsh economic shocks and crises. Blyth's work emphasizes what he calls the two key transformations in economics and economic policy that had global repercussions in the twentieth century: the first was the demise of the neoclassical method and the concomitant rise of the Keynesian approach to macroeconomic management during the Great Depression; the second was the downfall of state-led economic growth and Keynesian demand management after the international stagflation of the 1970s, the subsequent revival of neoclassical economics, and then the global ascendance since the 1980s of what came to be known as neoliberalism.[57]

The faces attached to such economic ideas and economic policy transformations in Latin America were, on the one hand, Raúl Prebisch, and, on the other, Friedrich von Hayek and Milton Friedman. Starting in 1948, Prebisch was the director of the UN's Economic Commission for Latin America, and between 1964 and 1969 he was the founder and director of the UN's Conference on Trade and Development. Prebisch's *dependencia* theory became the economic idea that legitimized a general move from market-led to state-led economic development, based on import-substitution industrialization between the 1940s and the 1970s—not only in Latin America, but also in the newly independent nation-states in Africa and Asia that were born during the years of decolonization between the 1950s and the 1980s.[58] In contrast, the ideas of the Austrian-school economist von Hayek and the Chicago-school leader Friedman were behind the economic-liberalization revolution that, to different degrees, swept through most of the Latin American countries. This was first implemented in Chile under the aegis of the Chilean economists known as the Chicago Boys, starting in 1975, and it later came to be called either neoliberalism or the Washington consensus in the 1980s and 1990s.[59]

DOMESTIC SPHERE

Conflicts based on antagonistic political ideologies and economic ideas and policy vary greatly according to time and place. Like contemporary political economists, I assume that as economic shocks/crises intensify and intergroup competition for scarce resources and opportunities increases in the short run, leaders of conflicting groups are likely to mobilize support, explain current ills, and propose solutions to their supporters and would-be supporters based not just on what dominant international trends say (for example, the embrace of electoral democracy and free markets since the end of the Cold War), but—first and foremost—on domestic conditions and the everyday experience of the majority of the population. Populism has been the prime mover in such incendiary conflicts between the haves and the have-nots throughout Latin America in the twentieth and twenty-first centuries.

Modern populism in Latin America arose in the 1920s and 1930s, and the background conditions that made it possible were increasing socioeconomic modernization (as evinced by growing rates of urbanization and industrialization) and the development of mass communications (such as radio broadcasting) and a mass car and truck transportation system around the world.[60] Populist leaders of the 1920s and 1930s rallied the masses against the dominance of foreign investors and their domestic elite allies; they inspired "a sense of nationalism and cultural pride in their followers, and promised to give them a better life as well."[61] The cultivation of nationalist themes by the founders of modern populism—such as Presidents Yrigoyen and Perón in Argentina, Vargas in Brazil, Alessandri and Ibáñez in Chile, and Cárdenas in Mexico; and populist leaders who never attained power, like Haya de la Torre in Peru—left behind a strong legacy that many subsequent populist leaders cultivated.

The nationalist tilt of early modern populism in Latin America, however, does not mean that nationalism and populism are necessary for one another's existence. As political theorist Ernesto Laclau famously put it, "populism is a concept both elusive and recurrent."[62] It is neither a specific ideology nor a movement. Populist leaders can create and develop or tap into both left- and right-wing political traditions. Some fit the reductionist portrait of scholars who have reduced populism to an expansive and unsustainable macroeconomic policy style.[63] But neither nationalist stridency nor fiscal profligacy is a constitutive element of populism. Instead, I follows Laclau's perspective, whereby populism is a political practice that historically has been linked to general social crises in which the opposition organizes effectively around an appeal to "the people" against the established order; such opposition is defined antagonistically, rather than in ways that accommodate or respect differences.[64] I look to other authors for the second basic element of populism in this book, the personal contact and personal relationship populist leaders have established and cultivated with the masses through mass communications, which has allowed them to keep appealing to the people.[65]

Even within my small subset of Latin American countries—Argentina, Chile, and Uruguay—one finds substantial variations in the incidence of populism. Thus, while Argentina has been widely regarded as a basket case, inasmuch as Presidents Yrigoyen's and Perón's personalist ruling styles established populism as a political practice that bred and helped to entrench institutional and economic instability, Chile's and Uruguay's experiences, though not devoid of leaders and governments with populist characteristics, came to be dominated by an aggregation of mass and popular interests through political parties that formed plural, competitive party systems, instead of through the *jefe en turno* (current boss) of the party in power, be it the Radicals (under Presidents Yrigoyen and Alfonsín) or the Peronists (under Perón himself or later under Menem, Kirchner, and Fernández de Kirchner).[66]

In terms of political ideologies in the domestic sphere, my analysis emphasizes the type and intensity of domestic ideological conflict during the harsh economic shocks and crises being studied, along with the concomitant rise (or not) of populism. I look at the contribution of these ideologies to the organization and exercise of pressures in favor of and against democracy. As for changes in economic ideas and policy domestically, I concentrate on those policies implemented as a response to harsh economic shocks and crises and their impact on economic and political conditions. Inasmuch as worsening economic conditions breed fear and despair, the likelihood rises for populist leaders to connect with the suffering masses through their radical critique of the status quo and their promise of justice and redemption through substantial short-term redistribution. But there is no specific economic policy repertoire for populist leaders. As scholars have emphasized, successful populist leaders have tended to be pragmatists who have revised their views and policies to accommodate changing circumstances.[67] Therefore, rather than the style of leadership (populist or institutional) in the Southern Cone countries, what matters for my analysis of economic ideas and policy is the mix of policies that can either contribute to or hinder financial and economic stabilization, adjustment, and reinflation in the face of economic free fall. If and when such policies are successful at stabilization and reinflation, I then consider their political windfall for the incumbents, be they democratic or non-democratic.

Financial shocks and economic crises are not necessary or sufficient causes for some actors to launch a fight against others over the basic political rules that should govern them. Nonetheless, the Great Depression, which was the greatest of modern economic crises, and Latin America, which is the region of the world that experienced the highest incidence of regime changes in the second half of the twentieth century, are a fitting time and place to start this general inquiry about the political effects (regime wise) of major economic shocks and crises.

PART ONE

Great Depression, 1929–34

The economic collapse of 1929–34 was unprecedented in its
depth and breadth. There had been cyclical crises before, but
never like this. The economies of the industrialized world
disintegrated for five years and more, as output dropped by
one-fifth and unemployment went above one-quarter of the
labor force almost everywhere. Financial and currency crises
ricocheted around the world in the space of weeks, binding
economies together as they plummeted downward. No major
nation was spared.

—Jeffry A. Frieden, *Global Capitalism*

CHAPTER TWO

Economic Crisis and Democracy during the Great Depression

While the earth-shattering events of the Great Depression form the basis for my examination of the effects of financial shocks and economic crises on democracy in the Southern Cone countries, it's useful to take a brief look at what was happening before then.

LATIN AMERICA PRIOR TO THE GREAT DEPRESSION

Until the global bust of 1930–34, domestic and international economic elites had strengthened their position and influence throughout Latin America during the years 1870–1914. Some economic historians refer to this period as the first globalization of (financial and industrial) capitalism.[1] In Latin America the main economic effect of this "liberal era of free trade under the golden standard"[2] and relative international peace under the Pax Britannica was a rise in export-led growth, underpinned by two engines. The first was a sustained boom in the growth of world trade. Latin America sold raw materials to feed European and US industrialization and, in turn, bought the fruits of this process: manufactured and capital goods. The second was the rapid growth of finance, accelerating world trade and generating rents for European and American investors. Latin American governments issued bonds that American and European banks sold to businesses and savers in their home countries, while the same banks lent capital to these Latin American governments to cover their foreign debt obligations and investments in economic modernization.

In fact, between the last third of the nineteenth century and the first third of the twentieth, Latin American growth outstripped that of the United States, helping to slow down the development gap between the two, which had grown exponentially during the first half of the nineteenth century.[3] This expansion occurred not only in terms of total products, but also in GDP per capita. Between 1820 and 1870, GDP per capita grew 1.38% annually in the United States, while it decreased 0.05% in Latin America; between 1871 and 1929, however, it grew 1.87% annually in the United States and 2.02% in Latin America.[4]

A second subperiod (1914–early 1920s) saw the dramatic collapse of the internationalist world order as a consequence of the First World War and its aftermath, which also negatively affected Latin American economies, particularly those linked tightly to Europe. In addition, the First World War had other consequences: ideologically (the fierce world-wide competition among liberal democracy, communism, and fascism for peoples' loyalty between 1918 and 1945) and institutionally (growing radical left- and right-wing movements proposed alternative political regimes—either utopian or totalitarian—to liberal democracy).

The last years of this era (1923–29) experienced renewed international economic expansion (hence their designation as the roaring twenties), which made it seem as if the confidence and exuberance of the prewar years could be reenacted. However, the strong, US-led international economic expansion started running out of steam in mid-1928, and a bull market in Wall Street imploded at the end of October 1929.

1929 SHOCK AND THE GREAT DEPRESSION

Like the subsequent major external financial shocks in Latin America analyzed in this book, the Wall Street collapse of October 1929 was preceded by a prolonged foreign credit boom. Using the terminology of Kindleberger, this dramatic credit expansion can be considered the *causa remota* of the economic shock that helped lead to the Great Depression.[5] The credit boom of the second half of the 1920s was propelled by American banks seeking new business opportunities overseas as the United States emerged as the largest global creditor after the First World War. Indeed, during these years the United States became the world's economic growth engine. At the same time, the Western European countries, ravaged by the Great War, gave up their claim as principal capital exporters to developing regions and, moreover, had to borrow heavily to reconstruct their economies.

Great Britain relinquished its place to the United States as the globe's preeminent banker and foreign investor. What was true for the world in general applied particularly in South America. British presence and influence had been paramount there since the 1820s, after the Spanish-speaking countries and

ECONOMIC CRISIS AND DEMOCRACY   49

Brazil gained their independence from their Iberian masters. The change in economic hegemony from Great Britain to the United States, felt globally, was therefore particularly strong in the countries of South America after the First World War.[6] New York replaced London as the financial capital of the world, and American banks plus the US government pursued an aggressive strategy of international credit expansion. This made sense in the short term, given that the inflow of Old World capital to Latin America had dried up since the beginning of the Great War. The United States was in a strong position to replace Britain and other European countries as Latin America's main source of credit once hostilities broke out in 1914. Moreover, US banks, which had been legally prohibited from investing in foreign subsidiaries until then, were also allowed to start making loans to foreign borrowers in 1914. Consequently, American banks set up many branch operations in Latin America.[7]

The boom in credit to Latin American governments by US banks occurred during 1925–28, although the wave of southbound credit expansion had started in 1922, and by 1928 it amounted to more than 2 billion USD in Latin American government bonds sold to North American investors.[8] The majority of investors back then were retailers, rather than the bigger institutional investors that came to dominate financial markets on the buying side in the 1970s and 1980s. The American bankers that mediated the relationship between North American savers (lenders) and Latin American governments (borrowers) have traditionally been depicted as aggressive loan peddlers to naïve Latin American leaders. The former were neither as aggressive, nor the latter as naïve, as is usually assumed. Latin American leaders, committed to the idea of national development that was born in the 1920s (governments should promote the mechanization of economic activity and the building of heavy infrastructure), in fact encouraged American bankers to supply them with large-scale credit.[9]

The United States accounted for about 50% of all new loans worldwide in the 1920s, London for 25%, and other smaller markets (like Amsterdam and Paris) together made up the remaining quarter. In this context, Latin America became highly indebted to American banks. Moreover, even though this region was not the main source of demand for US credit in the 1920s (European countries asked for and were given an average of 500 million USD annually for reconstruction between 1924 and 1928), Latin America borrowed more annually (on average 300 million USD) than Canada (200 million) or Asia (100 million). The international appetite for US capital was such that "in peak years there was nearly one-third as many foreign bonds floated on Wall Street as bonds of American corporations."[10]

US credit expansion in Latin America led to an economic boom in the region, which produced faster growth than in Western Europe and North America in the 1920s.[11] However, such credit-driven growth was also irregular, and it was only possible thanks to the accumulation of substantial levels of short-term foreign indebtedness.[12] To keep open access to new credit, Latin American debtors had to generate enough economic activity to earn the dollars that paid the interest on their outstanding loans. As long as they did this, and foreign credit lines remained open, Latin American borrowers could keep expanding their commitments to either continuing to invest in the growth of production or covering losses from investments that did not prosper. Lenders, in turn, benefited from the interest and principal repayments, as well as from any asset price appreciation on their direct capital investments in the Latin American countries. The end result was that investors and borrowers did well as long as their prospective earnings remained positive.

But what if foreign credit were to dry up suddenly? Neither American lenders and investors nor Latin American borrowers and investment hosts seemed to have considered very seriously the possibility of a sudden stop in the availability of credit. This is not really surprising because, as Kindleberger notes, "every mania (a situation in which capital investors are caught in a growing, self-reinforcing wave of asset price rises, which create incentives for speculation) has been associated with the expansion of credit."[13] A gradual but accelerating fall in the supply of foreign credit, however, started in the second quarter of 1928.

Global Imbalances and the Wall Street Bust

While the US economy had been booming in the second half of the 1920s, European and Asian economies fell into recession. Great Britain's economy slowed down dramatically after Winston Churchill, then Chancellor of the Exchequer, readopted the gold standard in 1925. The continental economies were sluggish, and uncertainty reigned, due to the draconian war reparations that the victors had imposed on Germany at Versailles. Moreover, it was not only Europe's economic growth that was seriously slowing down by the second half of the 1920s. Countries or colonies whose growth relied on the export of commodities and raw materials—which included most of those in Asia and Africa, as well as in Latin America—suffered a serious slowdown starting in 1928.

This slowdown was due to a global crisis from an oversupply of commodities and raw materials, which was caused by the continued operation of wartime production levels in a postwar international economic environment. Exporters of raw materials around the world continued to increase their annual production of agricultural, mining, and energy products in the 1920s as if they still had to satisfy an abnormally high and growing demand for such commodities. In fact, these three sectors started expanding after the war even in Europe and America, and the end result was that by the late 1920s there was a global oversupply in the commodity markets. As a consequence, commodity prices started falling, and this adversely affected the terms of trade and the growth potential of the commodity-exporting countries on the periphery, especially in Latin America.

As the rest of the world's economies slowed down in the late 1920s, the United States continued to boom. The economic mismatch between the US economy as creditor and the rest of the world as debtor accentuated the financial pressures that ended up causing Wall Street's collapse in the last quarter of 1929. (The global imbalances of the first decade of the 2000s were similar, except that they were characterized by growing current account surpluses and an aggressive accumulation of foreign reserves in China, Japan, South Korea, and the oil-exporting countries, counterbalanced by a steep rise in US trade and fiscal deficits.)

How did the 1929 collapse happen? The American boom attracted capital from the slowdown occurring outside the United States. Such capital repatriation created and fed the bull market in Wall Street that led to the Dow Jones Industrial Average almost doubling between early 1928 and September 1929. Given that US capital had fueled global growth in the 1920s, its return to New York "turned a mild recession elsewhere into a full-fledged crisis."[14] As US credit dried up, European and Latin American countries turned to short-term borrowing to keep meeting their obligations and financing their growing current account deficits.[15] Yet as investment positions continued to be liquidated overseas and invested back in New York's bull market, their prices kept falling and borrowers found it increasingly difficult to meet their short-term debt obligations.

The trigger for the 1929 collapse was the paralysis of the credit system, reached in October of that year, "because declines in the prices of many commodities and goods caused many borrowers to default on their loans."[16] In fact, this process was not unlike the growing mortgage default rates in the US subprime markets that started in 2007 and accelerated in 2008, leading to the toppling of once mighty deposit and investment banks in the United States and several Western European countries, and morphed into the now infamous Great Recession. The multiplication of suspended loan payments led to a deterioration in market sentiment and a pullback in further credit expansion. Central bankers now identify such periodic credit pullouts as part and parcel of the pro-cyclicality (rising asset values lead to more lending, while falling values lead to credit retrenchment) that "is embedded in the supply side of the markets-based financial system."[17]

Severity and Duration of the Great Depression

As leading scholars have noted, the stock market bust of 1929 need not have ended in the Great Depression.[18] It was only the absence of early countercyclical economic policy measures that set the scene for the transformation of an aggressive financial crisis into the onset of the deepest, longest, and most widespread depression of the twentieth century. Even contemporary critics who have questioned the achievements of state-led economic policy in the 1930s under the New Deal in the United States concur that debt deflation was one of the major causes of worsening conditions.[19] By early 1931, the self-reinforcing logic of deflation led to panic among both small and big savers; this triggered runs on banks, which, like falling dominoes, transformed financial difficulties into currency crises around the world. This process started in Europe—where the contagion spread from Austria to all Eastern European countries, Germany, Great Britain, and France—and then passed from Europe to the United States and Latin America in the second half of 1931. It was this process, rather than the Wall Street bust of October 1929, that caused the systemic crisis that then led to the severe breakdown of international financial and economic systems. The magnitude of this seizure is apparent if we contrast the four national banking crises around the world in the years 1924–29 with the thirty-three that occurred in 1929–34.[20]

GREAT DEPRESSION IN THE SOUTHERN CONE COUNTRIES

The democratic cause had more to win than to lose in Latin America when the Wall Street stock market collapsed on October 24, 1929. This had little to do with the inherent strength of democracy per se, and much to do, paradoxically, with its weakness. Back then there were only two democracies in Latin America—Argentina and Uruguay—while the rest of the countries in the region were ruled either by oligarchic or authoritarian regimes of different stripes. The strength of the democratic cause stemmed more from its potential than its reality.

The good news for democrats was that all the non-democratic regimes would have to find effective ways of dealing with the social and political consequences of the economic crisis, and that the worse living conditions became for Latin American populations, the better their chances would be of promoting democracy as an alternative to the non-democratic incumbents. As it turned out, however, the only two democracies in the region broke down—Argentina's on September 6, 1930, and Uruguay's on March 31, 1933. It would take a different type of international conflagration, the Second World War, for democratic regimes to be restored in these two countries (in Uruguay in 1942 and in Argentina in 1946) and to be installed in other nations in the region.

Chile was the only country in Latin America during the Great Depression that was able to shed an authoritarian regime (General Ibáñez was ousted on July 27, 1931) and, after a convoluted period that included a short-lived Socialist Republic, to successfully give birth to a democratic regime (after Arturo Alessandri was elected for a second time to the presidency on October 30, 1932). Democracy went on to rule uninterruptedly in Chile and Uruguay until 1973, when it broke down again in both countries. In sharp contrast, democracy in Argentina broke down in 1955, and thereafter civilian and military regimes alternated in power until 1983.

Following the discussion about recessions and depressions in chapter 1, figure 2.1 shows that the three Southern Cone countries experienced depressions in the early 1930s. (The annual GDP growth rates of Argentina, Uruguay, and Chile between 1927 and 1940 are given in 1970 purchasing power parity dollars.) Argentina's annual GDP growth, while it did not contract by 10% or more

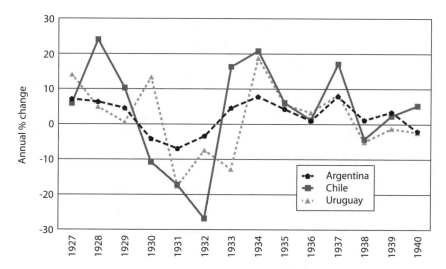

Figure 2.1. Growth trajectories in the Southern Cone economies, 1927–40

Source: Based on data from the *Oxford Latin American Economic History Database*, http://oxlad.qeh.ox.ac.uk/ search.php [accessed July 7, 2009].

in any of these years, experienced a four-year decline. Uruguay, while avoiding a decline of three years or more, suffered an annual contraction of GDP that was greater than 10% between 1930 and 1931. Chile's boom-and-bust growth trajectory in the years immediately before and after the 1929 shock illustrates the dramatic reversal of fortune it faced, due to its close financial links to the US economy (see chapters 3 and 4). Chile qualifies for a depression on both counts: three or more years of continued GDP decline, and a fall in annual product greater than 10%. The trough in growth for Argentina and Uruguay was 1931, and for Chile, 1932. This means that the regime changes we are studying within the Great Depression period occurred before the low point was reached in Argentina and Chile, but not in Uruguay. When compared with the annual GDP growth trajectories of the subsequent economic shocks/crises examined in this work, the 1930s remains in a class of its own. After the 1930s the evolution of annual growth in the Southern Cone countries varied substantially, but the troughs and peaks remained within −10% to +10% annual growth rates (see figures 6.1 and 6.2). It is as if the application of Keynesian reflationary policy since the 1930s narrowed the variation in economic activity without allowing (at least until now) a repeat of the Great Depression.

Foreign investors stayed away from Latin America in general and the Southern Cone countries in particular during the early years of the Depression, whose low point in the region was the year 1932. Reflationary economic policy enacted by the governments in the three countries thereafter helped to generate demand and kick-start their economies. A gradual recuperation in international economic activity after 1933 and, for Argentina and Uruguay, securing access for their beef exports to their main market, Great Britain, contributed to the economic turnaround.[21] Thereafter, foreign investment returned to the region, which helped to spark a seesaw type of economic recovery, characterized by a boom that led to a new peak in economic activity in the three countries in 1934, and thereafter to at least positive annual growth until 1937.[22] By 1938, a new international economic downturn hit foreign flows to Latin America, and most economies suffered a prolonged slowdown. Chile experienced negative growth in 1938, Argentina in 1940, and Uruguay throughout 1938–40. It took the start of the Second World War in September 1939, and particularly the entry of the United States into the theater of war in December 1941, to produce the international shocks that created a surge in demand for raw commodities that helped the Latin American economies, including the Southern Cone ones, turn their back definitively on the Depression.

CHAPTER THREE

Institutions

Polarized Domestic Conflicts and
Weak International Capacity

When the 1929 financial crisis struck, Chile was ruled by an authoritarian regime under Colonel/General Carlos Ibáñez (1927–31),[1] while Argentina and Uruguay were ruled by democratic regimes since 1916 and 1918, respectively. The inability of these governments to cope with the severity of the socioeconomic dislocations and political conflicts produced by the Great Depression led to the fall of the incumbent political regimes in all three countries—irrespective of their democratic or non-democratic form. Chile shed an authoritarian regime and was able to build a democracy during the Great Depression, while Argentina and Uruguay experienced the death of their democracies, which were replaced by authoritarian regimes.

Accounting for a common historical sequence of events in different countries is intellectually relevant, because it sheds light on the thorny issue of the direction of causality, which remains one of the central fault lines of debate between the social science scholars who use quantitative methods of inquiry and those who use qualitative ones. In the context of the Great Depression, the commonality for the Southern Cone countries—the shift in regime types—in no way ensures causation, but it raises its likelihood by showing that this sequence of events happened in three countries that, despite their common traits (early industrialization and democratization, in a Latin American context), were also quite different in terms of their size, material endowments, production structures, political institutions, and historical experience.

The main weakness of this explanation, however, is that it cannot account for either the variations in the pressures for and against democracy unleashed by the economic shock and crises of the 1930s or for the extent to which such variations contributed to the regime changes. It must be qualified and refined to yield a more nuanced understanding of the impact that specific domestic and international pressures for and against democracy had in shaping the breakdown of democracy and the construction of authoritarian regimes in Argentina and Uruguay and the breakdown of authoritarianism and the transition to democracy in Chile between 1930 and 1933.

DOMESTIC INSTITUTIONS-AS-RULES

The three countries had presidential forms of government on the eve of the Great Depression, but their constitutions contained very different rules about the way government should be organized, how it should operate, the way power should be contested electorally, and the territorial division of power.

Argentina

The largest country in the Southern Cone had an electoral system that favored the creation of artificial majorities through the use of first-past-the post, similar to that in Great Britain and the United States, but with the added rule that it assigned two-thirds of the lower house seats to the winning party and the remaining one-third of the seats to the runner-up. A president whose party had a majority in the lower chamber was potentially a force to be reckoned with.

The provincial oligarchies retained substantial autonomy from the central government, thanks to Argentina's federalism, a system enshrined in the country's 1853 constitution and its successive revisions. Provincial governors retained ample legal powers that, combined with the historical tradition of *caudillismo* (rule by strongmen) that developed since the wars of independence against Spain in the 1810s, allowed provincial elites to preserve and advance their privileges and power, because more often than not governors were members of the tightly knit politicoeconomic families that dominated life in the peripheral regions, away from the capitol. The degree of provincial autonomy was somewhat curtailed, because Argentine presidents tended to be influential in picking governors in many provinces.[2] Still, control of the Senate was an important institutional concession that enhanced the power that regional elites could exercise at the federal level, given the constitution's prescription whereby senators were elected by the provincial legislatures (dominated by the governors' henchmen). Thus the upper chamber remained a bastion of conservatism and a defender of the different provincial elites' interests. These interests were not necessarily similar, which meant that the Senate did not find it easy to bring its disparate members together to work proactively. Nonetheless, it was a powerful reactive force, because as long as a third of its members opposed any given law coming from the lower chamber or the president's office, it could stop it dead in its tracks.

The constitution did grant the federal executive a direct tool to check the power of provincial governments, as it allowed the president of the republic to issue an *intervención*, or intervention, (a clause copied from the US Constitution where, however, it was hardly used[3]) against a provincial government, on the grounds of national security. When called, *intervenciones* led to the suspension of provincial government authorities during the emergency period. Instead, a presidential envoy would run the province. Although used by presidents in the second half of the nineteenth century and first years of the twentieth, the Radical presidents, particularly Yrigoyen, resorted to federal *intervenciones* much more frequently than their predecessors. This was one of the reasons that helped convince the landowning elites and their allies in the armed forces that the existing political system (an electoral democratic regime) had come to represent a growing threat to the socioeconomic order.[4]

Argentina's political parties operated under a dominant party system led by the Radical Party (UCR), although this party was divided between the *personalistas*, who supported President Hipólito Yrigoyen's populism and winner-take-all governing style (he was president twice, in 1916–1922 and 1928–1930), and the *anti-personalistas*, who were pro-establishment. The *anti-personalistas* were led by Marcelo T. Alvear, whose family belonged to the oligarchy; he was president in 1922–28. The most distinctive feature of the Argentine party system was that, despite the strength and power of the country's oligarchy, its interests were not served by a strong national party. Rather, a collection of provincial conservative parties represented the interests of the local oligarchies. Authors such as Edward Gibson have emphasized the absence of a strong national party supporting their interests as a cause of the elites' repeated tendency to seek military support to overthrow their popularly elected adversaries.[5]

Socialists were divided between independents, who were moderates, and communists, who did not possess a mass following and were made up of middle-class intellectuals. Their influence was felt in the spheres of education and culture. Therefore it was more ideological than directly political, in the sense that the socialists had few representatives in the federal and provincial governments and therefore only weak bargaining power in shaping policy.

By the time Yrigoyen was elected for a second (nonconcurrent) presidential term in 1928, his party not only comfortably dominated the Chamber of Deputies, but was also pushing to overturn the provincial oligarchies' majority in the Senate. In the congressional elections of March 1930, the *personalista* Radicals tried to overturn the opposition's majority in the upper chamber by withholding recognition from the elected provincial conservative candidates from Mendoza and San Juan. For the provincial elites, this new instance of interference was even more outrageous than Yrigoyen's previous federal *intervenciones*, which he had resorted to repeatedly. *Intervenciones* at least were mandated by the constitution. Not recognizing legislators who had legitimately won elections was a blunt, heavy-handed political maneuver by President Yrigoyen to try to overcome at any cost the last institutional means the conservative opposition possessed to check the power of the federal executive. Although other factors came into play (such as Yrigoyen's apparent senility during his second presidency, or the populist urban political machine that he created, which kept expanding and demanding larger slices of the national income), the potential loss of control of the Senate—the last bastion of the conservative opposition to short-circuit national executive action—helped to crystallize the resolve of those calling for the fall of democracy. This broad opposition was probably not so much against democracy per se as a political regime, but rather against what the practice of democracy had become in Argentina under Yrigoyen. As a consequence, political and social polarizations had generated so much momentum that by 1929–30, democracy was on its last legs.[6] After the conflict over the congressional elections of 1930, the opposition gave up trying to check and contain Yrigoyen's power through institutional means. Thereafter, a growing chorus of civilian and military voices started demanding the president's overthrow.

Fear of a more centralized, more powerful presidency was reinforced by another feature of the Argentine governmental system, its tendency toward the personalization of power in the presidency. One of the Radicals' main critiques about the pre-1912 oligarchic system had been the concentration of power in *caudillo* presidents such as Julio Roca (1880–86 and 1898–1904). However, once in power, the Radicals were unable to check Yrigoyen's populism, his concentration of power, and his behavior (like the *caudillos* of old): rewarding his party supporters and alienating those who questioned his policies; intervening in provincial governments; and bypassing the armed forces' high command to advance officers who supported him, to the detriment of the military's professional criteria.[7] This was the root cause of the split in the Radical Party between *personalistas* and *anti-personalistas*. It was also at the heart of the elite's fear about *yrigoyenismo* in 1930, which led to the informal military-civilian alliance that toppled Argentina's democracy, a system they had come to think of as a populist tyranny.

Uruguay

The smallest Southern Cone country's electoral and party systems, along with its peculiar national executive branch, tempered the possibility of artificial majorities and, therefore, of winner-take-all politics, as had happened in Argentina. Uruguay's system was also based on full male suffrage, but it assigned legislative seats in both chambers on the basis of proportional representation, while the executive branch was run on the principle of coparticipation. The idiosyncratic system of coparticipation was institutionalized as a result of a settlement between the leaders of the country's two main parties, José Batlle y Ordóñez of the Partido Colorado and Luis Alberto de Herrera of the Partido Nacional, also known as Partido Blanco. This settlement allowed the creation of the 1918–19 constitution, whose main innovation was the formation of a collegial executive, or *colegiado*, following the Swiss example. This executive was made up of a president, who was popularly elected and in charge of foreign relations, external security, and internal order; and a Consejo Nacional de Administración (CNA), a nine-member body, also popularly elected, that was in charge of economic and social policies. The winning party automatically got two-thirds of the seats in the CNA, while the runner-up was allocated the remaining one-third. This system ensured that the opposition participated in the executive branch.

Batlle y Ordóñez had designed this system to lock in his pioneering socio-economic and nationalist reforms during his second presidency (1911–15; the first one was in 1903–7), which created the first welfare state in Latin America. By dividing the executive branch, Batlle y Ordóñez tried to ensure that no future president could unilaterally reverse these reforms. A collegial executive forced its members to deliberate and work out their differences before policy change could be enacted. Moreover, governmental coparticipation provided a source of patronage only for those parties represented in the CNA (the Colorado and Blanco parties), whose members were in charge of appointments; while it strengthened Uruguay's two-party system, it was detrimental to third parties.

Uruguay's electoral law was the other factor that helped to cement a two-party system. Introduced in 1910, the country's double-simultaneous-vote system was similar to holding a primary and a general election at the same time. Candidates within each of the parties could present their own candidates' lists (known as *sublemas*) and voters cast their votes for one of the lists. The votes for the different *sublemas* of each party (known as a *lema*) were then added together, and the winner was the candidate of the *sublema* that received the highest number of votes within the party whose *sublemas*' votes, once added together, also yielded the greatest number of overall votes. This system created incentives for the different factions of each of the parties to stay together, because the outcome of elections depended on adding the votes of all the *sublemas* under each *lema*. However, it also promoted factionalism, because party members were encouraged to form their own *sublemas* as an intraparty bargaining tool. Given that the Colorado and Blanco parties were evenly matched and the margins of electoral victories were small throughout the 1920s, leaders of *sublemas* that had received even a small number of votes could muster influence and negotiate concessions by threatening to remove their *sublema* from the final vote for the *lema*, which could jeopardize victory for their party. The end result was substantial intraparty fragmentation.[8]

In general the Colorados were more progressive and the Blancos were more conservative, but some Colorado factions were less progressive than some of the less conservative Blanco factions, while some Blanco factions were less conservative than some of the less progressive Colorado factions. The parties were therefore not highly ideological, and their social bases were made up of multiclass coalitions. Entrenched bipartisan competition was the norm in Uruguay, but the socialists—and especially the communists—were well established, thanks to a solid early presence among organized workers, intellectuals, and students. Their influence was evident in several areas: helping to organize trade unions, having a strong presence in labor markets, and remaining independent from either of the two main parties. The Uruguayan Left also had a significant role in shaping the discourse on higher education. It was a strong Left, given the Latin American context, but its main sources of power were still in the economic and social spheres rather than in the political sphere—at least in terms of electoral competition. The Left in Uruguay (as in Argentina) remained weaker than in Chile.[9]

Unlike Argentina, Uruguay had a unitary territorial division of power, made up of the capital city, Montevideo, and nineteen departments. The center/periphery and urban/rural cleavages were nonetheless as prevalent in Uruguay as in neighboring Argentina. Although both Blancos and Colorados had support in the countryside, adherents of the former tended to come from the more traditional and paternalistic landowners who still supported *caudillo* traits, while proponents of the latter came from landowners who believed in modernization, wanted to industrialize their sector by constructing meat-freezing plants (*frigoríficos*), and expected an aggressive expansion of their exports to the British market. In short, Colorado-supporting landowners saw themselves, as one scholar put it, more as businessmen than as seigneurial patrons.[10] Batlle y Ordóñez's Colorados, in turn, secured the backing of fast-growing Montevideo, thanks to high immigration rates from southern Europe in the early twentieth century.

This expanding urban support for Batlle y Ordóñez's modernization—nationalist, industrial, secular politics with a strong sense of social justice in their firm commitment to the redistribution of resources and opportunities—came head to head with both Blanco and Colorado factions in the countryside, who opposed *batllismo*. The seeds of irreconcilable conflict were sown in 1931 after the *batllista* and the *anti-herrerista* wings of the Colorado and Blanco parties, respectively, struck a deal "to expand the state through the creation of the Administración Nacional de Combustibles, Alcoholes y Portland—ANCAP [see chapter 4]—and secured the distribution of directive jobs in the growing public corporations for their political followers. . . . This was known as *el pacto del chinchulín* [the pork barrel pact]."[11] This pact strengthened the patronage and clientele power of the party factions that opposed both President Gabriel Terra of the Colorados (an anti-*batllista*) and Luis Alberto de Herrera, the patriarch of the most conservative and traditionalist Blancos, which emboldened these two leaders to forge their own informal alliance. In effect, a Colorado-Blanco coalition ended up fighting another Colorado-Blanco coalition, and the end result was the collapse of democracy in 1933.

Herrera used the 1931–33 economic collapse—which had created widespread discontent in Uruguay (as elsewhere)—to argue that the collegial executive was too cumbersome a decision-making mechanism to formulate the fast and radical policy changes the country needed to overcome the economic crisis of the early 1930s.[12] Such justification for a regime change was a sham, because the national government had implemented countercyclical policies to combat the economic crisis since 1931. President Terra used Herrera's argument as one of the justifications for the *autogolpe* (a duly elected leader taking on emergency powers above and beyond those normally granted to him or her) that he executed on March 31, 1931. In reality, the substance behind the coup was the *terrista-herrerista* alliance that was formed to counteract the growing patronage power of rival factions in their own parties. An important facet that also brought

Terra and Herrera together was their mutual opposition to and desire to put a stop to the rising influence of *batllismo* (a style of economic policy that prized the statization of increasing sectors of the national economy), especially since state-led solutions to the Great Depression were exactly the policies that leaders of advanced capitalist countries like Great Britain, the United States, and continental Europe embraced in the wake of the 1931 international banking crisis.

President Terra's personal ambition was an element in his coup, as well as the fact that a majority in the president's own party—the *batllista* Colorados—opposed his intention to stop the march of state-led socioeconomic modernization. This meant that the president could not count on majorities in the legislature to carry out his program.[13] After the coup, Terra assumed sole authority and crafted a new constitution, which was secured in 1934, along with Terra's reelection. This constitution eliminated the dual executive and gave the Terra-Herrera alliance an additional lease on power, until 1938.[14]

In Uruguay, as in Argentina, the nature of the country's existing political institutions was used to justify a coup against democracy in 1933. Herrera's and Terra's argument used the supposedly cumbersome decision-making process embedded in the multimember CNA to justify the cancellation of Uruguay's constitutional process. Likewise, in Argentina the traditional landowning elites feared that the country's majoritarian electoral system, coupled with the growing urban party machine that Yrigoyen had developed, would lead to their complete exclusion from decision making and therefore from domination of the policy process—particularly if the Radicals secured a majority in the Senate. Such fears were justified in the case of Argentina, where a Radical majority in the Senate would have erased the last sector where the conservative opposition could check the power of the federal executive; but they were not relevant to the situation in Uruguay, because the CNA had been implementing countercyclical economic policies since 1931. The proliferation of political conflict generated in part by institutions-as-rules in Uruguay, was due to the double-simultaneous-vote electoral system, which allowed the president to face crippling opposition to the implementation of his government program both in the legislature (by legislators from his own party as well as by those from the main opposition party) and in the executive branch (where one-third of the seats in the CNA were allocated to the opposition).

Chile

Unlike Argentina and Uruguay, where democracies succumbed during the economic crisis of the early 1930s, Chile was ruled by an authoritarian regime. In common with the other two countries however, this regime also was done in after General Ibáñez was forced to resign on July 26, 1931. Ibáñez's rule, although nominally based on the country's 1925 constitution (Ibáñez was elected to office by a special election held in May 1927, and Congress still functioned throughout his tenure), was dictatorial rather than democratic. His government demanded and obtained decrete powers, and Congress delegated some of its most important functions to the president's cabinet. Ibáñez's government was not based on a party or a coalition of parties. Instead, his style of leadership and his government were nationalist and populist. This meant that he railed against the conservative-dominated status quo and promised reforms that would lead to more socioeconomic inclusion and development. Ibáñez built significant labor support by using the Labor Code that the conservative-dominated Congress had been forced to pass in 1924, due to the intervention of the military. In exchange, the General demanded order and acquiescence; when it came to basic civil and political rights, he did not hesitate to institute press censorship, the banishment of opposition politicians, the repression and then the outlawing of the Communist Party, and coercion of the organized labor movement to force it into state-sanctioned unions that were vertically controlled.[15]

The 1925 constitution was restored after Ibáñez was toppled (although the turmoil that ensued between mid-1931 and late 1932 meant that stable constitutional rule was not guaranteed until after the election of former president Arturo Alessandri on October 30, 1932). The electoral system set up in the 1925 constitution was based on proportional representation, so the likelihood of winner-take-all politics in Chile, as in Uruguay, was lower than in Argentina. Moreover, Chile's voter participation was limited by literacy requirements (see chapter 1). In contrast to Argentina and Uruguay, Chile was effectively a limited democracy where, as Simon Collier and William F. Sater note, the "electorate did not seriously expand much before the 1960s."[16] Even if a proportion of the poor could read and write, those living in the countryside voted for conservative parties more often than not, because, as these authors observe, "the venerable tradition of vote buying continued until well into the 1950s." The big landowners exercised strong vertical control over peasants, and they lobbied governments successfully to ensure that electoral districts remained the same, regardless of population changes. The end result was that urban areas, where the leftist and centrist parties were stronger, remained underrepresented.

Like Uruguay, Chile's territorial division of power followed the unitary model. Similar to both Argentina and Uruguay, Chile's main political fault lines were also the center/periphery and urban/rural cleavages. Of these, the center/periphery split was more influential in deciding the balance of power in Chilean politics. Even though the remote northern and southern regions were the engines of export growth, and therefore of the country's economic expansion, most central governmental resources were spent in the burgeoning cities of Santiago and Valparaíso. It was therefore no surprise that, "benefiting from popular resentment of exploitation by the urban and rural elites of the central region, the Left's presidential candidates—in 1938, 1946, and 1958—registered their highest percentages of the ballots in the distant northern and southern provinces."[17]

Another feature that was central to deciding the balance of power in Chilean politics was the country's party system, correctly identified by many authors as the backbone of Chilean society.[18] The country boasted the liveliest multiparty system in Latin America in the early twentieth century, and, starting in 1932, its legislature had members from parties across the political spectrum, ranging from the Far Left to the Far Right. The main parties were the Radicals, the Liberals, and the Conservatives, as well as splinter groups from the last two parties, the Democrats and the Nationalists, respectively. An offshoot of the Conservatives—a subgroup whose members followed the Catholic Church's social doctrine—formed the Falange Nacional toward the end of the crisis-ridden 1930s. While this movement was not prominent electorally early on in its life (it was founded in 1938), it was one of the seeds of the party that came to dominate the centrists in Chile, the Partido Democracia Cristiana.

On the Left, Chile had relatively strong Socialist and Communist parties. Support for the Left was concentrated in the cities and the mining region in the north. In stark contrast to Argentina and Uruguay, the leftist parties in Chile had a broader appeal and mobilized workers much more effectively than their counterparts. An important difference among the leaders of the Left in the Southern Cone countries was that, while a majority of them were foreign-born individuals (primarily from southern Europe) who had emigrated to Argentina and Uruguay, where they became active in social and political organization and action, the bulk of their Chilean counterparts were native-born individuals, most of whom had become active in politics through the organization and mobilization of workers in the mining industry. The governments in Argentina and Uruguay defanged their respective labor movements through the deportation of foreign-born anarchists and other radical labor leaders, but this was not the case in Chile, which had a preponderance of native-born workers and their leaders. Therefore, left-wing leaders and movements in Chile continued to espouse more combative, less conciliatory positions in the 1920s and 1930s than their counterparts in Argentina and Uruguay (see chapter 4).[19]

Despite the relative prevalence of polarization in Chile's political culture, the historical precedent under the oligarchic regime known as the República Parlamentaria, or Parliamentary Republic (1891–1924)—where governments were generally made up of multiparty coalitions—also dominated the post-1932 presidential system, at least until the late 1950s. The structure of government was therefore more pluralist in Chile than in Argentina, and less clearly divided into two camps that shared the spoils, as in Uruguay. Even though the Chilean president's survival did not depend on majority support in the legislature, withdrawal of this support by parties that had originally pledged it meant that the president would find it very difficult to implement his program once his party was in the minority in Congress. The system seemed to force stasis and compromise. Therefore Chile had no fear of a winner-take-all system in which the presidency might not be checked by any institutional means, as was potentially the case in Argentina after the 1930 congressional elections. Nor did a sitting Chilean president face lame-duck status due to harsh opposition from his own party's legislators, as was the case for Terra in Uruguay in 1932–33.

Even though Chile and Uruguay had leaders who appealed to and governed in a populist direction (some scholars consider President Batlle y Ordóñez as a precursor—along with President Yrigoyen in Argentina and President Billinghurst in Peru—of 1920s–30s populism, while in Chile Presidents Alessandri and Ibáñez, and the leaders of the Socialist Republic between 1920 and 1932, such as Marmaduke Grove, had significant populist elements),[20] electoral rules and organizations channeled popular demands in an institutional direction through competitive, deeply rooted, multiparty systems.

In sharp contrast, in Argentina electoral disputes and the exercise of power developed in a personalist direction under President Yrigoyen and later under the quintessentially classic populist leader Juan Domingo Perón (who ruled in 1946–55 and 1973–74). This critical difference, planted and developed between the late 1910s and the early 1930s, had a structural, long-lasting effect that has been repeated time and again when these three Southern Cone countries have faced harsh financial shocks and economic crises. On the one hand, Chile and Uruguay formalized contestation through competitive multiparty systems, which has allowed these countries to process the acute distributional conflicts typical of harsh crises in an institutional direction, one subject to preestablished rules, procedures, and calendars. Argentina, on the other hand, has followed a zigzagging trajectory, where the process of contestation became personalized in the figure of the *jefe en turno* (current boss) since President Yrigoyen's first presidency. Especially during harsh economic shocks and crises, using such a personalized channel as the main means of handling elite and popular contestation short circuited, leading to an alternation of successive civilian-military regimes between 1930 and 1983. Democracy in Argentina since then has remained subject to the personalization of power in the figure of the president-in-turn, where an ineffectual capacity to manage severe, complex crises has resulted in two interrupted presidencies (in 1989 and 2001) amid social and economic chaos.

Chile's and Uruguay's highly institutionalized politics versus Argentina's personalized political process is a key difference between the three countries. While the structural changes in their institutions/interests/ideas (see the introduction and chapter 1), have raised the likelihood of democratic regime survival in periods of harsh economic crises, this basic institutional difference still lingers, making governability during such crises much more uncertain in Argentina than in Chile and Uruguay.

DOMESTIC INSTITUTIONS-AS-ORGANIZATIONS

The Chilean elites were as alarmed, if not more so, by the Depression as their Argentine and Uruguayan counterparts. After all, Chile was the country in the Western Hemisphere (along with Cuba) that was most deeply affected by the 1929 financial crisis and its aftermath.[21] The fall of authoritarianism after the economic shock hit, followed by the construction of what became a long-lived democratic regime in Chile—in contrast to what happened elsewhere—has to do with a key difference in what I call the realm of institutions-as-organizations: the role of the armed forces, in particular of elites' opposition to or support for a military takeover, as well as the internal unity or disunity of the armed forces themselves.

Argentina

The armed forces had expressed growing concern about the rise of left-wing politics since the strikes and workers' unrest that culminated in the 1919 *semana trágica*. This foundational confrontation in Argentina between organized workers and right-wing paramilitary organizations started as a labor dispute—in the context of a depressed international economy after the First World War—that became violent and spread through Buenos Aires. The capital was a no-man's-land for one week before the military reimposed order.[22] The clashes left about seven hundred dead and four thousand injured. Such large-scale violence traumatized the upper and upper middle classes in Buenos Aires. Equally critically, the military ended up having to clamp down and purge its own ranks.[23] Some military officers and rank-and-file troops started identifying with the plight of the working classes after the *semana trágica*, and radical activity (such as the formation of "soviets") was discovered and suppressed in at least two garrisons.[24] Therefore, a faction of the Argentine armed forces believed that the priorities of the military were quashing any dissent among their own ranks, defeating communists (particularly in light of the triumphant Soviet revolution in Russia in October 1917), and checking the spread of other international influences, including Anglo-American liberal capitalism. Their models were Primo de Rivera's and Mussolini's takeovers in Spain and Italy, respectively. The ultimate aim of the *nacionalistas*, as they were known, was to install a corporatist regime based on functional (rather than individual) participation and representation. General José Félix Uriburu (the leader of 1930 coup) was a prominent representative of this group.[25]

Another faction in the Argentine armed forces was more traditionally conservative, in the sense that its members looked back to the years of oligarchic rule prior to Yrigoyen's first presidency (1916–22), when elections based on political parties and individual voting were the norm, but the oligarchy's political domination was ensured through their control of the electoral process. In keeping with their support for the *status quo ante*, these military personnel were internationalist in economic outlook and continued to champion Argentina's primary exports-led growth and the long-term alliance between British capitalists and major Argentine landowners. Their undisputed leader was General Agustín P. Justo, himself a scion of an old aristocratic family. Crucially, General Justo served as the Minister of War in the government of President Alvear (1922–28), the leader of the *anti-personalista* faction of the Radical Party who, like Justo, was concerned about Yrigoyen's populism and patronage-driven politics. General Justo and the oligarchy that supported him agreed with the *nacionalistas* that *la marea roja* (the Red tide) had to be stopped; that worker activism and radical politics had to be tamed and controlled by the state; and, if these objectives could not be carried out, that these movements should be repressed and destroyed.

The provincial oligarchies and the capital city's elites and upper middle classes felt reassured that the two main factions in the armed forces believed in the control—legal or otherwise—of pressures from below. They were uncertain, however, about the creation of a corporatist regime along the lines of what Uriburu's *nacionalistas* wanted, because this would mean a substantial concentration of power in the armed forces, and the potential emergence of a charismatic leader like Mussolini. Instead, the Argentine elites wanted to go back to the past, a period of liberal oligarchic rule in which a growing international orientation for the country's food-exporting economy combined snuggly with the landowning provincial elites' control of elections and, therefore, of Argentina's politics.

Soon after General Uriburu's successful coup on September 6, 1930, the *nacionalistas* tried testing how broad their popular support was before launching their corporatist vision. They permitted elections in Buenos Aires province to go ahead in April 1931. The *nacionalistas* expected that the citizenry would support their transformational right-wing agenda. Instead, the Radicals won the election, and the military regime responded by nullifying the vote. Shunned by the public, General Uriburu's attempt to create a fascist regime did not prosper. He stepped down in favor of General Justo, who assumed the presidency after winning elections in November 1931, with the Radicals abstaining from participating in them. General Uriburu and the nationalists ruled under a state of emergency, while General Justo and the traditional conservatives returned to constitutional rule. Not only had General Justo's government dropped the idea of creating a corporatist regime but, through constitutionalism, it also restored the oligarchy's political and economic powers by resorting to a game of rigged elections. This is how the conservative civil-military alliance that would run the country between 1932 and 1943 (during the *década infame*) was put in place.

In short, the leading factions in the Argentine armed forces were right wing, one traditional and the other corporatist. Like the country's landowning elites, the leaders of both military factions were concerned with protest from below, particularly since the events of the *semana trágica*, and they wanted to clamp down on it. The end result was that after the military deposed President Yrigoyen, and particularly once the *nacionalistas* yielded the control of power to General Justo and the traditional conservatives at the end of 1931, there was a stretch where there was a communion of interests, values, and outlook among Argentina's socioeconomic elites and its military-backed rulers.

Chile

The armed forces in Chile became the main arbiters of the distributive conflict among the elites in the 1920s. On the one hand, the traditional aristocratic, land-based conservatives supported the status quo through the continuation of the Parliamentary Republic. On the other hand the reformists, headed by President Arturo Alessandri, whom some scholars (such as Paul Drake) have dubbed a populist precursor during his first term in office (1920–24/25),[26] advocated redistributive social reform to defuse pressures from below. In marked contrast to their Argentine peers, the Chilean armed forces were significantly divided. Adherents of both Marxism and fascism could be found within the ranks, and internal military divisions and conflict gave way to ruptures and open conflict in the years 1924–27 and 1931–32.[27]

Time and again Congress vetoed presidential proposals to amend the constitution so that a social reform package could be implemented. The armed forces intervened to break the deadlock in September 1924. They deposed President Alessandri but forced Congress to adopt his reform proposals, which became a watershed in terms of the legal empowerment of workers and the poor. The 1924 Labor Code was the seminal legal contribution in instituting basic social rights in the country: the prohibition of child labor; the creation of eight-hour workdays; the legalization of trade unions; and the formation of mechanisms for collective bargaining, occupational safety measures, and the settlement of industrial dispute. The military also passed an income tax law (absent before then) and demanded better wages and working conditions for the military. Institutionally, the legal reforms enacted by the military in Chile in 1924 were a watershed.

The armed forces' high command, more conservative in outlook than the younger officers who supported social reforms, tried to return power to the parliamentary elites. In reaction, the younger, left-leaning officers, such as Colonel Marmaduke Grove and Major Carlos Ibáñez, led a countercoup against their more conservative superiors and deposed the junta in January 1925. The reformist junior officers invited Alessandri to return from exile in Italy to finish off his presidential term, and they pledged to support his reforms. The scene was set for the passage of the 1925 constitution, which reinstated a presidential system where executive-sponsored redistribution to workers and the poor was much easier than under the previous oligarchic, parliament-dominated system that had thwarted social mobility and progressive redistribution.[28] Along with redistribution, the constitution facilitated the enactment of social legislation and state arbitration, all of which Colonel/General Ibáñez promoted assiduously and carried through quite comprehensively during his years of dictatorial rule (between 1927 and 1931). A labor-supportive position gave President Ibáñez wide, genuine mass support in the boom economic years of 1928–29. Such support turned against him after the 1930 economic collapse and the end of state-led redistribution through high levels of public spending and public investment in infrastructure.[29]

After General Ibáñez was toppled in July 1931, civilian rule was reinstated after elections in October of the same year, which Juan Esteban Montero, backed by the establishment (Radicals, Liberals, and Conservatives), won by beating Alessandri. Plotting by the main political camps continued unabated. Both *alessandristas* and *ibañistas* attacked the new government by alleging that it did not have a plan to overcome the deep economic crisis the country was experiencing. The *ibañista* reformist military also feared that President Montero's government would help restore the oligarchy's privileges and power. As a consequence, the reformist military, headed by now Air Commodore Marmaduke Grove (also identified as a populist leader)[30] and General Arturo Puga toppled Montero's government in June 1932. They established a junta and declared the birth of a Socialist Republic. Early on, the armed forces supported this move, because widely popular officers like Grove and Puga were among the primary coup leaders. However, disagreements among the junta members regarding the extent to which socialist measures should be pursued (in the triumvirate, Grove and Matte were inclined toward Marxism, while Dávila favored statism), and fear among the right-leaning sectors of the armed forces and the civilian elites, soon led to renewed military intervention, a new coup, and the toppling of the socialist experiment in September 1932.

This extraordinary sequence of events (three regime changes between July 1931 and October 1932) convinced both civilian and military leaders that the armed forces' intervention in government had run its course. As Frederic Nunn puts it, "between Ibáñez' resignation in 1931 and Alessandri's election in 1932— 17 months in between—the armed forces dissipated the support given them by civilians between 1924 and 1931 and lost [the] respect of the civilian sector. . . . The military organization fell prey to individualistic ambitions, rivalries which convinced civilian and military leaders that the armed forces should remain obedient to the Constitution."[31]

After the military brought down the Socialist Republic in September 1932, power was transferred to General Bartolomé Blanche, an *ibañista*, who immediately scheduled elections for October to restore civilian rule. At this point distrust about the intentions of the high command (some feared Blanche might try to return power to General Ibáñez) were so pervasive that civic leaders, supported by several commanding officers (including the head of the army, General Pedro Vignola) demanded the immediate reestablishment of civilian rule, and forced Blanche to step down and transfer power to civilians (the president of the Supreme Court, Abraham Oyanedel, assumed the office) before the elections.[32] Arturo Alessandri went on to win the 1932 elections, inaugurating a civilian regime that operated uninterruptedly until General Augusto Pinochet's coup of September 1973.

The triumph of civilian rule and constitutionalism over military intervention amid a deep economic crisis in Chile is in stark contrast to the case of Argentina, where the 1930 military coup inaugurated a six-decade period in which the armed forces intervened time and again to depose civilian rule. Nothing was preordained to ensure that civilian rule would triumph in Chile, while it would be defeated repeatedly in Argentina. Civilian politicians and military leaders were certainly as power-hungry in Chile as they were in Argentina, as the plotting of *alessandristas* and *ibañistas* against the legally elected Montero government in 1931 shows. The crucial difference between the two countries was that, on the one hand, the elites in Chile feared the continuation of military involvement in politics, given their mixed and often poor record in power since 1924. "Progressive military officers had been involved in the coup of 1924–25, the fall of Ibáñez, and the declaration of a socialist republic in 1932, [all of which heightened the] elite's fear of the Left and strengthened its identification of revolution with the military."[33] On the other hand, the elites in Argentina did not face the threat of credible, sizeable, radical left-wing supporters in the country's armed forces, which were purged of left-wing officers in the early 1920s. In fact, the two leading factions in Argentina were right wing (one corporatist, the other traditional conservatives), and they both believed in clamping down on pressures from below. The elites therefore not only supported the military takeover in September 1930, but they established a close, informal, civil-military alliance during the presidency of General Justo, which allowed the oligarchy to remain as the dominant politicoeconomic power between 1932 and 1943.

In short, the decision to support or oppose democratic arrangements in Argentina (in 1930) and Chile (in 1931–32) hinged on what the military would do once in power. Faced with the potential creation of a right-wing corporatist regime, a broad spectrum of Argentine forces, which included traditional conservatives, democrats, and socialists, chose to oppose General Uriburu's nationalists. Instead, these forces settled for General Justo's attempt to restore the *status quo ante*, where electoral competition existed but was limited, thereby ensuring a preponderance of the oligarchy's interests. For the Chilean elites and for many in the upper middle class, "socialism and military presence . . . had become if not synonymous, equally obnoxious. [Consequently, they preferred the] reestablishment of traditional constitutional normalcy."[34] This normalcy meant the acceptance of the 1925 constitution, which the elites had opposed a decade earlier. This was surely preferable to them than the potential for a military-led, left-wing transformation of the country. It was fear about this possibility (and, in the case of Argentina, uncertainties and fear regarding a potential fascist regime) rather than civic duty or a strong commitment to democracy that led the mainstream political forces in both countries to embrace their different versions of electoral competition in 1932: unfree but fair in Chile, and free but unfair in Argentina.[35]

Uruguay

In contrast to Argentina and Chile, where the armed forces were prominent political actors in the 1920s–30s, in Uruguay their participation in politics had been tamed—or at least channeled institutionally—since the presidency of General Máximo Gómez (1880–86), when he created what went on to be a long-term, tacit alliance between the armed forces and the Colorado Party. This mediation of the military's interests by the leading party in the country helped to ensure that the military remained loyal to democratic institutions and civilian authority.[36] Thus, despite his authoritarian creed, President Gabriel Terra, a conservative Colorado, kept the military outside of partisan politics during his years in power (1931–38), dismissing General Sicco, the army's Inspector General, after he expressed electoral ambitions.[37] When authoritarianism came to Uruguay, civilians remained in charge of the regime. Some observers consider that a dictablanda was in place in Uruguay in the years 1933–42, particularly when contrasted with the harsher dictatorships of General Uriburu in Argentina and General Ibáñez in Chile.

Even when leaders of one or the other of the two main Uruguayan parties during the authoritarian years (1933–42) tried to strengthen their power by bringing some of the forces of state coercion more closely under their control, such as when the Partido Nacional tried to decentralize the police (which would have given them a say in the staffing and organization of police forces in their electoral strongholds), such measures did not prosper, because each party required substantial support from its counterpart to enact legislation.[38] Still, given the decisive role that the armed forces can play in imposing political regime outcomes by virtue of their use of force, it is reasonable to assume, as other authors have, that they at least acquiesced in the shutdown of the constitutional process in Uruguay in 1933.[39] In sum, while the armed forces were a key factor in deciding political regime outcomes in the cases of Argentina and Chile, they were not Uruguay.

INTERNATIONAL RULES AND ORGANIZATIONS

From our privileged position as early twenty-first century observers of the interwar years, the most surprising feature of the 1920s and 1930s is the absence of an international institutional architecture capable of promoting or defending liberal capitalism and democracy. The UN system and the Bretton Woods international financial organizations, which were born in the wake of the Second World War, were game-changers in many respects. Economically, they led to the creation of effective international rules and organizations capable of having a substantial influence on the transnational management of economic shocks and crises that could otherwise easily spark domestic political crises, particularly in developing countries. The contrast between the absence of an effective politicoeconomic international infrastructure in the interwar years and its presence after 1945 cannot be emphasized enough.

Staying with the previous era for now, the main international organization of the interwar years was the League of Nations. It came into existence with the Versailles Treaty of 1919, which formally ended the First World War. The League's rules included lofty ideals, such as the prevention of war, the diplomatic resolution of conflicts, and the improvement of human conditions around the world. The League's real impact on the international scene, however, was quite limited. For one thing, the strongest emergent world power after the war, the United States, could not ratify its membership in the League, due to opposition in the US Senate. Of the larger Latin American countries, Mexico was not invited to join; Argentina withdrew in late 1920, after it was unable to modify Article 21 of the Covenant, which considered the Monroe Doctrine to be a "regional understanding"; and Brazil withdrew in 1926, after it failed to promote the idea of equal treatment between big and small powers. Without the United States, Mexico, Argentina, and Brazil, "the representation of the American continent was indeed weakened."[40] Nonetheless, the number of states from the Americas constituted close to one-third of the nations in the League.[41] Uruguay was one of the founding members, while Chile, Argentina, and four other countries had been invited to join in early 1920. The main reasons why the League would have been unable to do much in the presence of threats to the democracies or the economies of Latin America were twofold. First, it did not possess an explicit mandate to promote or defend democracy, or to intervene to try to temper financial shocks. Second, the bulk of the issues it did tackle were concerned with the postwar order in Europe and the Middle East, rather than with the Western Hemisphere.

An inter-American system had been born and developed in the New World, thanks to a series of international conferences, starting in 1889. This early system, however, which was based on periodic conferences attended by officials of the Western Hemisphere countries, had a very limited remit. Its main administrative unit was the Commercial Bureau of the American Republics, under the US State Department in Washington, DC, whose primary function was to collect and distribute commercial information. Its size and functions grew in an ad hoc manner, depending on the pressing international issues of the day. The Bureau was renamed the Pan-American Union in 1910, but despite its increased activities and responsibilities, it never created the legal, political, or economic bases to promote or defend democracy. For example, Article 6 of the Convention, which established the Union's functions, opened with a statement that entrusted the governing body and the Pan American Union as a whole to "discharge the duties assigned by this convention subject to the condition that they shall not exercise functions of a political character."[42] Likewise, despite establishing some bases for cooperation among the Western Hemisphere countries in Article 3, such as to "assist in the development of commercial, industrial, agricultural, social, and cultural relations,"[43] these bases were so general that it was impossible to envisage anything remotely like the specific arrangements that helped to regulate the international economic order created by the 1944 Breton Woods conference and the international financial system it created. The Union's only international economic anchor was adherence to the gold standard, a rule that contributed to the worsening of the downward spiral after 1929 in the advanced as well as in developing economies. Indeed, Jeffry A. Frieden goes so far as to say that "the gold standard is the key to understanding the Depression." The rigidity it imposed on monetary authorities was the main constraint that precluded countercyclical measures. As a consequence, economic "recovery proved possible . . . only after abandoning the gold standard."[44]

The absence of relatively effective international institutions like the ones crafted after the Second World War does not obviate the fact that some bilateral relations were important enough either to help support or oppose the political regimes of the Southern Cone during the Great Depression. This was particularly the case with smaller (and therefore more dependent) countries, such as Uruguay. The execution of their 1933 coup against democracy was influenced by the 1930 coups in neighboring Argentina and Brazil. Terra's authoritarian regime also received diplomatic and economic support from fascist Italy and national socialist Germany. Likewise, the eventual return of democracy was influenced by the Uruguayans' admiration for President Franklin D. Roosevelt's New Deal (the American president visited the country in 1936, and President Terra spoke admiringly of the United States).[45] Moreover, while the more conservative *herreristas* wanted to retain the 1934 constitution and authoritarian politics, President Alfredo Baldomir (1938–42) used the entrance of the United States into the Second World War after Pearl Harbor as a justification for breaking with the *herrerista* Blancos and aligning Uruguay with the Allies. Baldomir wanted his country to be totally identified with the inter-American war effort led by the United States.[46] Thus in early 1942 he separated himself politically from Herrera, broke off Uruguayan diplomatic relations with the Axis countries, and executed a new *autogolpe* to rid the country of the 1934 constitution and return to democracy. These events, regarded as the "good coup," had the tacit support of the United States as well as the *batllistas* in the Colorado party.[47] Democracy, thus restored, survived uninterruptedly until 1973, when the military executed a coup.

All in all, without international bodies similar to the UN Security Council or the IMF, the politics and economics of the 1930s were likely to produce a much broader range of outcomes (in terms of domestic ruling arrangements and economic conditions) than would have been the case had these organizations existed then. This is not to say that simply transposing the international arrangements of the post-1945 world order to the 1920s and 1930s would have prevented the rise to power of non-democratic regimes or avoided the Great Depression. It does mean, however, that the severity and duration of these and other extreme political and economic events during those decades might have been somewhat different had there been international institutions that could apply effective pressure against extreme political behavior and act as a lender-of-last-resort to economies facing financial shocks. In short, without such means to affect actions in domestic contexts, the international sphere had little capacity to raise the costs for the exercise of pressures against democracy, as was the case during the subsequent economic shocks and crises in the early 1980s, in the late 1990s and early 2000s, and since 2008–9.

CONCLUSION

The analysis of institutions in the domestic sphere of the three Southern Cone countries during the Great Depression highlights three points. First, even though the specific institutions-as-rules in each country helped to structure political conflict (and therefore pressures for and against democracy) differently, there is an important similarity in that most of the conflicts leading to regime changes had as their focal point the balance of power between the executive and legislative branches of government. The only case in which social mobilization resulted in regime change was when the urban working and middle classes took to the streets and forced General Ibáñez to resign in Chile in 1931 (see chapter 4). All other cases were, to greater or lesser degrees, instances of politicians fighting each other.

Second (and also related to institutions-as-rules), the development of mass contestation through stable, competitive multiparty systems in Chile and Uruguay resulted in relatively institutionalized processes of crisis management in times of harsh economic fallouts. This was in marked contrast to Argentina, where a personalized form of mediation between elites and the masses— inaugurated by Yrigoyen and developed and consolidated in its most distinctive of expressions anywhere in Latin America by Perón and his movement from the 1940s—led to the absence of an institutionalized process of crisis management where its main effects were recurrent civilian-military regime changes and erratic policymaking, particularly during harsh financial shocks and economic crises.

Third, regarding institutions-as-organizations, the military had the capacity to further its political regime choice—either through interventions (as in Argentina and Chile) or through its acquiescence (as in Uruguay)—but such capacity was strongly mediated by the elites' perception of what the armed forces would do if they came to power, as is suggested by the elites' support for their intervention in Argentina in September 1930, and their opposition to their continuation in power in Chile after September 1932. In short, democracy's chances were not good, given the prevalence of executive-legislative conflict and the military's capacity to be a decisive factor in supporting or changing a political regime during the 1930s in the Southern Cone countries. Still, lasting democracy was not impossible, as the reestablishment of civilian rule in Chile under Arturo Alessandri toward the end of 1932 showed.

The international sphere possessed neither the rules nor the organizations and resources that would have been required to raise the costs for the exercise of pressures against democracy in domestic political contexts in the crisis-ridden 1930s. Given the extremely polarized and uncompromising character of political ideologies during those years (see chapter 5), and the sense of urgency and need for decisive action that the dominant and negatively affected economic interests called for (see chapter 4), it remains highly unlikely that even as well-populated and developed an international sphere as has existed in more recent times (particularly since the end of the Cold War) would have been capable of raising the costs enough to deter strong, uncompromising pressures against democracy.

CHAPTER FOUR

Interests

---

*Foreign Capital and Domestic Coalitions
against Democracy*

The second factor to examine is the way international and domestic interests raised or lowered the likelihood that actors organized and exercised pressures in favor of and against democracy during the Great Depression in the Southern Cone countries. My comparative historical analysis explains their political regime outcomes in a way that is generally consistent with that of contemporary political economy scholars, who have emphasized that conflict over alternatives to political regimes are—first and foremost—part of a redistributive struggle among competing economic interests.[1] Nonetheless, my argument qualifies the perspective of these authors. The cases of Argentina and Uruguay in the early 1930s can be seen as illustrations of their viewpoint: capitalists, particularly those tied down by fixed assets (the bulk of foreign investment in the Southern Cone countries in the 1920s and 1930s was in fixed assets, such as infrastructure, utilities, mining, and energy), decide to cast their lot against democracy when, in their perception, the risk of nationalization or confiscation increases (the situation with energy policy and foreign companies operating in that sector in both Argentina and Uruguay).

On the other hand, what happened in Chile is at odds with that story. Foreign investors and the domestic elites and middle classes supported General Ibáñez's dictatorship during good economic times, but they surprisingly did not back his reinstatement after spreading urban protests in the midst of the 1930–31 economic meltdown forced Ibáñez's fall from power in July 1931, despite the fact that a large proportion of the capitalists' investments were held in fixed assets, particularly mining. Starting in 1927, foreign and domestic capitalists supported dictatorial rule in Chile as long as it yielded control and profits, but they stood on the sidelines when the tide decidedly turned and social mobilization threatened to become widespread in the summer of 1931. The key difference with Argentina and Uruguay was not so much a predominance of capitalists with fixed or liquid assets per se, but rather the foreign and domestic elites' perception of great danger in Chile, due to the threat of a left-wing military revolution from above, particularly when the Socialist Republic was installed in June 1932. Given that such an outcome was a real possibility, the elites cast their lot with the return of democracy and of Arturo Alessandri to the presidency in October 1932, despite the fact that less than a decade earlier he had seemed to them to be a radical populist whose progressive reforms had to be resisted at all costs.

Organized labor was relatively weak in Argentina and Uruguay at that time, and it did not play a role in trying to defend democracy in those countries in 1930 and 1933, respectively. In contrast, in Chile organized labor and the middle classes mobilized, and the protests and violence that ensued forced the fall of General Ibáñez.

INTERNATIONAL SPHERE: AMERICAN AND BRITISH ECONOMIC COMPETITION

The Iberian countries had held the biggest economic stakes in Latin America since the establishment of the Spanish and Portuguese colonies in the sixteenth century. After Spanish-American and Brazilian independence in the 1820s, however, the expanding British Empire became the dominant foreign economic force south of the Rio Grande. A subsequent change took place as a consequence of the rise of US hegemony in the Western Hemisphere after the Spanish-American war of 1898, although British foreign investment continued to dominate in Argentina, Brazil, and Uruguay until the 1930s. At the turn of the twentieth century, British and American private businesses, and support from their national governments, were the main foreign sources of economic competition throughout the subcontinent (the British in South America and the Americans in Mexico, Central America, the Caribbean, and western South American countries like Chile and Peru), although by then and until the First World War, Germany and France also had a substantial banking and direct investment presence in the region.[2]

The competition among British and American investors for this Latin American economic activity was fierce in the years leading up to the Great Depression, yet American foreign investment grew much more rapidly than British investment in every country in the region. Figure 4.1 shows the ratio of US

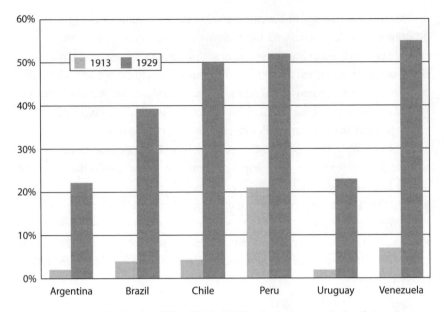

Figure 4.1. Racing ahead: ratio of US to US plus UK foreign investment in South America
Source: Based on data from Thorp, "Latin America," 64.

foreign investments to the sum of US plus UK investments in the years 1913—
the year before the First World War started—and 1929, the year of the Wall
Street crash. In Thorp's words, "British investment barely increased while US
investment soared."[3] Even though UK investors remained the dominant foreign economic force in the Southern Cone countries in terms of nominal investment (except in Chile) on the eve of the Great Depression, this was an economic force that had been in retreat since the First World War, and the
Depression gave it the coup de grâce.

American investors became the biggest stakeholders in Chile. Their investments were concentrated in mining and were led by tycoon Daniel Guggenheim, who committed substantial amounts of capital in the country's northern
desert, the seat of massive nitrate and copper deposits. The British were heavily
involved and remained the biggest foreign presence in Argentina and Uruguay,
whose economies depended on the meat, meat-packing, and wool industries.
The British also ran large portions of the basic infrastructure, such as railways
and utilities, in both countries. However, the United States pushed into these
economic areas in the late 1920s. For example, after American investors bought
the rights to supply electricity to the cities of Buenos Aires and Montevideo and

telephone services in Uruguay from the British, leading British businessmen worried that natural gas companies and the railways would be next, and reckoned that Americans could make offers to buy out all the British companies operating in Latin America.[4]

Transformation of the transport system is a case in point. A struggle between the extant railways and the new roadway system took place around the world, starting with the United States itself.[5] This conflict helped to catapult big American companies ahead of their British peers; while the latter had developed and dominated the age of the railways in the Southern Cone countries during the second half of the nineteenth century, American banks and companies developed and came to dominate the age of mass automobile transportation.[6] The end result was that on top of the financial expansion led by American banks in the 1920s, the US economy grew its capital goods export sector in Latin America at similarly high rates. In fact, the US financial and capital goods sectors acted in a complementary way. US corporations exported their wares (automobiles; tires; machinery to build road infrastructure; oil-based products such as gasoline and engine oils for vehicles, and tar for laying out roads) at the same time that US private banks extended credit to Latin American governments—particularly in more advanced economies like the Southern Cone's—to pay for modernizing the transport sector.

Most Latin American economies benefited, at least in the short term, from expanded US economic activity in the region. This also applied to Argentina and Uruguay, despite their heavy economic dependence on Great Britain.[7] However, the good fortune of being closely linked to the US economy during the years of cheap expansion of credit backfired and became a major liability once the US market imploded in late 1929.

Chile

This country was doubly vulnerable, due to its deepening dependence on US trade as well as credit. Growing proportions of both Chile's imports and exports became tied to the US market in the 1920s. On the export side, the countries affected the most after 1929 were those that, like Chile, relied heavily on mining exports to the United States (other such countries were Bolivia, Peru, and Mexico). At the nadir of the Depression in 1932, Chilean "exports had tumbled to less than 12 percent and imports to less than 20 percent of their 1929 value."[8] In contrast, Argentina, Uruguay, and other countries that "produced a range of foodstuffs and agricultural raw materials, the demand for which could not be so easily satisfied from existing stocks," experienced a less radical decline.[9] Chile's economy was also overreliant on the export of a single commodity, nitrates. Even though German synthetics started eating into Chilean nitrate exports after the First World War, Chile still controlled more than 50% of the world nitrate market by 1928. The 1929–31 financial shocks and economic crises that morphed into the Great Depression devastated Chilean nitrate mining, and by 1931 the country only accounted for about 10% of the world market. The copper industry, emergent in the 1920s, also suffered a huge drop in the early 1930s.[10]

Chile had also tapped US financial markets and borrowed 1.76 billion USD during the 1920s; by 1930 it faced annual debt payments of around 400 million USD.[11] US financial inflows and businesses helped to prop up General Ibáñez's authoritarian regime during the late 1920s.[12] For example, the Guggenheims and President Ibáñez created a joint venture known as Compañía de Salitres de Chile (COSACH), whose mission was to revive the market for natural nitrates through capital-intensive exploitation. The run up to the Great Depression had been good for foreign business in Chile, because the Ibáñez regime had exercised political control and repressed organized labor and other dissidents. Thus, while COSACH promised higher foreign-exchange earnings, this was done at the expense of mining jobs, which bred discontent in that sector. The catch was that the Ibáñez regime became dependent on the plentiful availability of short-term credit supplied by American banks and businesses to keep propping up an economic boom that had been based on aggressive state expansion into the economy through the growth of both public employment and major public works (such as infrastructure). Extensive public investment represented a good opportunity for foreign and domestic contractors, as well as for the creation of employment in areas other than nitrate mining, so the main players with economic interests in Chile supported the government while the going was good. Robust economic performance and an image of technocratic efficiency helped to sustain General Ibáñez's authoritarian regime in what was otherwise a country with a long tradition, if not of full democracy (given the literacy barrier to enfranchisement for regular competitive elections), at least of constitutional government and, up until the military intervention of 1924, of civilian supremacy over the armed forces.

Changing economic conditions for US investors at home proved to be decisive for the fate of the Ibáñez regime. American credit started to dry up in mid-1928, after many international investors left peripheral markets to buy into the bull market in New York. After the 1929 shock, this financial collapse fed into the real economy, leading to a dramatic fall in world trade between 1930 and 1932. Depressed demand at the capitalist core severely affected the Chilean government, because taxes from trade made up close to 50% of the country's fiscal revenue.[13] In addition, the demand for raw materials dried up, devastating the American companies operating in Chile. US mining giants Kennecott and Anaconda, whose copper-mining activities in Chile had absorbed more than 200 million USD in investments, experienced a drastic collapse in the value of their outputs, which went from 111 million USD in 1929 to 11 million in 1932.[14] The Guggenheim's investment in COSACH, which had led to significant worker layoffs thanks to their introduction of capital-intensive mining and refining techniques, also soured as the crisis accelerated, and this eventually led to the collapse of the public-private venture.[15] The double whammy of credit (to refinance short-term debt) drying up and real economic activity (which was heavily dependent on mining) falling pushed the Ibáñez regime up against the wall.

Without the continued distribution of material benefits to various social sectors, a growing number of them demanded that General Ibáñez step down. Starting in 1930, economic collapse led to the organized workers deserting and turning against him. Public demonstrations and protests escalated. By the middle of July in 1931, a broad front that included university students and other middle-class groups (such as professional associations) took to the streets in droves. The police clamped down on the protesters, killing at least a dozen. The July disturbances were the catalyst that accelerated the fall of General Ibáñez, because by then all his sources of support—foreign and domestic businesses, the middle classes, and organized workers—had turned against him after the economy soured. In the words of two leading historians of Chile, "the movement became uncontrollable. For the first time in Chilean history, a government was forced to yield to civil protest."[16] Ibáñez was compelled to resign and go into exile in Argentina.

The Ibáñez regime came to depend on both liquid and fixed foreign assets— the former as the main source of financing to create and sustain an economic boom based on public spending; the latter, dominated by foreign-owned mining, to generate foreign exchange and employment, although capital-intensive mining in fact eliminated many workers' jobs. Of the three countries studied here, the connection between the short-term deterioration of international economic interests operating in a given country and the fate of the host country's political regime was strongest in Chile in 1931: "the Depression and the COSACH debacle helped topple Ibáñez from power."[17] The Chilean case is therefore at odds with the thrust of this work's general argument, which is that pro-democracy forces faced higher costs to organize and act than anti-democracy forces in the 1930s. This should lead to the expectation that General Ibáñez's dictatorship should have survived the crisis. Instead, the external resources on which the legitimacy and performance of his non-democratic regime came to depend dried up, and the rise and spread of working- and middle-class mobilizations and protests eventually led to the collapse of the regime.[18]

Argentina and Uruguay

Deteriorating conditions for international economic interests also affected Argentina and Uruguay, but the downfall of democratic regimes in these countries in the wake of the Depression was not a function of a sudden collapse of economic activity, as it was in Chile. Rather, foreign economic interests helped to fuel the domestic-based political conflict that led to the collapse of democracy in Argentina (1930) and Uruguay (1933). It would be erroneous to think that the depth and breadth of foreign interests' opposition to democracy was uniform. Despite the fact that two disparate sets of activities—railways, utilities, and general infrastructure, on the one hand, and oil exploration and production, on the other—both operated with fixed assets, and that potential losses were higher in the former than in the latter, due to a longer investment history, it was the oil sector that became the epicenter of foreign business opposition to democracy in Argentina and Uruguay.

This opposition was sparked less by the amount of fixed assets held by foreign investors in the different sectors than by which sector became politicized as a consequence of domestic leaders' calls for the nationalization of foreign-owned assets. In terms of infrastructure, historian Luis Alberto Romero notes that British owners were unafraid of potential nationalization of the railway system, and even wanted to sell it to the Argentine state, because of steeply falling profit margins from growing competition by the flourishing highway transportation sector.[19] It was the smaller but fast-growing energy sector that became the target of nationalization in the course of the 1920s. America's Standard Oil and Britain's Royal Dutch Shell were the largest energy firms in Argentina and Uruguay. These companies grew concerned as they watched the rise of nationalism and the birth of state-owned hydrocarbon companies in Argentina (Yacimientos Petrolíferos Fiscales [YPF] was created in 1922) and in Uruguay (Administración Nacional de Combustibles, Alcohol y Portland [ANCAP] was created in 1931).

Populist nationalism became a winning political formula, taking off through-out Latin America in the 1920s (see chapter 5). This was not a region-specific phenomenon, but one with both local and foreign roots—think of US isolation-ism after the First World War, and the rise of xenophobia and other forms of violent nationalism during the interwar years in countries like Germany, France, and Italy. Part of the nationalist agenda included expropriating foreign assets to enhance the economic independence of nation-states. In Latin Amer-ica, politicians peddling populist causes married nationalist economic policies with the fight against the informal economic empires that Great Britain and the United States had established in the region. This style of politics engendered an impassioned allegiance "at least [for] the minority of alert Latin Americans, [who regarded anti-imperialism as] not only a popular cause but almost a duty of conscience and salvation."[20]

In contrast to the Chilean case, where the US recession after 1929 contrib-uted directly to knocking out the Ibáñez regime, the foreign oil companies' fears of expropriation in Argentina and Uruguay predated the economic shock of 1929 and the Great Depression by several years. Pressures for nationalization gathered momentum in the context of the economic crisis (Yrigoyen's expro-priation push in 1928–30 and the creation of ANCAP in Uruguay in 1931), but the nationalist impulse had longer political roots (not just economic emergency ones). These grew during the first presidency of Hipólito Yrigoyen (1916–22) in Argentina and in the nationalist creed in Uruguay developed by President José Batlle y Ordóñez in his second term in office (1911–15). In the end, while US credit and economic activity became the lifeline for Ibáñez's government in Chile, and the collapse of both variables after 1929 sounded the death knell for his authoritarian regime, in Argentina and Uruguay neither the activities of foreign oil companies nor the role trade policies played in the meat, meat-packing and wool industries had such direct effects.

ENERGY: CONFLICTS WITH FOREIGN OWNERS OF ILLIQUID ASSETS

Argentina. Yrigoyen made the nationalization of the oil industry the corner-stone of his platform when he ran for election to the Argentine presidency for a second time in 1928. The strategy worked out, for the old Radical patriarch gar-nered close to 60% of the votes in that election. Interestingly, Yrigoyen aimed his expropriation strategy against the US's Standard Oil, not against British Shell; this, as well as his general pro-British stance between 1928 and 1930, were due to his fear of retaliation, given the preponderance of British economic in-terests in Argentina.[21] The president's caution has to be seen in the context of economic conditions at that time, as the economic crisis in Argentina (starting in 1928) predated the United States' 1929 shock. By 1930, Argentina's GDP growth had fallen consecutively for three years.

President Yrigoyen tried to stay on the offensive, introducing legislation to carry out his electoral pledge to nationalize Standard Oil's assets. The bill passed in the Chamber of Deputies (where the Radicals enjoyed a majority) but stalled in the Senate, which was still dominated by conservative provincial interests. After all, the governors of oil-producing provinces like Salta and Jujuy benefited from revenue-sharing agreements with the foreign oil companies operating in their territories. Yrigoyen decided to concentrate his firepower on subnational politics, to subdue opponents and raise the likelihood that the Radicals would win a majority in the upper chamber. The president and his followers tried to preempt the continuation of the opposition's majority in the Senate by withholding recognition of the conservative candidates from Mendoza and San Juan provinces who won in the March 1930 elections. In fact, one of the justifications by the military and their conservative civilian allies for executing the September 6, 1930, coup that brought down democracy was precisely the fear that Radical majorities would allow President Yrigoyen to consolidate a winner-take-all system in which he had absolute control over patronage. Rural landed interests were not scared as much by Yrigoyen's economic policies (since there was no serious effort to affect land tenure through redistribution) as by his monopolization of political power.[22] Foreign interests feared his policies because he had targeted the oil sector for nationalization after his 1928 campaign. In particular, September 1930 was going to be a key month, because (Senate majority permitting) the government planned to proceed with its campaign pledge and try to pass the oil nationalization bill in the upper chamber. At the same time, the director-general of YPF, General Enrique Mosconi, had arranged an alternative line of supply for crude oil for Argentina with the Soviet company Iuyamtorg, in case of cuts by Western companies.[23]

Did the foreign oil barons push Yrigoyen out, or at least contribute to his ouster? An in-depth study of the events leading to the September 6 coup argues that, while there is indirect evidence that the foreign oil interests benefited from it—for example, several of the ministers appointed by General Uriburu, the leader of the coup and later president, had served as legal advisers to Standard Oil as well as to Shell—a smoking gun that could tie such interests directly to the breakdown of democracy has not been found. The study concludes that any participation by the oil companies "was a peripheral factor and that the Yrigoyen government's campaign against Argentine federalism convinced the opposition that its alternatives were to either permit one-party Radical rule or to remove the president from office."[24]

Other works by leading historians of Argentina concur with this interpretation. Romero argues that the 1930 coup was not carried out to quash widespread mobilization from below by workers and radical political activists, as had been the case with the government's military and police brutality during the *semana trágica* of 1919. In fact, since 1928 the economic crisis had weakened the workers' capacity for contestation, and trade union leaders had become disillusioned with Yrigoyen's personalist style of politics. In Romero's view, the coup was also not in answer to the international economic crisis, since this factor was largely absent from the political debate of the time. Rather, the coup was carried out against what democracy—at least as it was practiced in Argentina—had come to represent: a personalist style of rule centered on the president-*caudillo*, with all its accompanying vices, such as unbridled patronage and populism to cement middle- and working-class loyalty, and the use of force to subdue opponents and undermine authorities who dared to disagree with the president.[25]

Uruguay. Historians like Juan Oddone have opined that just because there is indirect evidence of foreign oil companies' support for the 1930 Argentine coup, with the accompanying temptation to infer their participation in the 1933 coup in Uruguay as well, we should not jump to conclusions.[26] Other historians, like Raúl Jacob, assert that the creation of ANCAP in 1931 can be considered to be the straw that broke the camel's back, since it emboldened conservative politicians, as well as some domestic and foreign businessmen, to confront the dominant *batllistas* in the Colorado Party and their policy of statism and hostility to foreign capital.[27]

The foreign oil interests were concerned about the Uruguayan government's plan to build a petroleum refinery, which would give ANCAP substantial leverage over downstream activities, and perhaps even legal authority to become the monopolist distributor of liquid fuels. Having observed the crude-oil supply agreement that YPF in Argentina had signed with the Soviet Union, the Anglo-American companies were concerned that the Uruguayan government would take the same route. The evidence even points to the fact that, similar to the situation in Argentina, once President Gabriel Terra executed the *autogolpe* in Uruguay on March 31, 1933, he appointed managers to the helm of ANCAP who had done business with the Western oil companies and were positively inclined toward their interests.[28]

Oddone agrees with Jacob in noting that the foreign oil interests were clearly aligned with those conservative Uruguayan sectors that favored a political regime change.[29] Still, both authors conclude that there is no direct evidence that links the foreign oil companies with the 1933 coup itself. Rather, the creation of the state-owned hydrocarbon entity represented only one chapter in a broader and deeper conflict that divided Uruguayans into *batllista* and *anti-batllista* camps over the country's future socioeconomic trajectory: the former statist, and the latter led by private business.[30] As such, and similar to the situation in Argentina, institutional and ideological factors in Uruguay, as well as the personal ambition of some political leaders (see chapter 5), were more directly responsible for the breakdown of democratic institutions than the economic shocks and crises of the period, whereas the latter was the case in Chile in July 1931.

TRADE POLICY: RISE OF PROTECTIONISM

As the economic crisis deepened in the core capitalist countries, their governments pursued protectionist measures to safeguard their producers, and this move severely damaged Latin American economies. The United States passed the Smoot-Hawley tariff (on foreign imports in general) in 1930 and a specific tariff on copper imports (which hurt Chile considerably) in 1932.[31] The British passed protectionist measures in 1931, which culminated with the adoption of the British Commonwealth Preferences during the Ottawa Conference of 1932. This preference system gave a competitive edge to imports from the Empire's territories and dominions, which could savage Argentina and Uruguay's exports.

A high level of dependence on the Anglo sphere forced the Argentine government to make trade and financial concessions in exchange for the maintenance of Britain's beef-importing quota (the 1933 Roca-Runciman Treaty). Uruguay followed suit with a similar treaty in 1935. Argentina and Uruguay gave much more than Great Britain provided in return. For example, after having enacted heterodox monetary measures (such as foreign-exchange controls and the non-convertibility of their local currencies into gold) to slow down the drainage from foreign exchange, the Argentine and Uruguayan governments then ended up granting British firms full repatriation for their profits and committed themselves to continuing to honor the payment of their external debt obligations. Argentina was one of the few countries in Latin America that regularly continued paying its external debt obligations with foreign exchange; Uruguay also committed itself to keep paying, but it did so in local currency. These measures led to a net outflow of resources that both countries' governments might otherwise have devoted to public expenditures to promote quicker economic recuperation.[32] In stark contrast, Chile and most of the rest of the Latin American countries adopted a moratorium on external obligations during the Great Depression.

The main question here is the extent to which the adoption of protectionist measures by the United States and the United Kingdom contributed to the collapse of political regimes in the three Southern Cone countries. Concentrating on the timing of the adoption of such measures helps to highlight that both the tariff on copper implemented by the United States and the imperial preference system created by the United Kingdom started operating some time *after* the fall of the Ibáñez authoritarian regime in Chile and the democratic regime in Argentina. The adoption of the British imperial preference system, however, predated the fall of democracy in Uruguay. The years 1931 to 1933 saw the worst performance in Uruguay's growth. Indeed, historians suggest that this nation's sense of hopelessness deepened in 1932 after the introduction of British tariffs (85% of the country's exports were tied to the British market); this fed into the polarization of politics and, in particular, emboldened the conservative sectors of both the Blanco and Colorado parties to call openly for a change of political regime.[33] President Terra, who had assumed power after a clean democratic election in 1930, acquiesced and went on to assume the mantle of authoritarianism by executing an *autogolpe* in March 1933.

DOMESTIC SPHERE: ELITES AND UPPER MIDDLE CLASSES COME OUT ON TOP

The exporters of raw materials (and their foreign partners) were at the heart of the dominant domestic economic interests in Latin America. The local elites were not monolithic, but most of the long-established ones derived their social and economic preeminence from landowning, mining, and trade, and their political dominance from their control of the state. This had been the case at least since the *criollos* (individuals who had been born in the Americas but whose parents were Spanish) kicked out the *peninsulares* (those born in Spain who migrated to the New World) in the 1810s–20s.

The leaders of the traditional public institutions (the military, the Catholic Church, and the state) were also members of the elite. In fact, many younger sons from the landed elites pursued successful careers in these institutions. The main difference between the traditional public institutions was that the military and the Church were relatively open to talent from below, which made them the main institutional avenues for upward mobility in these rigidly hierarchical societies, while the state remained relatively closed, because participation in government tended to be restricted to the socioeconomically dominant, a very small minority everywhere. Economic and social power begat political power, strengthening the oligarchic character of Latin American societies during the years of high levels of economic growth and the integration of the region into modern industrial capitalism during the belle-époque (1870s–1914). Unfortunately for the export-oriented elites, the Great Depression wiped out their material base throughout Latin America. The resulting crisis from the commodity-export-led growth model brought down oligarchic regimes in a majority of Latin American countries (the notable exception was the Central American republics) in the space of a few years, starting in 1930.[34]

The Latin American elites benefited enormously by backing the Anglo-American model of capitalist expansion until the Great Depression, and this process also strengthened the middle and working classes, particularly in more advanced countries like those in the Southern Cone. The combination of fast growth and socioeconomic modernization during the 1870–1930 period meant that growing urbanization, incipient industrialization, and higher literacy rates created conditions that stimulated a rise in economic and political influence of the middle strata, made up of professionals, bureaucrats, tradesmen, and artisans. Their relative power was enhanced by their physical location, especially in capital cities, which became the nerve centers for politics as economic modernization, the transportation revolution, and the growth in urban amenities (with their demand for labor) brought increasing numbers of people together, presaging the rise of societies dominated by the masses in the 1920s and 1930s.

Urban workers were better organized and had a greater chance of engaging in collective action than rural workers. The strength of trade unions and labor-based political parties was a function of a country's level of capitalist development. Moreover, "the working class was the most consistently pro-democratic force. [This] class had a strong interest in effecting its political inclusion and it was more insulated from the hegemony of dominant classes than the rural lower classes."[35] Still, however strong a given organized labor movement seemed to be, its political influence was limited in the 1920s and early 1930s. Even in countries with the earliest and most combative labor organizations in Latin America, such as the Southern Cone countries, Rueschemeyer and colleagues note that "in the 1920s and first half of the 1930s the labor movements in Argentina and Chile were greatly weakened by repression, unleashed by an alliance between economic elites and the middle classes or the military. In Argentina heavy repression came in the aftermath of the *semana trágica* in 1919, and in Chile under Ibáñez. In Uruguay labor organization stagnated during this period."[36]

Despite the differences in the relative strength of the social classes in each of our three countries (in the early 1930s labor was better organized, more politicized, more inclined to public displays of collective action, and had forged closer links to leftist political parties in Chile than in Argentina and Uruguay), the class coalitions formed as a reaction to the breadth and scope of the Depression were similar in all three nations. The elites and influential groups in the upper middle classes (the managerial classes in both the public and private sectors) supported regime changes to the right of the governments that were in place in the three countries (Uriburu, and later Justo, instead of Yrigoyen in Argentina; *terristas* and *herreristas* instead of *batllistas* in Uruguay; the short-lived restoration of democracy with the triumph of Montero after the fall of Ibáñez in Chile, as well as the restoration of limited democracy in that country, starting with Alessandri's presidential victory in late 1932 after the fall of the Socialist Republic). The only instance of a temporary regime change to the left was the fall of President Montero, followed by the birth of the Socialist Republic in Chile in June 1932.

While the majority of regime changes to the right were not preordained, they can be understood in the context of a substantially weaker organized labor movement, with a more limited reach, in the Southern Cone countries than in Western Europe during the post–First World War years or in the United States on the eve of the New Deal. Labor had been stronger and more combative in Argentina, Chile, and Uruguay in the 1910s and early 1920s than in the late 1920s and early 1930s. The critical years 1918–21 had seen the triumph of the Bolshevik revolution in Russia and the post–First World War international economic bust. These events mobilized and radicalized labor movements across the world, but, as Rueschemeyer and colleagues have observed, in the Southern Cone countries (as in many others), labor was tamed by a combination of state repression and cooptation that aborted the possibility of a workers' revolution anywhere in Latin America.

Of our three countries, the only one where popular mobilization and its consequences (violence, destruction of property, people injured and dead) exercised decisive pressure to force a regime change was Chile, after General Ibáñez was forced out in July 1931. Multiclass popular pressure began with working- and middle-class protests, which catalyzed protests by university students and professional associations, provoked their bloody repression by the state, and thereafter led to General Ibáñez's untenable position.[37] In contrast, worker participation was very weak in Argentina and Uruguay, where not even the middle classes came out to defend democracy before its breakdown in these countries in 1930 and 1933, respectively.

Argentina

Yrigoyen's political gamble to generate support among both the middle classes and the oligarchy through resource nationalism (both classes espoused anti-Americanism and declared their opposition to *yanqui* imperialism) worked in the short term, as he was elected again in 1928. Thereafter, the members of both classes waited for the promised economic bonanza that resource nationalism would bring. In 1930, after two years of economic crisis, frustrated expectations, and spending cuts dented patronage and clientelism (the modus operandi of *yrigoyenismo*), the government became very unpopular; university students, the press, and members of right-wing movements like the Liga Republicana protested and agitated in the streets, asking for the president's fall.[38] When the military executed a coup on September 6, no civilian group—upper, middle, or working class—came out in the government's favor. Democracy died an unmourned death that, thanks to the benefit of hindsight, historians have interpreted as a case of not valuing something until it has been lost.[39]

Uruguay

Similar to the case in Argentina, there was barely any resistance to the *autogolpe* of President Terra on March 31, 1933. The show of force, however, was much less robust in Uruguay than in Argentina, with the police (but not the military) participating in the closure of the General Assembly in Montevideo. *Anti-batllista* Colorados, Blanco *herreristas*, and large landowners supported the president's move to cancel the constitutional process. Moreover, the "Foreign Office was delighted, and Terra received the immediate congratulations of the British minister in Montevideo."[40] Despite the presence of a strong ideological conflict between *batllistas* and *anti-batllistas*, this did not translate into any meaningful mobilization and pressure from below to force the restoration of democracy. Terra's authoritarian regime did exercise press censorship, persecuted some political groups, and exiled opposition leaders, "but the repression was in general as mild as opposition to the coup had been muted."[41]

Chile

This country suffered through three instances of regime change between July 1931 and October 1932. Of all the regime changes in our three countries, the fall of Ibáñez was the one where pressures from below played a decisive role. Mobilization by organized workers started in 1930, and the middle classes joined in as the economic crisis bit deeper. Growing protests and state repression were catalysts in the breakdown of public order and the eventual fall of Ibáñez's dictatorship. In contrast, the next two regime changes included decisive participation by the military. When President Montero fell in June 1932, reformist officers like Grove and Puga executed the coup that established the Socialist Republic. In the case of the coup against Dávila, most military officials supported the demise of the Socialist Republic in September 1932.[42] The end result of military reformism in Chile was that both the upper and upper middle classes, including civilian and military leaders and their close followers, saw civilian government—even if this form of governance tended toward deadlock and inertia—as the lesser of two evils. As a result, civilian as well as military elites opted to harness the armed forces strictly to their legal role, as prescribed by the 1925 constitution.

CONCLUSION

During the Great Depression, there was a continuum in the Southern Cone countries, going from a strong connection between economic crisis and political regime collapse in Chile to a weaker correlation in Uruguay and an even weaker one in Argentina. Chile, which was the country that was hit hardest by the international economic collapse of 1929–34, was also the country whose short-term economic performance relied most heavily on the short-term evolution of three international prices (nitrates, copper, and US interest rates), over which it had no control. The regime was left exposed when these prices suffered a downturn, and neither its foreign nor its domestic business partners, who had supported General Ibáñez when the going was good, defended it. The organized working class and then the urban middle classes took to the streets and forced a political regime change.

The economic decline in both Argentina and Uruguay was neither as pronounced nor as long lasting as in Chile. Paradoxically, this was due at least in part to the then unpopular trade and financial concessions both countries' governments extended to their main trading partner, Britain, in 1933 and 1935.[43]

Such responses were at least partly due to the political influence of the economic backers for the authoritarian solutions—the major landowners and their merchant partners (both foreign and domestic)—most of whom were very concerned about their potential loss of political power and economic clout in the convulsed climate of the early 1930s.

The dominant anti-democracy coalitions were the military high command and the *oligarquía*, associated with the principal landowning families in Argentina, which ran the state, the party, and the electoral systems during the *década infame*; and the *anti-batllista* Colorados and *herrerista* (Nationalist) Blancos in Uruguay, who backed President Gabriel Terra's *autogolpe* in 1933. Foreign businesses, particularly the Anglo-American owners of illiquid assets in the energy sector, supported these coalitions and joined the chorus of dissatisfaction with the way democracy was practiced in both Argentina and Uruguay. The creation of the British imperial preference system in 1932 worsened economic conditions in both countries, but Argentina was already under authoritarian rule, while democracy was still limping along in Uruguay, which suggests that in the latter country, trade protectionism might have helped strengthen the case that those organizing to exercise pressures against democracy made in the run up to the 1933 *autogolpe*.

Finally, a common element in Argentina and Uruguay was the relative absence of organized working-class participation in the overthrow of political regimes in 1930–33. Organized labor, having initially experienced a surge in the wake of the Soviet revolution, the end of the First World War, and the international economic crisis of the late 1910s and early 1920s, later had been repressed and coopted in both countries, reducing the likelihood that major political change could come from below. On the other end of the spectrum, even though the Great Depression destroyed the material bases of the domestic elites and their foreign business partners, for the time being they remained on top in Argentina and Uruguay. In contrast, the elites in Chile had to increase redistribution to the well-organized, mobilized labor and middle classes, starting with General Ibáñez's authoritarian regime, continuing during the 1931–32 interregnum, and remaining in place after Arturo Alessandri returned to the presidency at the end of 1932.

CHAPTER FIVE

Ideas

---

*Extreme Ideological Conflict and the Rise
of the State in the Economy*

Let us now turn to the third of my three pillars—political ideologies and economic ideas and policy—to ascertain how they affected the costs of organizing and exercising pressures for and against democracy in the Southern Cone countries during the Great Depression.

INTERNATIONAL SPHERE: CONFLICTING POLITICAL IDEOLOGIES AND BIRTH OF KEYNESIANISM
Political Ideologies

Latin America is by and large the ideological offspring of the West. The region has been dubbed "the 'other' West,"[1] meaning the area of the world where changing politicoeconomic ideas and cultural heritage are partly pre-Columbian but predominantly Western European or, more generally, Atlanticist, given the mutual influence between the Americas and Europe and Africa since the sixteenth century. Politically, not only the French Revolution and British and Spanish liberalism, but also the influence of US political practice and institutions since the American War of Independence were of particular relevance in early nineteenth-century Latin America. Liberalism and conservatism—with their varied roots in the British, French, Spanish, and American versions of these ideologies—became the backbone of politics throughout the Latin American subcontinent during the first two-thirds of the nineteenth century. The last third of that century and first decade of the twentieth saw the dominance of positivism in the region. Positivism was a doctrine expounded by the French forefather of sociology, August Comte, whereby human history is characterized by progress, and the highest level of progress can only be achieved by applying the scientific method to solve all problems, both natural and human.

For the Latin American ruling elites, the application of this doctrine meant a technocratic approach to government, where the top priority was material modernization (railways, shipping, and factories) through foreign investment and partnerships. Following Herbert Spencer rather than Comte himself, the ruling elites in Latin America came to believe that the best way to promote progress was through the competition engendered by laissez-faire.[2] The free movement of factors was advocated only for relations between countries, however, rather than within them. Thus peripheral countries supplied the raw materials that the core capitalist nations transformed into manufactured goods, but few efforts were made to connect regional markets within countries to create true national economies. Given the highly stratified character of Latin American societies, in domestic politics the positivistic approach was paternalistic and authoritarian; it fostered loyalty through material dependence. Therefore, the elites not only enforced their control through coercion and violence, but they also tried to rely more generally on patronage and clientele networks, practices that later made populism seem almost a natural development of some of the paternalistic practices born during the later nineteenth century.

Positivism was superimposed on the main, long-established political cleavage of liberalism versus conservatism in Latin America. Like their related doctrines in Europe and the United States, these two ideologies had conflicting views about the role of the church in politics, the extent to which the state should be centralized, and the degree of social change that could be imposed through sheer political will and design, among others. Notwithstanding these deep differences, the late nineteenth-century version of the political dogma of both camps, which was fed either by a positivist faith in science and industry or by opposition to it, remained the preserve of the Latin American elites. Economic and social power begat political power, which in turn preserved (and if possible enhanced) socioeconomic power, which then strengthened political influence, and so forth.

Pressures for participation from below had to wait until anarchism and socialism were transplanted from Western Europe to Latin America in the last third of the nineteenth century. The radical Left grew substantially in the context of high export-led growth during the belle-époque years, but labor's strength was patchy, given the wide range of local variations in Latin America. In the earliest industrializing, urbanizing countries (like the Southern Cone ones), trade unions and organized labor had their moment of political relevance in the period of uncertainty following the First World War. The triumph of the Soviet Revolution in 1917 sparked the rise of Communist, Fascist, and National Socialist movements and parties throughout the world, including Latin America. Both right- and left-wing varieties of nationalism became a powerful political ideology throughout the world in the 1920s. As a result, politics came to be characterized by fierce and uncompromising ideological conflict everywhere.

By the time the Great Depression started, radical leftists and rightists alike called into question the liberal capitalist order represented by the United States and Great Britain and their elite Latin American business partners. The Anglo-American system was widely perceived as being incapable of reining in and taming the excesses associated with the roaring twenties type of international capitalism. Communism criticized liberal capitalism for its exploitation of the laboring masses and its tendency toward monopolistic rents, both of which were byproducts of the system of private ownership. Fascism's critique was not based on the disavowal of private property, but instead repudiated internationalism, as represented by American and British high finance. Given that most of Latin America's externally linked economic activity was with British and American firms and governments—and therefore with their diplomatic and business philosophies—capitalism and liberal democracy suffered an important credibility crisis in the region during these years. This credibility crisis sparked political conflicts, which were particularly acute in the Southern Cone countries, the part of Latin America where capitalism had developed the most.[3]

It is worth adding that the credibility crisis that liberal democracy confronted in Latin America after the 1929–31 international financial and economic busts was ameliorated by a key US foreign policy change by President Franklin D. Roosevelt. FDR and his advisers were aware that leaders in periphery countries pinpointed the origin of the global economic collapse in the greed of Wall Street speculators. Sound familiar? A further surge of resentment and opposition was ignited after nations with advanced economies, starting with the United States and Western Europe, implemented across-the-board trade protectionism to insulate their populations from the Depression, and exporters throughout Latin America and other periphery regions were badly hit. The Latin American backlash against Anglo-American interests was fairly visible, ranging from the actions of leaders to mass-based movements such as trade unions, professional groups, and (of course) left-wing parties protesting in the streets of the major South American cities. A regional attempt to cut trading links with the United States in 1932 was a wake-up call for American leaders during a presidential election year. South American leaders tried to form a power bloc that would include Argentina, Brazil, Chile, Peru, Paraguay, and Uruguay "as a means of enabling these republics permanently to sever most of their economic ties with the United States."[4] The formation of such a bloc would not have been straightforward, given the competing political and economic interests among these countries. However, what really defused this idea in the short term was President Roosevelt's formulation of the Good Neighbor Policy.

When he came into office in 1933, FDR abolished the unpopular gunboat diplomacy of selective intervention in Latin American countries that predominated in the administrations from Presidents Theodore Roosevelt to Herbert Hoover, and implemented the Good Neighbor Policy, which became very popular among Latin American leaders. FDR's promotion of this new diplomacy resonated strongly in South America, because it promised "to cooperate with these countries as equals in the attempt to modify the practices of capitalism so that it might be transformed into a system that would benefit all classes and restore dignity and purchasing power to those who had lost or never adequately possessed them."[5]

The irreconcilable, escalating tripolar competition among the political ideologies of liberal democracy, communism, and fascism helped produce an international environment that weakened the chances for democracy and for democratization throughout the world in the 1930s, particularly in regions that were tightly linked to Anglo-American capitalism, such as Latin America. In the Southern Cone nations, international demonstrations of what these ideologies could produce had a strong impact on political leaders from the left, the center, and the right. The Soviet regime's high-speed electrification and industrialization of semifeudal Russia became the example that radical leftists wanted to emulate. Likewise, the economic recovery, discipline, and political control that Mussolini and Hitler achieved in Italy and Germany became examples that radical rightists and some traditional conservatives put forward as solutions.

The Spanish Civil War became a particular sore point among the adversarial political groups in Latin America in the second half of the 1930s. Leftists and civilians in favor of republicanism threw in their lot with the Spanish Republic, while conservative Catholics, corporatists, and fascists supported General Francisco Franco and his nationalists' onslaught against the republicans. For example, the trauma of the Spanish Civil War strengthened what became the only effective Popular Front government in Latin America, in Chile.[6] Even though fascism was never implanted as a governing system in Uruguay, on multiple occasions President Terra declared his adherence to Mussolini's regime and to national socialism, as well as his sympathy for Franco's nationalists in Spain; the alliance between *terristas* and *herreristas* was reinforced by their mutual admiration for European fascism; and Terra's government broke diplomatic relations with the Spanish Republic and with the USSR.[7] In Argentina the civil war in Spain sharply widened that country's ideological divide. "On the right . . . conservatives, nationalists, filo-fascists, and Catholic integrists [experienced] a common reaction against liberal democracy. The opposite block of [political] solidarities was also consolidated [and encompassed] radicals to communists, and between these [were] socialists, democrat-progressives, students, and trade union leaders under the CGT [Confederación General del Trabajo], and a large sector of independent public opinion, which included prominent members of conservative liberalism."[8] International competition among the three dominant political ideologies acted like a magnifying glass that intensified rivalries in the domestic sphere by giving adversarial leaders repertoires to illustrate their points of contention, that is, sets of ideas, values, and analytical tools they could use to interpret the prevailing political and economic climates and gain adherents for the remedies they offered.[9] For example, both communism and fascism identified the death of liberal democracy as a precondition for their implementation, so as to avoid in the future the corrupted politics and market economies that, according to them, had led to the Great Depression.

While domestic actors—such as government and party leaders, military officers, business elites, middle-class intellectuals, labor and peasant leaders, and the rank and file—were the ones who primarily carried out the fight for or against democracy, the ideologies they invoked to promote and justify their collective actions were variants on one of the main competing political ideologies that had come to Latin America from Europe, particularly after 1917–18. Thus the core capitalist countries (the United States and Western Europe) exported not only institutional models and economic interests, but also political ideologies and economic policy concepts to the periphery, including Latin America. In the 1920s and 1930s, irreconcilable ideological competition led to uncompromising political conflict internationally. By acting like a magnifying glass and enlarging the scope of the arguments beyond local borders, international ideological competition lowered the costs for and fed into the organization and exercise of pressures against democracy in domestic political contexts, not only in the Southern Cone countries, but more generally.

Economic Policy Ideas: Pre- and Post-Keynes

Latin American governments during the first third of the twentieth century followed the neoclassical framework that dominated economic debates and policymaking in the advanced capitalist countries. The advent of the First World War, and with it the general mobilization for total war, did propel the state in warring countries into the role of general planner, coordinator, and executioner of economic policy. Once the general conflagration ended, however, there was no corpus of economic ideas that could provide the intellectual justification for state intervention during short-term downturns or for longer-term state-led development in liberal democracies with capitalist systems.

Although a return to the *status quo ante* dominated by laissez-faire was not possible, given the advent of state provision for war veterans, widows, and orphans as well as the creation of systems of mass education and public health even in the most pro-market countries like Great Britain and the United States, the aggressive expansion of state intervention in the economy came to be associated first and foremost with the rise of communist and fascist regimes in the 1920s. The American and British governments saw this development as a frontal and uncompromising opposition to John Locke's principles of life, security, and property—bedrocks of the Anglo-American system of liberal capitalism and representative government. For defenders of liberal democracy, the takeover by the state of both the economic and political spheres in countries that followed communist or fascist paths became twin menaces that had to be confronted and, if possible, rolled back.

In the context of the onset of the Great Depression, the main consequence of the battle between economic systems (John Maynard Keynes first advocated reflationary policy for Great Britain in 1923) was that at least until 1931, a contractionary economic policy response prevailed in the core capitalist economies, which accentuated the pro-cyclicality of the downturn. The pro-cyclical policy response in the United States under President Herbert Hoover was particularly pernicious. It was not until President Franklin D. Roosevelt was inaugurated in March 1933 that the US government embraced the idea of a state-led countercyclical economic policy. Until then, previous governments had "another idea of what to do about price declines: nothing. Received wisdom and prewar experience said that the recession would correct itself. . . . The Fed [Federal Reserve System] turned to the usual monetary tools to impose a sharp and quick bout of austerity. . . . This policy of liquidationism aimed to force down prices and wages so that excess stocks of labor, food, and goods would be liquidated . . . but the results were troubling not only in the United States but in virtually all the developed world."[10]

Pro-cyclical economic policy dominated in the United States during the Hoover years, although his administration and the Federal Reserve did engage in some countercyclical measures. Nonetheless, they were modest and were reversed in the short term. The economic crisis in the United States had an immediate international spillover effect because the country's economic activity had become the main engine of international growth after the First World War. In contrast, President Roosevelt's New Deal helped revive demand and became a blueprint of state-led economic management that inspired governments throughout Latin America and elsewhere. That a state-led response to the economic crisis could also be implemented in a liberal democracy offered an important counterbalance to the radical left- and right-wing movements and parties in Latin America that expressed a growing admiration for and wanted to emulate such state-led economic experiments as Mussolini's Italy, Stalin's Soviet Union, and Hitler's Germany.

Therefore, the most important difference regarding economic policy ideas between pre- and post–Great Depression shocks and crises is that the earlier ones could not count on a sanctioned recipe for reflationary economics, while post–Great Depression busts benefited immensely from the lessons learned in the 1930s. This later response came in the form of countercyclical monetary and/ or fiscal policies (the type of demand management associated with Keynes), which became the standard way to address subsequent crises.

It is not as if this economic policy approach was a silver bullet that did away with recessions without producing potentially disastrous side effects, such as the creation of new asset price bubbles, a rise in general prices that could culminate in a price-wage spiral of entrenched and growing inflation, or higher future borrowing costs in the face of deep fiscal deficits. The bottom line, however, is that reflationary policies such as lowering interest rates, creating exemptions or lowering taxes, and increasing public spending helped put a floor on decreasing economic activity and falling prices, which stopped the process of debt deflation that had ravaged economies around the world in the early 1930s and kept them from continuing and accelerating.

Avoiding the side effects of expansionary monetary and fiscal policies is a high-wire act that can lead to the premature withdrawal of a stimulus that could reignite an economic downturn (as happened in the United States in 1937 or in Japan in 1997), or to an overextension of a stimulus that could translate into new asset bubbles and/or a more general inflationary process (as was the case in advanced capitalists countries in the mid- and late 1970s with the onset of stagflation). The inherent difficulty in calling an end to or beginning to halt an expansionary economic policy has been especially apparent since the financial and economic bust triggered by the Lehman Brothers' bankruptcy in September 2008, as illustrated by the absence of consensus among politicians, international bureaucrats, economists, and policymakers regarding when to start reining in countercyclical economic policies.[11]

Still, the bottom line remains finding a floor that the process of debt deflation can use to bounce back. From this perspective, pre- and post–Great Depression shocks are fundamentally different. Since the early 1930s, and as a direct result of the ravages of debt deflation during that horrendous conflagration, governments around the world have instead used countercyclical policies to establish floors on declining economic and credit activity and falling prices. The end result has been that by implementing countercyclical policies, governments in countries experiencing harsh economic shocks since that era have at least bought themselves time and potential credibility if they are successful in stabilizing an economy that is in crisis. These tools can then help to defuse distributive pressures against the incumbents—be they in a democratic or an authoritarian regime—and reduce domestic and international conflict from above and below in the face of falling economic activity. How countercyclical macroeconomic policies affect the costs for pressures in favor of and against democracy is, in turn, a function of the type of regime in place in a country battered by economic shocks and crisis.

DOMESTIC SPHERE: DEMOCRACY BEING SQUEEZED
Political Ideologies

To an early twenty-first century observer, it is hard to imagine the intensity of competition over political loyalty that liberal democracy, communism, and fascism engaged in between the two world wars in the growing cities of Latin America. In the 1920s and 30s, this region, which did not suffer the human cost of total war, experienced "signs of accelerated population growth, expansion of urban populations, growth of nationalism, and the beginnings in some cases of mass politics."[12] Structural changes, such as fast population growth and urbanization, forced all actors—domestic and foreign elites, the growing middle classes, and organized labor—to shift their calculations about how politics and political power operated. The rise and spread of mass communications in the 1920s, accompanied by accelerating urbanization, permitted the rise of populism and populist leaders, who tapped the sense of crisis and uncertainty that accompanied the mass movements of migrants from rural backgrounds to the big cities of South America. Scholars note that "a generalized sense of rootlessness and malaise, that sociologists call anomie, afflicted many city dwellers. . . . Conditions were ripe in Latin America for leaders who could give the masses a sense of belonging, provide a semblance of representative government, and undertake changes that would improve daily life. These leaders did emerge and took the initiative in urban politics. Their style of campaigning and administration was later dubbed populism, after its earlier counterpart in the United States."[13]

The rigid ideological division pitting liberal democracy, communism, and fascism against one another sat uncomfortably with successful populist leaders, because they usually had no specific ideology and tended to be pragmatists who would alter their views and their policy according to changing circumstances.[14] Growing Far Left and Far Right movements questioned and tried to destroy liberal democracy, but populist leaders like Alessandri, Ibáñez, and Grove in Chile (between 1920 and 1932) and Yrigoyen in Argentina (in 1916–22 and 1928–30) found it hard to accommodate the extreme groups. Adherents to fascism might have sympathized with General Ibáñez's regime, but the General himself had to keep a watchful eye on his reputation (and that of his government) in front of more traditional conservatives, such as foreign businessmen, representatives of foreign governments, and other so-called respectable members of society, who would have been skeptical about fascism.

Anti-democratic movements did not preach just to the choir. Rather, they experienced growth as people's livelihoods everywhere deteriorated considerably in the face of the implosion of the international economy in the early 1930s. At the same time, the structural conditions that had lowered the costs of collective action in the cities facilitated social and political conflict, which was partly structured by the warring ideological systems of communism, liberal democracy, and fascism.

In the Southern Cone countries, the stakes for the main contenders in the fight for or against democracy were high, because political ideologies, state actors, parties, movements, and (in some cases) populist leaderships were all well developed by the second and third decades of the twentieth century. Communist, socialist, and anarcho-syndicalist alternatives populated the Left; while democratic, liberal, republican, and moderate nationalist and conservative groups occupied the center and the center right; and radical nationalists, Catholic integrists, fascists, and national socialists populated the Far

Right. Bureaucracies and public employment had mushroomed in the Southern Cone nations, thanks to the promotion of state-led growth and development by Presidents Yrigoyen, Ibáñez, and Batlle y Ordóñez. In relative terms, the weight of these two institutional sectors was heaviest in Uruguay, where a large share of this country's politics was dedicated to securing public positions for the adherents of the two main parties. The main state actors in each of the three countries, though, were the armed forces. Their size, training, equipment, and firepower were most formidable in Chile, followed by Argentina, and then Uruguay. Particularly in Argentina and Chile, the military was a decisive political force. Thus the tactics, strategies, and actions of groups on the left and right extremes of the political spectrum, and the way the military reacted to them, established the limits of potential outcomes (ranging from a communist revolution or the anarchist liquidation of the state to a quasi-medieval corporatist Catholic polity or a totalitarian fascist dictatorship) that the mainstream political forces had to consider in their fight for or against democracy during the Great Depression.

THE LEFT

On the Far Left, the most distinctive characteristic in the Southern Cone was the strength of the anarcho-syndicalist movement. This was due to mass immigration from southern Europe, particularly Spain and Italy, where this ideology had strong roots among intellectuals and the laboring masses. In Latin America, anarcho-syndicalism was strongest in the eastern seaboard countries, such as Argentina, Brazil, and Uruguay, but it also had a presence in Chile, Peru, Bolivia, Venezuela, Nicaragua, Mexico, and Cuba.[15] In terms of worker organization, anarcho-syndicalists were influential in the rise of the earliest trade unions in the Southern Cone countries, in the 1880s and 1890s.

Unlike traditional workers' parties (such as the Socialists), which tried to broaden the power and influence of the state as a prerequisite for promoting labor's political and economic inclusion, the efforts of the anarcho-syndicalists were directed "at restricting the activities of the state and blocking its influence in every department of social life wherever they [saw] an opportunity."[16] Thus, as opposed to their socialist and (later) communist counterparts, they rejected collective bargaining and state mediation between workers and employers. Instead, their main weapons were direct action (rather than working through parliaments): strikes, boycotts, sabotage, and anti-militarist propaganda.[17] Deployment of these tactics led time and again to violent confrontations between workers and state forces. According to one author, "from 1900 to 1920 [such confrontations] virtually reached the proportion of an undeclared civil war."[18]

Anarchist-led collective action in Chile led to the worst confrontations between workers and the state's forces of coercion: "Valparaiso strike/massacre (1903), looting and massacre of Santiago (1905), Antofagasta massacre (1906), Iquique miners' massacre (700 plus dead) in 1907, and then the turmoil and further massacres of the post-WWI period into the 1920s and more in the 1930s."[19] Nor was Argentina unscathed, as it endured the *semana trágica* in 1919.

Anarcho-syndicalists lost strength once the Soviet revolution triumphed in 1917 and some workers turned to communism. However, the main labor federations retained some of their anarcho-syndicalist roots, such as distrust of the state and infighting (due to their inherent abhorrence of the principle of authority). According to some authors, these features were partly responsible for preventing the organized workers' movements from being able to mount an effective opposition to the coups against democracy in Argentina in 1930 and in Uruguay in 1933.[20]

Communists capitalized to some extent on the waning influence of anarcho-syndicalism, particularly after the Communist International (Comintern), also known as the Third International, was born in 1919. The Communist parties in Argentina, Chile, and Uruguay were born as offshoots of prior Socialist parties.[21] A Socialist Party had existed in Argentina since 1896, and the first Socialist to be elected to a national legislature in Latin America, in 1904, came from this party. A Socialist Party arose in Uruguay in 1910. Likewise, the Partido Obrero Socialista (POS) was created in Chile in 1912. Communist splinters appeared in 1918 in Argentina and 1920 in Uruguay. The POS became the Communist Party in Chile in 1922. As a result, Socialist parties lost votes, since they competed for the same pool of voters as the Communists. A significant exception was the formation (in 1933) and subsequent strengthening of a new Socialist party in Chile, the Partido Socialista (PS).[22]

Contrary to received opinion, Communist parties were not necessarily bent on overthrowing the regimes in the Latin American countries where they operated in the 1920s and 1930s. To start with, most of the founders and leaders of the Communist parties in the region were foreigners, "a symptom of the congenitally alien character of Marxism in Latin America,"[23] which made it difficult to attract the laboring masses. In addition, the Comintern "discovered" Latin America relatively late. This region lacked priority in the early 1920s, and it was not until the Sixth Congress in 1928 that it was seen as a potential weapon against imperialism, through attacks on US interests.[24] However, even where this might have been possible, thanks to strong party organization in Chile and Uruguay, operating within the system trounced the revolutionary path. This was particularly the case after the Seventh Congress of the Comintern in 1935, when Moscow made a policy U-turn and decided to support the construction of Popular Fronts, that is, alliances with non-fascist bourgeois parties, to fight the Far Right. The end result was a watering down of the Communists' revolutionary instincts by their willingness to support democratic institutions as a way to promote a Popular Front. In Latin America, such tactics not only called off the fight against imperialism, but also went so far as to actually "include American imperialism as an ally."[25]

Chile. This policy was successful in Chile, where the Communists and the Socialists participated in the creation of a Popular Front with centrist parties. The Popular Front went on to win the 1938 presidential elections with Radical Pedro Aguirre Cerda (1938–41), and Communist leaders participated in cabinet positions.

Argentina. Even though the Popular Front tactic did not prosper in Argentina, and the electoral game was rigged after 1930, the Socialists and the Progressive Democrats legitimized the system by participating in elections; moreover, they accepted cabinet positions in General Agustín P. Justo's government (1932–38).[26]

Uruguay. Here, the Left was divided. The Communists followed Moscow's directives and supported the formation of a Popular Front. Failing this, they were in favor of cooperating with Terra's successor, General Alfredo Baldomir (1938–42). The Socialists rejected the idea of the Front or any cooperation with President Baldomir's government because, after all, he was related by marriage to Terra and had been Montevideo's chief of police when police forces took over and shut down the General Assembly on March 31, 1933, breaking apart Uruguayan democracy.[27]

—⚬ ⚬—

All in all, confronted with the possibility that fascism could take hold in their respective countries, most of the parties and movements from the Left decided to throw in their lot with the mainstream political forces. In Chile, socialists and communists participated in the triumphant Popular Front, formed in 1936 and victorious in the presidential election of 1938. In the other two Southern Cone countries, elections and some measure of civil liberties, however restricted they remained—in Argentina from General Justo's presidency to the election of Colonel Juan Domingo Perón in 1946, or in Uruguay from President Terra's *autogolpe* in 1933 to President Baldomir's own coup in 1942—seemed preferable to the potential development of right-wing totalitarian regimes.

THE RIGHT

The Far Right movements, which also developed in the course of the 1920s in the Southern Cone, were bitterly anti-communist and suspicious about internationalism. Paradoxically, the Far Right criticized liberalism and the capitalist system, as did communism. However, its angle of attack was different. Fascists and Catholic integrists did not identify the original sin of capitalism as being situated in private property, but in the perceived excesses of international high finance. Frieden writes that "at least some of the anti-Semitic bent of the fascists was related to the fact that in Germany and much of Eastern Europe, many of the internationally oriented businesses were owned by Jews."[28] As a consequence, in the view of scholars of the Far Right, anti-Semitism became a substitute for class struggle.[29] The Far Right supported closing the economy (autarky), nationalizing enterprises, creating cooperatives, and restricting immigration. In contrast to the ups and downs inherent in liberal capitalism, the Far Right set forth a protected, disciplined, state-led society, which attracted the loyalty not only of many of the elites and the upper middle classes, but also those among the lower middle classes and the working classes. All the Southern Cone countries experienced variations on this ideology.

Argentina. Right-wing nationalism was strongest in Argentina. The nationalists' critique of liberal democracy extended to their being against the idea of political parties and electoral participation, preferring to take power by fiat through the armed forces, where they were influential. This influence had grown, along with the concerns about the rise of left-wing politics, in the wake of the strikes and workers' unrest that culminated in the 1919 *semana trágica*, after which radical activity (such as the formation of soviets) among soldiers and noncommissioned officers in two garrisons had been discovered and suppressed.[30] Officers responded by creating the Logia General San Martín, whose purpose was "to eliminate from the Army all partisan political activity. . . . Unfortunately, in the effort to eliminate partisan politics the Logia members surrendered themselves to politics of another sort. [They took control of other influential military organizations, such as the Círculo Militar,] as a means of pressuring the government to be less tolerant to the political Left."[31] Right-wing civilians reacted to the events of 1919 by forming the Liga Patriótica Argentina, which advocated safeguarding the nation from the Left. Even though the Liga initially tried to bridge the growing Argentine class divide by reaching out to the working class and the lower middle classes, it "gave way to virulent 'nationalist,' anti-liberal, and anti-Semitic groups, which recruited major intellectuals and reached a crescendo in the years 1927–30."[32] The end result was that military personnel and civilians from these 1920s groups went on to support enthusiastically General José Felix Uriburu's 1930 coup. The new military regime also endorsed the creation of the Legión Cívica, a civilian paramilitary group entrusted with the promotion of the conservative revolution.

The right-wing nationalist movement's view of the world was Manichean: virtue was associated with manliness, Catholicism, rural life, and the countryside in general; while vice and decadence were linked with effeminate cosmopolitanism, secularism, city life, and all things associated with it.[33] This world view prompted nationalist leaders to "reduce all of their enemies to one: high finances and imperialism combined with the Communists, the foreigners responsible for national disintegration, and also the Jews, all of them united in a sinister conspiracy. [They] demanded the establishment of new governing elites that were nationalist and not beholden to foreign interests."[34] Despite this credo, which resonated with segments of the upper and upper middle classes, the nationalists were unable to create a corporatist regime. They could not gain the loyalty of a majority of the traditional conservatives, who remained skeptical about ceding ultimate control to the military. Instead, they preferred to return to a system such as the pre-1912 one, characterized by parties and elections, but where competition was limited, the oligarchy prevailed, and the military enforced the status quo.

Chile. The Far Right did not come as close to achieving power in Chile as it did in Argentina after General Uriburu's September 1930 coup. The Chilean National Socialist Movement (MNS) was born in April 1932 in the turmoil surrounding the fall of General Ibáñez in July 1931. The MNS remained a fringe movement, but its tactics of public unrest and violence gave it considerable public visibility and influence. Much more so than in Argentina and Uruguay, extremist groups on both the left and the right carried their quarrel to the streets of Santiago, Valparaíso, and other Chilean cities, where they fought pitched battles. Public unrest became worse as a consequence of the 1930 economic collapse, but it had initially appeared and then grown uninterruptedly since the late 1910s, when the production of synthetic nitrates had decimated the Chilean mining industry. Unemployed miners and their families migrated south to the cities in search of work, and activist trade unions, under the Federación Obrera de Chile, capitalized on these conditions to push for redistribution during Alessandri's first presidency.

The armed forces, among whose ranks could be found adherents to both Marxism and fascism, became the main arbiters of the distributive conflict between the elites, who supported the status quo through the continuation of the Parliamentary Republic, and the reformists, headed by President Alessandri, who advocated remedial measures to defuse pressures from below. The ideological divisions that characterized Chilean officers—with their strong left- and right-wing factions—meant that, unlike the situation in Argentina, the victory of right-wing doctrines imposed by the military was not a foregone conclusion. In fact, the political instability created by the repeated replacement of populist-reformist and conservative regimes between 1924 and 1932 led the principal elite and popular leaders to compromise and support the return of civilian rule under (restricted) democracy after Alessandri's October 1932 presidential victory.

Uruguay. Because of the dominance of bipartisan civilian politics over military intervention in Uruguay, the stakes for mainstream political actors there were not as high as in Argentina and Chile. While the Left, by and large, was willing to continue acting through established institutions (which was also the case in the two other countries), the Far Right was much weaker than in Argentina and Chile. This weakness was not self-evident. After all, Uruguay was sandwiched between Argentina and Brazil, where right-wing nationalism and integralism, respectively, had acquired strong political influences after the 1930 coups in both countries. Still, in Uruguay fascist ideology "did not crystallize in a party or significant current of public opinion. . . . There was no fascist government project between 1933 and 1938. [What existed was] a strongly conservative politics, supported by influential sectors of the bourgeoisie who looked with admiring eyes toward fascism."[35]

Thus, even though some sectors supported the idea of creating a corporatist regime through the 1934 constitution, the mainstream political forces and, crucially, even the *herreristas*—the most right-wing Blanco faction—opposed it. In place of fascism's critique of multiparty democracy as leading to obstruction and inaction, they argued that "parties effect a stabilization of social forces and of the interests of the state. . . . The parties avoid more dissolution than they create."[36] Herrera himself argued that "there is simply the deep desire to stay close to these historic groups (the two main parties) and to permit the one victorious in the urns to rule, while the other controls its action. . . . What we have desired is simply to affirm the principle that in the government of Uruguay, exclusivism is not permitted."[37]

—◌ ◌—

In short, despite the fact that the international sphere acted like a magnifying glass by expanding domestic ideological conflicts and situating them in the global arena in the 1920s–30s, the historical evidence suggests that by and large the Far Left in the Southern Cone countries did not engage in a fight to the death against capitalism in the context of the Great Depression. More often than not, left-wing parties continued participating in politics through institutional channels and threw in their lot with the bourgeois system, if only to resist attempts by far-right military and civilian advocates who wanted to destroy both the Left and liberal democracy. The Far Right exaggerated the threat from the Left, and the image of an expanding "Red tide" taking over power was used as a justification for clamping down on dissent in the aftermath of the Great Depression.

This finding confirms the general observation made by Juan Linz in the context of democratic regime breakdowns in Europe and Latin America in the 1920s–30s and 1960s–70s: "most of the breakdowns have been counter-revolutionary, in that they have aimed at preventing radical changes in the social structure, even though they often culminated in decisive changes."[38] During the Great Depression, left-wing ideas in the Southern Cone countries led to decisive regime changes, not through civilian movements or parties, but only when they took root among a critical mass in the armed forces, as was the case in Chile between 1924 and 1932, when its dictatorship was overthrown. On the other hand, whether from the Far Left or the Far Right, ideologies that explicitly rejected liberal democracy and positioned themselves as substitutes for it lowered the costs for the organization and exercise of pressures against democracy (from civilian as well as military individuals and groups) and, at least in Argentina and Uruguay, contributed to its breakdown.

Economic Policy Ideas and Crisis Management

Regardless of their own ideological inclinations, all the governments in the Southern Cone countries (and elsewhere) faced a fait accompli regarding economic management after the implosion of the international economy in 1929–31. A consequence of resource scarcity was that every government—conservative, liberal, or populist—gradually had to violate orthodox economic policy as they confronted real problems, such as the possibility of defaulting on debt obligations, the establishment of exchange controls to prevent serious gold outflows, or the installation of price controls and subsidies to cushion the costs of adjustment borne out by most groups in society. As a result, heterodox, reflationary economic policy was not so much designed by plan before being implemented, but rather grew up as the collection of government responses to the practical socioeconomic and political dislocations produced by the Great Depression.

These responses were in no way limited to the Southern Cone countries or to Latin America more generally because, as Thorp has observed, "international trends also favored the move towards a stronger role for government.... The Soviet . . . Italian and German [state-centered systems] had a clear influence on Vargas in Brazil, Cárdenas in Mexico, and Perón in Argentina. U.S. New Deal policies of the 1930s and the increased role of planning and controls in wartime were added influences."[39] The state-centered polities that Presidents Batlle y Ordóñez and Ibáñez created in Uruguay and Chile, respectively, can be added to this list.

In short, with both the international and domestic spheres reinforcing heterodox economic policy, even conservative governments that espoused a philosophy that was anti-statist and orthodox in its macroeconomic management—such as President Justo's in Argentina and President Terra's in Uruguay—ended up furthering the gradual process of urbanization, industrialization, and expanded state-led economic directives. In Chile, the military had introduced radical change in the direction of state-led economic policy and development since the 1920s, so even though "the Socialist Republic had failed . . . socialism in one form or other was now very firmly on the agenda."[40] Hence the economic policy norm in the Southern Cone countries (as elsewhere) became variants on state-led economic nationalism through heterodox economic policy.

ARGENTINA

General Justo's government abandoned the orthodox, contractionary policy that had been implemented in the country since President Yrigoyen had run out of options to try to pump up the economy in 1929–30. In mid-1933, Justo appointed Federico Pinedo, who had worked with Raúl Prebisch, to the Ministry of Finance. This change led to greater state intervention and the gradual closure of the Argentine economy. Control of the financial sector was enhanced by the establishment of the central bank in 1935; banks that failed after the economic shock were liquidated in an orderly way. Regulation was brought to bear on the commercialization of agriculture, and minimum prices for producers were guaranteed.

Argentina's economy was led by foodstuffs exports, but in the midst of the deep crisis the Justo government and its backers had to go against their own ideological instincts and accept the promotion of industry in order to stimulate the economy. This was facilitated by the heterodox economic policy tools (e.g., exchange controls, an income tax, and tariffs) that the government had introduced since 1931 to cope with the crisis.[41] The only area where the government stuck with orthodoxy was in its commitment to keep meeting its external debt obligations punctually, which (despite its unpopularity) was considered a key lifeline; officials and landowners feared that a suspension of payments would invite retaliation from Great Britain, on whose markets Argentina depended. Thus Minister Pinedo also was committed to strengthening Argentina's economic links with Great Britain.[42]

Heterodox economic policy and official support for industrial growth helped to turn around the economy and, in so doing, reinforced the new status quo in Argentina. This changed equilibrium, however, contained the seeds of its undoing. The interests of the landowning elites were restored politically by the military coup of 1930 and the "civilianization" of the regime after Justo assumed the presidency, but the context in which this happened (the state took over economic growth and development) and its measures (an industrial policy and the strengthening of urban economic activity) weakened the interests of *el campo*— the concept that Argentines have used to identify the big landowning interests—relative to the growing urban-based popular pressures that went on to become the backbone of *peronismo*, the nemesis of *el campo*.

CHILE

Effective crisis management and the appeasement of contending economic interests were important factors that helped to account for the success of politicoeconomic stabilization during the second presidency of Arturo Alessandri (1932-38). The government accomplished this task by its commitment to embrace economic heterodoxy, carried out under the effective management of Minister of Finance Gustavo Ross. Alessandri had an advantage in that the previous regime (the Socialist Republic) had tried to push radical economic change, which made his own measures seem much less extreme. Still, President Alessandri raised levies and introduced exchange controls in the copper industry; more than doubled general tariffs; strengthened the protectionist pattern of quotas, licenses, and the control of foreign exchange; promoted public works; established price controls over basic staples for consumers; fostered a loose monetary policy by the central bank; and refused to pay the interest owed on the external debt between 1931 and 1935, during which time Chile defaulted on its foreign obligations.[43]

As in Argentina, the government's policies boosted urban and industrial activity and interests, and there was a substantial redistribution from the countryside to the cities. Although heterodox policy would end up creating structural problems for the Chilean economy, such as a persistently high inflationary record between the 1940s and the early 1970s, in the short term it promoted a vigorous economic recovery.[44] As in Argentina, the economic upturn strengthened the hand of the new status quo. What was different was the status quo itself: an authoritarian regime under civilian and electoral garbs in Argentina (*la década infame*), and a limited democracy (due to literacy barriers to enfranchisement) in Chile.

URUGUAY

However much President Terra wooed the supporters of regime change (the big *estancieros* and British businesses) by vowing to put a stop to the growth of statism and nationalism embedded in *batllismo*, he could not roll back state intervention in the Uruguayan economy. Faced with a stringent economic contraction between 1931 and 1933, Terra could not make good on his promises to return to orthodoxy and market discipline. Instead, after executing his *autogolpe* at the end of March 1933, he went on to declare the partial suspension of foreign debt obligations.[45] He put this into practice by establishing that interest payments would be deposited in local banks and would be made in local currency, rather than in gold. Likewise, despite their ruralist rhetoric, President Terra and his ministers pursued a policy of industrial protection (as did Argentina and Chile), which transferred income from the countryside to the urban economy.[46] These two measures negatively affected the interests of Terra's main backers. Furthermore, the government established minimum prices for farmers' products, imposed import controls, and devalued the local currency.[47] These actions protected different aspects of both the rural and the urban economies, but the main point is that they were heterodox policies that ran counter to the ideological and philosophical orientation of the governing *terrista-herrerista* coalition (as was the case for the Justo government in Argentina). Paralleling what happened in Argentina and Chile, the weight and influence of urban, industrial activity and interests increased relative to the countryside.

Heterodox economic policy measures in Uruguay, as in Argentina, ended up strengthening urban interests, which were the enemies of the conservative, non-democratic regimes established in these countries in 1933 and 1930, respectively.

CONCLUSION

The interaction of the international and domestic spheres in the realm of ideas acted like a magnifying glass in the Southern Cone countries, as it did elsewhere during the Great Depression. In terms of political philosophies, the main consequence of this effect was the amplification of ideologically fueled conflict, although populism and populist leaders, well known for their pragmatism rather than for their ideological rigidity, also came of age and thrived for a time in countries like Argentina and Chile in the 1920s. As for economic ideas and policy, the main effect of the 1929–31 global financial and economic busts was the spread of the type of reflationary macroeconomic policies thereafter associated with John Maynard Keynes. This is not to say that heterodox economic policy would have not existed without Keynes. A recent book analyzing the personalities and decisions of the central bank presidents of the United States, Great Britain, France, and Germany during the 1920s and early 1930s notes that in the United States, both President Herbert Hoover and the Federal Reserve engaged in fiscal and monetary easing in 1930 (although not in a systematic and continued way); and Hjalmar Schacht, returning to the presidency of the Reichsbank in Germany under Hitler's first government in 1933, also engaged in economic stimulus "even before Maynard Keynes had fully elaborated his ideas."[48] Authorities simply had no choice but to respond to the challenges of crisis management and redistributive conflict during the early 1930s by breaking off with orthodoxy as problems escalated.

Expanding a bit on the topic of political ideologies, the growth and intensity of left- and right-wing critiques of liberal democracy lowered the costs for organizing and exercising pressures against democracy in the Southern Cone countries, as was the case more generally throughout Latin America and Europe. Regarding our three nations, in Chile left-wing military officers appealed to populism as a way to fight the oligarchy and its conservative ideas (which were associated with the Parliamentary Republic) between 1924 and 1932, when a limited democracy was restored. The growing urban machine of President Yrigoyen and his populist approach fought the landowning elites in Argentina between the late 1910s and 1930, when the military brought down democracy and restored the *status quo ante* by reestablishing the elites' control of the electoral process and, therefore, their access to power and decision making. Finally, *anti-batllista* Colorados and *herrerista* Blancos fought the secular, nationalist modernization carried out by the *batllista* Colorados in Uruguay since the late 1910s, and the former two factions took over after executing a civilian *autogolpe* that suspended democracy between 1933 and 1942. From the perspective of political ideologies, a reasonable conclusion is that democracy was more exposed and vulnerable in the 1930s than during any of the other periods analyzed in this work (the early 1980s, the late 1990s–early 2000s, and since 2008).

Two conclusions can be made regarding the realm of economic ideas and policy. First, the adoption of reflationary economic policies—implemented initially by advanced capitalist governments and then employed by countries on the periphery, such as our three Southern Cone cases—helped stabilize and reactivate economic activity. This, in turn, helped stabilize and strengthen the status quo: fostering a return to limited democracy during Alessandri's second presidency in Chile; establishing the basis for the system of phony elections and control of the political process by the elites in the *década infame* in Argentina; and allowing the *terrista-herrerista* coalition to remain in power until 1938 in Uruguay. As such, economic stabilization through heterodox policy helped bolster whichever type of regime was in power when effective stabilization was implemented. It therefore raised the costs (at least in the short term) of pressures in favor of democracy in cases where there was successful economic stabilization under authoritarian rule (Argentina and Uruguay), and lowered such costs when successful stabilization occurred under restricted democratic rule (Chile).

Second, the adoption of economic heterodoxy as the backbone of macroeconomic policy, which first and foremost meant privileging domestic economic activity at the expense of international activity, enhanced urban, industrial activity and interests relative to those of the countryside. The relative weakening of the traditional landowning elites (compared with urban industrialists, white-collar and blue-collar workers, politicians, and bureaucrats) was of particular importance for the balance of power in each of these three societies. This change gave impetus to the enemies of the conservative, non-democratic regimes in Argentina and Uruguay. In Chile, which had experienced state-led growth and development under Ibáñez since his takeover in 1927, the application of a heterodox economic policy during Alessandri's second presidency likewise strengthened urban, industrial activity and interests.

The end result of the adoption of heterodox economic policy and state-led growth and development in the Southern Cone countries (as elsewhere)—with its accompanying urbanization, industrialization, and high literacy rates—was that politics became more mass based after the state took over the economy in the face of the 1929-31 financial and economic implosions. Regardless of their ideological and/or interests-based orientations, individuals and groups in charge of the state—be they conservative-ruralist groups or, more logically, liberal or progressive urban-based ones—had to prioritize mediation between growing urban-based economic activity (and the satisfaction of its interests) and the more entrenched, land-based oligarchic ones.

PART TWO

Economic Crises and Democracy in the Late Twentieth Century

The forces for global capitalism at the end of the twentieth century proved extremely powerful, as they had been at the end of the nineteenth. Earlier economic globalists weathered the Great Depression of 1873–1896, with its mass populist movements and recurrent debt crises. The recent course of globalization [since the 1980s] survived global recession, persistently high unemployment in Europe, social disintegration in the former Communist countries, and contagious [financial] crises in Asia and Latin America. Technological advances, the power of internationalist economic interests, and trends in global politics reinforced the globalizing trend.

—Jeffry A. Frieden, *Global Capitalism*

CHAPTER SIX

1982 Debt Crisis and 1997–2002 Emerging Markets Crises

The Bretton Woods system delivered relative international financial stability between the aftermath of the Second World War and 1971. The system's anchor was pegging member countries' currencies to the US dollar, which was credible, given the free convertibility of dollars into gold at $35 an ounce, a parity that had been established in 1934.[1] This anchor did not prevent national financial crises from happening—and, when they did happen, countries had the option to borrow funds from the IMF, which had not been the case in the Great Depression years—but it helped to contain the potential contagion and spread of a given national financial crisis into an international one. After all, holders of US dollars anywhere in the world knew that they could redeem them for solid gold. Therefore, the international dominolike financial crises that came to be common around the world after 1971 were rare during the years when the US dollar was convertible to gold.

1982 SHOCK AND DEBT CRISIS
Global Imbalances in the 1970s

The first shock to the international system was US president Richard Nixon's decision to take the dollar off the gold standard in August 1971 in the face of growing trade and fiscal deficits amid a decelerating economy. These conditions had led economic agents to dump dollars in the expectation of dollar devaluation before the 1972 presidential elections. By breaking the dollar-gold parity, the US government was able to devalue its currency to restore macroeconomic equilibrium in the face of sustained overspending, due to the Vietnam War and the social expenditure commitments incurred by the federal government in the 1960s through redistributive programs like the War on Poverty and the Great Society. Excess dollar liquidity internationally had also given way to what came to be known as the Eurodollar market as international banks, stuffed with US dollars, tried to find borrowers. An early spurt in demand for foreign credit in Latin America therefore occurred between the late 1960s and early 1970s, when international private banks joined the fray. Most credit until then had been channeled through official sources: bilateral ones, such as the US Export-Import Bank (Ex-Im Bank) or the US Agency for International Development (USAID); or multilateral ones, such as the IMF, the WB, and the IADB. Lending by these private banks accounted for almost half the increase in the public external debt incurred in Latin America between 1966 and 1972.[2]

The main consequence of these changes in the international monetary system that affected the independent variable of my analysis (financial shocks) was that, as Frieden puts it, once the dollar was taken off gold, "short-term investors— speculators, to use a loaded term—could move money in response to differences in national monetary conditions and could threaten the independence of national macroeconomic policy" in the context of governments' growing indebtedness.[3] End result? Out with international financial stability and in with a brave new world of currency exchange arbitrage that profited from betting against the capacity of national governments to keep up (or down) with a rough peg to the US dollar, which was now a floating currency.

INFLATIONARY TAKEOFF AND PUZZLE OF STAGFLATION

Without the straitjacket of automatic adjustment forced by fixed exchange rates, governments gained a degree of autonomy in monetary and fiscal policies. One outcome was that governments in both advanced and developing countries turned to expansionary policies to stimulate growth, and the international economy surged between 1970 and 1973. This surge was nonetheless inflationary, because rather than being a function of rising productivity, it was the consequence of sharp growth in both the money supply and public spending. Economic stimulus in the advanced countries created higher demands for commodities and raw materials, which (in the short term) benefited exporters of these goods, such as a majority of the Latin American countries.

However, expansive growth—courtesy of a commodity boom—was short lived in the face of a second shock to the system. In tandem with the end of dollar-gold convertibility and the rise of expansionary, inflation-producing policies, the Organization of Petroleum-Exporting Countries (OPEC), the oil cartel that had existed since 1960, called an embargo during the Arab-Israeli

War of October 1973. This shock led to a quadrupling of oil prices in a few weeks (from just above 2 USD per barrel to 5 and then 12 USD), and the embargo lasted from October 1973 to March 1974. The steep rise in oil prices dramatically altered international financial currents by creating huge inflows into oil-exporting countries and equivalent outflows from the main oil-consuming countries: industrialized nations such as the United States, Western Europe, and Japan. Advanced economies fell into recession as oil-exporting countries rapidly accumulated foreign exchange. The recession in the advanced capitalist world was the worst since the end of the Second World War. Post–oil shock economic conditions altered some of the basic economic policy assumptions that had come to be taken for granted since the rise of Keynesian macroeconomic policy management in the 1930s.

In particular, the Phillips curve (where the rate of inflation and the rate of unemployment are inversely related), which helped policymakers fine tune economies into full employment conditions in the 1950s and 1960s, broke down. In the post–oil shock world, price increases and mounting job losses went hand in hand. The problem came to be known as stagflation, and it gave plenty of ammunition to critics of the Keynesian consensus, which had reigned supreme in the sphere of economic policy ideas until then (see chapter 9). Advocates of the monetarist school, with a strong base at the University of Chicago, extolled neoclassical economics by reiterating that free market discipline was more effective than government intervention in the economy. In the context of accelerating inflation, Friedman's quantity theory of money, where general price changes were a function of changes in the supply of money, gained traction.

To add to the stubborn rise of inflation and the shedding of industrial jobs in advanced economies, the stock markets in New York and London suffered a collapse in 1973–74 (US stocks declined by 50% in that bust),[4] which meant that significant deterioration occurred not only in the real economy (investment, output, employment, and consumption), but also in the world of money and, therefore, in future credit conditions and the potential for economic growth. In the years 1974–75, the world economy "plunged into the steepest recession since the 1930s."[5] The world economy faced a peculiar type of imbalance. On the one hand, oil-exporting developing economies, awash with cash from the petrodollars they received during the oil shocks (a second oil shock took place in 1978–80), did not possess deep domestic financial systems or diversified economies. On the other hand, the advanced capitalist countries, which did possess these features, lacked short-term capital that they could invest to stimulate growth. The end result was that the Middle Eastern recipients of petrodollars recycled them in search of yield and investment opportunities through London and New York banks.

Investment opportunities did not look promising in economies suffering from stagflation, such as those in the United States and Western Europe. In contrast, conditions were ripe in Latin America, where governments in both democratic and authoritarian regimes were eager to access credit markets for two reasons. First, these governments had to keep servicing their external debt in order to obtain further credit, but debt service was already relatively high from the external debt commitments they had made since the second half of the 1960s. Debt service equaled around 25% of the region's annual exports by 1973.[6] Second, between the late 1960s and early 1970s, governments in the region tried to give a final push to import-substitution industrialization through state-led development concentrated in large-scale projects (which explains their willingness to tap into the Eurodollar market earlier); therefore they required further access to capital. It would take the region's 1982 economic implosion to hammer the last nail in the coffin of Latin America's long dream of becoming a leading region economically through import-substitution industrialization.

Still, the point for my analysis is that the 1982 bust was made possible—like its predecessor in the 1930s and its heirs in the late 1990s–early 2000s and the one since 2008—thanks to a prolonged foreign credit boom. The prime motivator for what Kindleberger calls the *causa remota* of Latin America's 1982 economic collapse was the massive accumulation of dollar-denominated foreign loans that were available after 1973–74 through London- and New York–based private banks, which channeled billions in petrodollars to credit-hungry public and private sectors around Latin America.

It is important to highlight that both the state *and* private businesses in the Latin American countries tapped into foreign credit. What varied was how much debt each sector contracted in the different countries. For example, most of Chile's foreign indebtedness in the years 1977–81 came from private-sector groups known as the *conglomerados* (see chapter 8). More than two-thirds of the foreign debts accumulated by these groups were originally not backed by public guarantees, because government officials wrongly assumed that private borrowing would be used efficiently, making an exchange rate crisis only a remote possibility.[7] The need to secure fresh credit lines once international loans dried up in 1982 was what forced the Chilean military regime to extend guarantees and therefore socialize massive private losses. Thus, while the proportion of the country's public debt before the financial crisis in 1981 was 36% of the total, it soared to 86% by 1987, given the socialization of private external debt.[8] Chile's private-driven foreign indebtedness was in sharp contrast to what happened in Brazil and Mexico, where the bulk of their external debt was originally contracted by the state and therefore was public debt. In Argentina, both the public and the private sectors had acquired foreign debt.

International banks concentrated their lending in the region's largest economies (Brazil, Mexico, Argentina, Chile, and Venezuela), although small, well-to-do economies (such as Uruguay, Costa Rica, and Panama) also tapped into private markets. Latin American economic agents preferred private capital sources to official ones, because the former did not contain conditionality provisions (policy commitments to adjust macroeconomic variables and restore equilibrium through demand-contraction measures). The change in the official/private debt profile was striking. Up until 1968, official sources of Latin American public external debt accounted for 60% of the total; by 1982 this had been reversed, and private banks accounted for close to 58%.[9] Outstanding loans to Latin America went from an annual average of 5.4 billion USD in the years 1966–70 to 29.2 billion in the years 1978–81.[10] High foreign indebtedness was sustainable for Latin America in the context of good terms of trade for its commodities and low interest rates for its loans. In fact, borrowing in international markets made great sense, because *real* interest rates were negative in the face of growing inflation.

But this could not last forever. Greater financial inflows than outflows started moving in reverse as a consequence of the second oil shock (1978–81), which was caused by severe disruptions to world oil markets from the Islamic revolution in Iran and the invasion of that country by Iraq in 1980. Both nations were leading world oil exporters. According to some economic historians, such as Bulmer-Thomas, this new shock—the result of partly ideological, partly geopolitical, and partly economic factors—represented "a watershed in global economic management."[11] It affected advanced as well as developing economies. The former, in the throes of stagflation since 1974, suffered a further hit, which reinforced growing inflationary pressures that were coupled with a worsening economic recession and more layoffs. Recession in the capitalist core affected Latin American terms of trade, as the demand for commodities slowed down.

More importantly in the short term, President Jimmy Carter appointed Paul Volcker—undersecretary of the Treasury under Nixon in 1969–74 and president of the Federal Reserve Bank of New York in 1975–79—chairman of the Federal Reserve in August 1979.[12] Mr. Volcker decided to slay the dragon of stagflation with the sword of deepening and prolonging the international recession by tightening US monetary policy. US short-term interest rates skyrocketed from 11% in 1979 to close to 22% in 1981.

This monetary-policy shock produced a dramatic reversal of fortune for the highly indebted economies in Latin America. An index for the region's net barter terms of trade, which equaled 100 in 1982, fell to 87 in 1983 and 79 in 1986. Moreover, the extra amounts of interest that had to be paid on foreign loans contracted since the early 1970s also skyrocketed. The ratio of external debt payments to exports exploded from 26.6% in 1975 to 59% in 1982, lowering the likelihood that countries could continue to service their debt. A bigger and rapidly growing bill for their foreign debt commitments forced governments throughout the region to acquire increasingly shorter-term, higher-interest loans, simply to continue paying interest on the principal. The sum total of Latin American debt jumped from 184 billion USD at the end of 1979 to 314 billion in the late summer of 1982.[13] In late 1981, Latin America was borrowing 1 billion USD weekly just to keep access to further credit open.[14] Financial conditions during this time were not unlike previous credit expansion manias. Thorp asserts that "echoes of the 1920s resound. Both the 1920s and the 1970s witnessed debt boom subject to the classic overshooting that follows from the tendency in such situations to underestimate risks."[15]

Mexican Moratorium, Regional Bust, and the Fall of Authoritarian Regimes

Mexico wielded the pin that burst the debt bubble in August 1982 when its Treasury Secretary, Jesús Reyes Heroles, announced that the federal government did not have the cash to meet its short-term debt obligations and therefore declared a three-month moratorium on payments. The tide of southbound credit unleashed by American, Canadian, and British banks quickly ebbed. The pullback was indiscriminate, and it can be accurately described by Kindleberger's anatomy of crises: when signs of financial distress appear during speculative booms and prices start declining, investors reach a point—and reaching this point is sometimes gradual and at other times quite sudden—when they switch to selling, in anticipation of further and faster falls in prices. Borrowing a term from nineteenth-century observers of market behavior, Kindleberger noted that the onset of revulsion begins when this point is reached: "The race out of real or long-term financial securities and into money may turn into a stampede. . . . Revulsion or discredit may lead to panic . . . as investors crowd to get through the door before it slams shut."[16]

Thus, after Mexico announced its debt moratorium, the credit tap ran dry for everyone else in Latin America as foreign banks froze lending throughout the region. The flow of capital, which had been favorable for Latin American borrowers for more than seven years, turned in the opposite direction within a few months. Frieden observes that while annual dollar flows to and from Latin America were favorable to the region—at 20 billion USD—in 1981, by 1983 Latin America suffered a net outflow of the same amount. The bursting of the external debt bubble then "ushered in a debt crisis of 1930s proportions."[17]

The real economies of all countries—including those whose governments (like Colombia's) had been prudent and refrained from the 1970s foreign-debt mania—suffered severe, prolonged credit and growth contractions, leading to the common description of the years 1982–90 as Latin America's lost decade of growth and development. Frieden aptly summarizes the cataclysm, where "income per person declined by 10 percent, real wages fell by at least 30 percent, and investment fell even further, while inflation rose above 1,000 percent in many countries."[18] Thorp adds that per capita social spending remained 6% lower in 1990 than it had been in 1981, while the number of households living below the poverty line increased to 41% in 1990, compared with 35% in 1980.[19]

Debt Crisis in the Southern Cone Countries

Paralleling the potential effect of the 1929–31 financial shocks and their aftermath on democracy, the democratic cause had more to win than lose in Latin America in 1982 after Mexico's debt moratorium led to a financial stampede that bankrupted most of the region's economies. In 1982 (as in 1929–30), favorable prospects for democratic governments were based on their potential, rather than on their prevalence on the ground. Democracy was not as rare in 1982 as it was in 1929, when Argentina and Uruguay had the only democratic regimes in the region. Still, according to Smith's political regime chronology and classification of nineteen Latin American countries, when Mexico's debt moratorium triggered the international debt crisis in August 1982, this area had just six democratic regimes: Colombia, Costa Rica, the Dominican Republic, Ecuador, Peru, and Venezuela.[20]

Unlike the 1930s, however, when the only two democracies in the region collapsed and just one country was able to transition to a democracy that was long lived, the 1982 debt crisis and its aftermath, the lost decade, seem, if not to have triggered, at least to have helped augment pressures in favor of ousting authoritarian regimes and transitioning to democracy. In commenting on this radical change in political regime landscapes, Frieden notes that "in 1980 there were two elected civilian governments in South America; by 1990 there were no dictatorships left." He goes on to infer that "the crisis led to more democratic rule in dozens more countries outside Latin America, from South Korea to Thailand, from the Philippines to Zambia."[21] Other authors have also seen the expansion of the third wave of world democratization as partly due to the economic crises of the 1980s that wreaked havoc not only in the United States, Western Europe, Latin America, and the Far East, but also in the Soviet Union and the Central and Eastern European countries under its aegis.[22]

There seems to be little doubt that financial shocks and economic crises in the 1980s rocked political regimes of all types (democratic, authoritarian, and totalitarian) around the world, and that the third wave democratization and the embrace of free market capitalism accelerated and spread to all continents. The extent to which such shocks and crises led to political conflict, however, centered on political regime survival/change, and how this conflict played out varied greatly, according to contextual factors. Our three Southern Cone countries went into the whirlwind of the 1982 crisis sharing three important similarities: (1) economically, they were highly indebted, like most of the rest of the Latin American countries; (2) politically, they had been under the rule of military regimes (Chile and Uruguay since 1973, and Argentina since 1976); and (3) financially, they underwent their worst economic crises since the Great Depression as a consequence of the 1982 fallout. Figure 6.1 shows the changing trajectories of annual GDP in these three countries during these years, and their economic and political similarities went even further.

First, in terms of economic policy, the military regimes in the three Southern Cone countries implemented what amounted to neoconservative economics.[23] As Joseph Ramos observes in his classic work, the extent to which the military juntas implemented orthodox stabilization, made adjustments, and then initiated a move toward market liberalization in different sectors varied greatly in the three countries. Between 1975 and 1982, Chile was the only country where a comprehensive implementation of what in the 1990s would come to be known as the Washington consensus took place. In contrast, even though the governments in Argentina and Uruguay attempted orthodox stabilization and adjustment to deal with spiraling inflation, they in no way engaged in any privatization, trade liberalization, or deregulation of domestic markets;

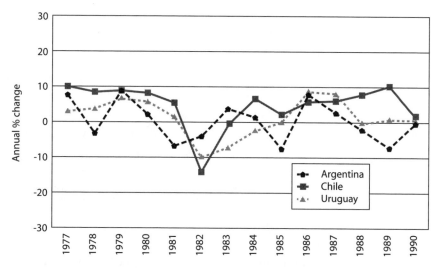

Figure 6.1. Growth trajectories in the Southern Cone countries, 1977–90

Source: Based on data from the *Oxford Latin American Economic History Database*, http://oxlad.qeh.ox.ac.uk/ search.php [accessed July 7, 2009].

instead, both military regimes remained committed to nationalist, inward-looking industrial growth.[24]

The free market experiment in Chile did not go unnoticed in the core capitalist countries. Later champions of what was known in the 1970s as neoconservative economics (and which later came to be identified popularly as neoliberalism), such as Margaret Thatcher in Great Britain and Ronald Reagan in the United States, made their case for rolling back the state and spurring progress by allowing the markets to sharpen competition by pointing to General Pinochet's turnaround of the Chilean economy. That was, of course, before the 1982 regional economic collapse, which swallowed Chile's economy, along with the economies of most of the rest of Latin America. In fact, just as in the early 1930s, Chile suffered an economic depression in 1982–83 (see table 6.1).

Still, surveying the international economic landscape at the turn of the decade (1980–81) before the busts, the neoconservative, or neoliberal, experiment in Chile was regarded internationally as an example that could be emulated to defeat stagflation, move away from state-led economic policy, and (in some ways) return to the type of international economy that had prevailed and spurred the advanced stage of the industrial revolution during the first globalization years (1870–1914). In other words, exit Fabians and New Dealers, re-enter Herbert Spencer and the free market philosophy of America's gilded age.

TABLE 6.1
Macroeconomic indicators, Chile, 1980–85

	1980	1981	1982	1983	1984	1985
GDP growth	7.7	6.7	–13.4	–3.5	6.1	3.5
Inflation	35.1	19.7	9.9	27.3	19.9	30.7
Unemployment	11.7	9.0	20.0	18.9	18.5	17.2
Fiscal balance (as % of GDP)	5.4	2.6	–1.0	–2.6	–3.0	–2.3
Current account (as % of GDP)	–7.2	–14.5	–9.5	–5.6	–11.0	–8.6
Capital account (as % of GDP)	0.4	3.6	–2.0	–1.7	4.4	1.3

Sources: International Monetary Fund, "International Financial Statistics (IFS)" database, www.imf.org/external/data.htm#data; and Economist Intelligence Unit, www.eiu.com/public/ [both accessed July 28, 2010].

Second, an important similarity in the political sphere in the Southern Cone countries in the years leading to the 1982 economic collapse was that they shared (to different degrees) a type of authoritarian rule that Guillermo O'Donnell identified as bureaucratic-authoritarian regimes:[25] military regimes that had come to power between the early 1960s and the mid-1970s, in the wake of growing radical pressures from below (ranging from militant labor movements to guerrilla movements that pledged to bring down bourgeois capitalism and institute socialism or communism). Bureaucratic-authoritarian regimes were installed to quash such pressures from below and ensure the continuation of economic growth and development along capitalist lines. These regimes had a strict and sophisticated division of labor to accomplish these objectives. The military took care of controlling and, if necessary, destroying pressures from below—a process that gave way to the infamous "dirty wars" in the Southern Cone countries. The economic sphere was delegated to civilian technocrats (many of whom were US-trained PhD economists), who tried to steer their economies from state-led to market-led paths. On the eve of the 1982 economic shock and the subsequent severe economic crisis, harsh military rule and harsh economic restructuring along free market lines had gone hand in hand in the Southern Cone countries for seven or eight years.

A GLOBALIZED ECONOMY AND 1997–2002
EMERGING MARKETS CRISES

The end of the Cold War heralded the triumph of liberal capitalism and the res-olution of the 1980s debt crisis through a new boom in portfolio capital flows from the United States and Europe to Latin America, as well as the introduction of newly born capitalist societies in what had been command economies in Central and Eastern Europe. Net private capital flows to emerging market economies in 1989 totaled 18.19 billion USD, and by 1993 this had skyrocketed to 181.87 billion.[26] Foreign investment was predominately portfolio investment, which could be pulled at a moment's notice, and doing so led to successive financial shocks and economic crises in countries in Latin America and East Asia.

The fever that caught investors from the rich countries, given the environment of low interest rates in the early 1990s, resulted primarily from the creation of a secondary market for credit swaps of the foreign-currency-denominated debt that developing countries had amassed in the second half of the 1970s and early 1980s. The Brady Plan, launched in March 1989 by US Secretary of the Treasury Nicholas Brady, was the platform used to create this secondary debt market. According to this plan, "countries were to implement market liberalizations in exchange for a reduction of the commercial bank debt, and, in many cases, new money from commercial banks and multilateral agencies."[27]

Mexico and the "Tequila Effect"

Mexico provides an example of the opportunities and challenges for developing countries in this new wave of capital inflows. On the positive side, "existing loans could be swapped for 30-year debt-reduction bonds that would provide a discount of 35 percent of face value. . . . Existing loans could also be swapped for 30-year par bonds that would effectively reduce Mexico's debt service on those loans through a below-market interest rate of 6.25 percent. Banks could also provide new loans at market interest rates over a four-year period of up to 25 percent of their 1989 exposure, taking into account any discount or par bounds obtained."[28] On the negative side, domestic as well as international events could shake the confidence of foreign investors, and the renewed expansion of credit could go into reverse. This is exactly what happened in Mexico. Having experienced a boom in new capital inflows from 1991 to early 1994, a series of unforeseen events that year, some domestic (the January 1 uprising of the Ejército Zapatista de Liberación Nacional [EZLN] in Chiapas; the assassination of PRI presidential candidate Luis Donaldo Colosio on March 23; and the assassination of PRI Secretary General Francisco Ruiz Massieu on September 28) and some international (a cycle of tightening interest rates, started by the

Federal Reserve in early 1994) led to market turmoil and later on to panic, which culminated with runs on the Mexican peso that forced the incoming government of President Ernesto Zedillo to devalue it.

The foreign-denominated debt of both domestic companies and the government exploded. Staggering under a combination of this enormous pressure and rising inflation, many businesses collapsed, setting off a chain reaction where foreign investors got spooked and pulled out from other emerging markets. This situation, which came to be known as the "tequila effect," showed that the interconnection of capital markets could spread financial shocks to other countries. Thus Argentina's economy, which had expanded rapidly in 1992–93, experienced negative growth (−2.84%) in 1995. Likewise, that of Brazil, which had grown 5.85% in 1994, suffered a significant deceleration (to 2.76%) in 1996. Uruguay, given its economic dependence on Argentine and Brazilian activity, also experienced negative growth (−1.75%) in 1995.[29]

The Mexican financial and economic implosions should have created some restraint and critical thinking among policymakers and investors, but this did not happen. According to one author, "if anything, the Mexican case gave the High Command [Washington Consensus] an overblown sense of its power to manage such situations. Only after the much more widespread gyrations and perturbations of the late 1990s did the system's lack of governability begin to hit home."[30] Only two years after the Mexican crisis, a new financial storm broke out in Southeast Asia.

Emerging Market Crises in East Asia and Russia

In 1997, the high-growth economies of the Asian Tigers were not obvious candidates for financial and economic meltdown. According to Frieden, "Korea, Thailand, Malaysia, and Indonesia were models of financial orthodoxy and conservative social policies: minimal inflation, small budget deficits, low levels of social planning, and few labor rights." The downside of such robust economic health was that "this safety of the Asian Tigers beckoned the investors from the world's financial capitals, tripling Thailand's debt to ninety billion USD and doubling Indonesia's to fifty billion USD in 1996."[31] Massive capital inflows ended up stoking inflation. Rising inflation and the prospect of devaluation attracted speculators looking for quick profits from shorting currency. The full force of the crisis was first felt in Thailand in the summer of 1997. This country, which had pegged its currency, the baht, to the dollar, was forced to depeg due to rising inflation. Frieden noted that the pullout of investors, which began in

Thailand, spread quickly to Indonesia, Malaysia, and South Korea. Asia saw capital flows of 62.5 billion USD in 1996 drop to –19.73 billion in 1997, and bottom out at –45.23 billion in 1998.

The attacks on currencies by international bankers contributed to the spread of devaluations in Southeast Asia and revealed once again the high-wire act of managing financial flows in the globally interconnected world of capital markets. For the economies in East Asia, "the fifty billion dollar annual inflow of the early 1990s turned into an outflow of over 230 billion USD between 1997 and 1999. Stock prices collapsed by 80 and 90 percent from their 1993 high. After years of extraordinary growth—10 percent a year was common—the economies of Indonesia, Thailand, and Malaysia contracted by 15, 10, and 8 percent, respectively, in a matter of months."[32]

The panic did not end there. The Asian crisis put a match to the tinder in the global financial markets; the next victim was Russia in 1998, and eventually Brazil succumbed in 1998–99. Like the Asian Tigers, the Russian economy relied on the confidence of foreign investors. Moreover, the crisis in Asia contributed to the slowdown of the Russian economy, since "the recession in Asia's biggest economies dampened world demand for oil and gas, Russia's most important export, causing the price of crude to fall by nearly half from the early 1997 level."[33] Fears grew about the Russian government's deficit and the pullout by investors forced it to default on its bonds; unlike the situation in Asia, the IMF and the global community refused to offer their support.

Emerging Market Crises in South America

Lack of support for Russia and the previous contagion in Asia raised fears that other emerging markets would be next. The attention of what journalist Thomas Friedman called the electronic herd began to shift to Latin America's largest economy, Brazil.[34] In a series of events similar to those that preceded the Asian collapse, Brazil became a prisoner of its reliance on sustained capital inflows. The Brazilian economy had been in turmoil between the early 1980s and 1993–94, experiencing several episodes of hyperinflation. Finance Minister Fernando H. Cardoso implemented the Plano Real in early 1994, which stabilized the domestic currency by pegging it to the dollar and helped combat the entrenched phenomenon of inertial inflation. Successful economic stabilization allowed Cardoso to run successfully for the presidency, and the country experienced large capital inflows in 1994–95. A fixed exchange rate, coupled with inflationary pressures, led to gradual currency appreciation that, similar to the cases of Mexico in 1994 and (later on) Argentina in 2001–2, subsequently shifted to mass capital outflows, devaluation, and a Brazilian economic crisis in early 1999.

The crisis could have started anywhere, but it wasn't until it reached Brazil that Argentina and Uruguay became ensnared in the menacing, self-reinforcing process of capital pullout. Figure 6.2 shows the growth trajectories of the three Southern Cone countries. Chile experienced a recession in 1999, but thereafter it experienced high, sustained growth rates. Argentina and Uruguay instead suffered economic depressions (economic contractions for four consecutive years) from 1999 to 2002, although they bounced back strongly in the short term and their GDPs rose rapidly over the next five years. This was in marked contrast to the seesaw recuperation trajectories of these economies during both the Great Depression and the lost decade of the 1980s.

Argentina and Uruguay experienced one of the most severe economic shocks in their respective histories between 1999 and 2002. This included rising unemployment, fiscal deterioration, and balance of payments crises, as shown in table 6.2.

Several factors precipitated the Argentine collapse. Argentina's fixed exchange rate under the Convertibility Plan of 1991 (see chapter 7) became a major liability after Brazil's financial crisis of 1998–99. Brazil was Argentina's main

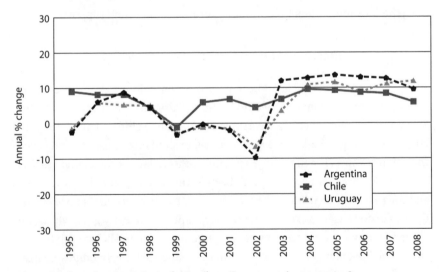

Figure 6.2. Growth trajectories in the Southern Cone countries, 1995–2008

Source: For the years 1995–2000, based on data from the *Oxford Latin American Economic History Database*, http://oxlad.qeh.ox.ac.uk/search.php; for 2001–8, based on data from the IMF's "World Economic Outlook database" [both accessed July 7, 2009].

TABLE 6.2
Macroeconomic indicators, Argentina and Uruguay, 1998–2004

	1998	1999	2000	2001	2002	2003	2004
Argentina							
GDP growth	3.9	−3.4	−0.8	−4.4	−10.9	8.8	9.0
Inflation	0.9	−1.2	−0.9	−1.1	25.9	13.4	4.4
Unemployment	12.9	14.3	15.1	17.4	19.7	17.3	13.6
Fiscal balance (as % of GDP)	−1.4	−1.7	−2.4	−3.2	−1.4	0.5	2.6
Current account (as % of GDP)	−4.8	−4.2	−3.1	−1.4	8.6	6.3	2.1
Capital account (as % of GDP)	1.4	3.1	0.9	−3.6	−16.1	−7.9	1.3
Uruguay							
GDP growth	4.5	−1.9	−1.9	−3.8	−7.7	0.8	5.0
Inflation	10.8	5.7	4.8	4.4	14.0	19.4	9.2
Unemployment	10.1	11.3	13.6	15.3	17.0	16.9	13.1
Fiscal balance (as % of GDP)	−0.8	−3.7	−3.4	−4.7	−4.0	3.2	2.0
Current account (as % of GDP)	−2.1	−2.4	−2.8	−2.7	3.1	−0.8	0.0
Capital account (as % of GDP)	0.7	2.2	2.4	1.6	−38.7	8.5	1.7

Sources: International Monetary Fund, "International Financial Statistics (IFS)" database, www.imf.org/external/data.htm#data; and *Economist Intelligence Unit*, www.eiu.com/public/ [both accessed July 28, 2010].

trading partner, and currency devaluation in the former led to a significant slowdown of exports in the latter, given the Argentine peso's peg to the US dollar. Even before the financial busts at the end of 2001, Argentine GDP contracted 4% in real terms between 1998 and 2000.[35] In addition, fiscal profligacy during President Menem's two terms also helped to set the stage for Argentina's downfall. Uruguay joined Mercosur in 1991, which deepened its ties (and linked the fate of the country's economy) to those of Argentina and Brazil. Its reliance on these economies, with their later collapse, made it almost inevitable that Uruguay would suffer, too. The main reason for Uruguay's financial and economic downfall was a run on its banks by Argentine depositors, who pulled out following the debacle in their country. Chile was the sole Southern Cone nation to remain relatively unscathed after its neighbors' financial and economic collapses. One reason was that only 38% of the Chilean debt was dollar denominated, which was in stark contrast to Argentina, where this figure was close to 80%. Likewise, capital controls prevented the large capital inflows seen in Argentina and Brazil. Having described the main features of both the 1982 debt crisis and the emerging markets crises of the 1990s and early 2000s and summarized their global effects, I now turn to the role of institutions, interests, and ideas in the Southern Cone countries regarding these more recent episodes of economic shocks and crises.

CHAPTER SEVEN

Institutions

---

*Demise of Military-as-Government
and Higher Costs for Action*

The Great Depression led to the breakdown of the existing regimes in the three Southern Cone countries. What was different about the situation in and effects of the 1982 and 1997–2002 crises that allowed democracy to eventually survive?

1982 DEBT CRISIS: RETURN OF A RESTRICTED DEMOCRACY IN CHILE

As recently as early 1978, there were only three democratic regimes in Latin America (Colombia, Costa Rica, and Venezuela).[1] When the financial and economic shocks of 1982 took place, the entire southern half of South America remained under military rule (Argentina, Bolivia, Brazil, Chile, Paraguay, and Uruguay). So, just as it did on the eve of the Great Depression, the democratic cause in 1982 had more to win than to lose in Latin America, based on its growth potential. (Remember that it was their weaknesses, not their potential, that caused Latin America's only two democracies to fail during the Depression.) Given the baseline for comparison in this volume, the 1930s, it makes sense to concentrate on Chile for the 1982 crisis, since this country was under military rule on the eve of both the financial shocks of 1929–31 and 1982. In contrast, Argentina and Uruguay were democracies just before the Great Depression but were under military rule prior to the 1982 financial shock.

In Chile, the authoritarian regime headed by General Ibáñez was brought down by middle-class protests in mid-1931, but the military regime under General Augusto Pinochet was not, despite the fact that the country's military regime faced a broader multiclass mobilization against its mismanagement of the economy in 1982–84 than in 1930–31. The question here is, Why did Chile experience different regime outcomes in the face of these two economic shocks and crises? As pointed out in the introduction, this outcome is at odds with the general argument in this volume, according to which dictatorship should have survived or been installed during the early 1930s, while it should have collapsed in the early 1980s.

Several factors could have contributed to these outlier, or unexpected, outcomes. For example, an economic viewpoint could highlight the difference in the sheer magnitude of the collapse. In the 1930s, annual GDP in Chile declined four years in a row and accumulated more than 50% of its annual growth between the peak and the trough (1928–34); in the bust of the early 1980s, annual GDP declined three years in a row, but it amounted to just over 20% of annual growth between the peak and the trough (1979–82). Still, if we follow the criteria spelled out in chapter 1 regarding the difference between recessions and depressions, the busts in both the early 1930s and the early 1980s produced depressions in Chile.

A political perspective could highlight the unity and cohesion of the army under General Pinochet, and the fact that the regime over which he presided established institutional bases through the 1980 constitution, which generated a relatively widespread core of support among the upper and middle classes.[2] In contrast, in the late 1920s and early 1930s the army remained fiercely divided between radical left-wing supporters of the Socialist Republic, reformist-populist *ibañistas*, and traditional conservative officers. General Ibáñez did not create a new constitutional order; instead he pretended to ground his rule on the 1925 constitution. The regime was based on Ibáñez's strongman, populist control style in a society undergoing rapid urbanization and industrialization. As president, Ibáñez generated substantial working- and middle-class support, but he lost the support of the professional middle and upper classes once the economy fell off a cliff in 1930–31. His foreign backers either could not or decided not to fight in support of his continuation or reinstatement in power.

My own analysis contains a mixture of political and economic factors. Concentrating first on institutions, I argue that in the domestic sphere, the costs for organizing and exercising pressures in favor of a shift to full electoral democracy remained high in Chile—the military regime was willing and used force systematically to clamp down on the explosion of social mobilization that followed the 1982 economic collapse[3]—while the 1980 constitution provided the institutional means that lowered the costs for engagement between the regime incumbents and the opposition. The opposition's strength crystallized, however, in the revival of Chile's traditionally strong parties and party systems in the aftermath of the harsh 1982 financial shocks and the economic crisis that followed. The end result was an engagement between the military regime and its civilian opposition, which led to the creation of a restricted, or tutelary, democracy.

In the international sphere the costs for exercising pressures against democracy increased substantially. While there was only a thin international system in terms of institutions (both as rules and as organizations) in the 1930s (see chapter 3), the settlement after the Second World War resulted in the birth of a robust political and diplomatic international network under the UN system and regional regimes such as the OAS, and the Bretton Woods economic conglomerate (the IMF as a lender-of-last-resort and the WB as a promoter of development). By the early and mid-1980s, although this international system pulled in different directions—the UN criticized military rule in Chile, while the IMF, the WB, and (within the OAS) the IADB supported it through the extension of credit and guarantees—it raised the costs for anti-democratic action in Chile, thanks to a change in US foreign policy toward Latin America, which now proposed waging civil wars by proxy in Central America while supporting pro-democrats in the last countries still ruled by the military in South America, namely, Chile and Paraguay (see chapter 9).

Aside from the fundamental change in multilateral engagement since the end of the Second World War, there was also a substantial growth and proliferation of non-state actors, such as the Catholic Church and the more recent human rights and other transnational civil society organizations, which were established in the 1960s–70s and exerted pressure on multilateral organizations, governments in the United States and Western Europe, and leaders of non-democratic regimes throughout the world. These transnational pressures also helped to raise the costs for anti-democracy actions, thus contributing to efforts to force the Chilean military regime to stick to the transition calendar of the 1980 constitution and accept the adverse voting results of the 1988 plebiscite.

Domestic Institutions-as-Rules

For institutions-as-rules, the primary elements here are constitutions and electoral laws.

CONSTITUTIONS

Many authors have highlighted the centrality of the 1980 constitution in the Chilean transition to democracy, as it provided the institutional means of engagement between the regime incumbents and the opposition.[4] The constitution was drafted by political conservatives and neoclassical, or neoliberal, economists. This foundational document secured the interests and ideas of the outgoing military and their civilian allies (see chapters 8 and 9) by creating institutional veto points—voting by a minority (say, in Congress) that stops legislative action by a majority to change a given status quo—that allowed appointed authorities (in the Senate, the Supreme Court, the Constitutional Tribunal, and the National Security Council) to limit the actions and legislation of elected authorities (the president and majorities in Congress).[5] The military retained relative autonomy from civilian authorities by allowing Pinochet to remain as commander-in-chief of the armed forces until 1998. Crucially, the constitution also contained a transition calendar, which structured the coordination of political engagement by lengthening the negotiators' time frames while helping them build mutual trust as the successive procedures spelled out in the calendar were met by both sides between October 5, 1988, when the military lost the plebiscite regarding its continuation in power, and March 11, 1990, when the military stepped down and democratically elected Patricio Aylwin assumed the presidency.

First and foremost, the harsh 1982 financial shocks and economic crisis reactivated opposition to the military regime in Chile. Among the opposition, strong supporters of democracy would have liked to force the military out and install a full electoral democracy, while regime diehards would have preferred not have to engage the opposition at all. With the 1980 constitution as an institutional means for engagement, moderate leaders, who were in the majority in both groups, opted for negotiation rather than rupture and thus gave up some of their claims in exchange for a second-best outcome. Pinochet's supporters committed to abide by the electoral results; they would step down and allow the return of civilian rule if their side lost in free and fair elections. In turn, the opposition to the military regime accepted the 1980 constitution, which meant acknowledging that Chile would have a restricted democracy in the foreseeable future.

ELECTORAL LAWS

Electoral law change during the Pinochet years transformed democratic representation in Chile. Up until Salvador Allende's presidency (1970–73), Chile had used a system of proportional representation, which gave way to a vibrant plural electoral system that leaned toward polarized pluralism.[6] Pinochet's constitutional advisers set out the case for a binomial electoral law that would force parties into a clear-cut bipolar pattern of competition and representation. The binomial system ensured this outcome by setting up sixty legislative districts, each having two seats. In order for a party or a coalition to win both seats in any district, it had to double the vote of the party that came in second. The likelihood of this happening was low, given Chile's polarized pluralism. In short, the binomial system favored the runner-up, meaning the Chilean Right.[7]

This was another key institution-as-rule, ensuring that the interests and voice of the outgoing regime and its supporters among the upper and middle classes was secured institutionally once democracy was reestablished, while allowing the pro-democracy camp to benefit from the return of civilian politics and civilian rule in Chile (although under a restricted democracy). The end result has been a very stable pattern of representation in Congress since the return of democracy in 1990, one in which two coalitions, a center-left and a center-right, dominate representation and smaller, out-of-center parties (such as the Communists) have been systematically excluded. This forced aggregation, although criticized by pluralists, has delivered a stable pattern of governance since Chile returned to democracy in 1990. The main problem for this system is that in many districts there is no real competition anymore—out of nine districts for the election of senators, only four have a chance of being competitive, while in the other five everyone knows in advance who is going to win. This has particularly disenchanted young Chileans, who have an abnormally high rate of nonparticipation in politics (up until the 1970s, Chile was highly politicized among the young). This trait of disaffection and disengagement is similar to what has happened in some of the richest democracies, from the United States to some Western European countries.[8]

Domestic Institutions-as-Organizations

For institutions-as-organizations, the two main factors are the armed forces, and political parties and party systems.

ARMED FORCES

The demise of the military-as-government in the early 1980s throughout Latin America came about through a combination of factors: opposition to this type of governance on the grounds of democratic theory and practice, as well as mass human rights abuses, and the collapse of its credibility as an economic manager. Human rights abuses and corruption went hand in hand, with the military killing thousands of opposition and presumed opposition members at the same time as they stuffed their pockets. The crisis of military rule in Latin America in the early 1980s was therefore due to moral issues, economic policy, and basic accountancy fundamentals. The military regimes in Latin America were bankrupt in the broad sense of the term.

Among all of the Latin American military regimes, General Pinochet's was the best positioned to remain in at least partially in place, not only by dictating terms but also by transmitting its institutional politicoeconomic system to Chile's new (albeit restricted) democracy. But even such a self-assured regime as that of Pinochet and his allies was not monolithic, nor did its members agree on everything. In the run up the October 5, 1988, plebiscite that would ratify or reject eight more years of military rule, the armed forces were divided, with the heads of the air force and the *carabineros* (national police) in support of a civilian, conciliatory figure, while the navy, the army, and the regime's allies supported General Pinochet.[9] By the late 1980s, with Pinochet aging and the military regime in Chile left as the only viable one remaining in South America (alongside the embarrassing company of General Alfredo Stroessner's three-and-a-half decades-old dictatorship in Paraguay), the heads of the other armed services also stuck with following the transition calendar in the constitution and, when the time came, they supported the triumph of the "No" option, which derailed the plan of keeping Pinochet in power at least until 1996. That Pinochet's peers sided with the actual result of the plebiscite, even though it meant the defeat of their *primus inter pares*, suggests that had the top brass not backed the official results of the 1988 plebiscite, Chile's return to democracy might have ended up being more uncertain and could have taken longer.

POLITICAL PARTIES AND PARTY SYSTEMS

The dynamics of political parties and the entire party system in Chile changed with the formation of a binomial electoral system. Unsurprisingly, the bipolar pattern of competition established during the process leading to the 1988 plebiscite (with its "Yes" or "No" votes) persisted once elections started in 1989 under this system. Political parties, traditionally the backbone of Chilean politics, revived in the wake of mass protests in 1982 against the regime's economic management. In August 1983, the leaders of the Democracia Cristiana (DC), the Radicals, renovated socialists (the Partido por la Democracia, or PPD, and the Partido Socialista, or PS), and some center-right moderates reached a partial settlement with the elites by launching the Alianza Democrática as a platform to oppose the regime.[10] In reaction, in September 1983 the close allies of General Pinochet created the Unión Democrática Independiente (UDI) to defend the government dominated by the armed forces, while more traditional conservatives created the Unión Nacional, a party later renamed the Renovación Nacional. Thus the current Chilean party system was largely forged in the wake of the 1982 economic collapse and Chilean society's protests. Of particular importance was the historic rapprochement between Christian Democrats and the renovated socialists, a second partial settlement with the elites to form the majority bloc that ruled Chile uninterruptedly between 1990 and 2010,[11] when the Right (under Sebastián Piñera) won the presidential elections for the first time since 1958. The binomial system ensured representation of and spoils to the major parties in the system by lowering the costs for the incumbents and the opposition to engage by means of the status quo, namely, the 1980 constitution and the restricted democracy it created.

International Institutions

Institutions-as-rules in the international sphere involve the post–Second World War international legal architecture that created, at the multilateral level, the UN (1945) and Bretton Woods (1944–46) systems and, at the regional level, the Inter-American system and its pillars, the Rio Treaty (1947), the charter of the Organization of American States (1948), and the charter of the Inter-American Development Bank (1959). Institutions-as-organizations encompass (1) the main organizations created by the post-1945 international legal edifice, and the dominating influence of the US government in them; and (2) the role of international non-state actors.

LEGAL SYSTEMS

In this respect, the most important difference between the Great Depression and the post-1982 debt crisis was that the former happened at a time when the international system was thin and ineffective, and countries therefore did not have access to the concerted diplomatic, political, and economic support that the post-1945 international institutions provided to those involved in the 1982 debt crisis. Early on, the UN Charter recognized and sanctioned regional organizations. Between the 1950s and the 1970s, the UN tended to defer to the Inter-American system regarding disputes in the Western Hemisphere. An important change took place in the early 1980s, when the UN system (along with the

Catholic Church and human rights activists) took the initiative in the wake of the civil wars in Central America, and a David-and-Goliath dynamic ensued. For example, in 1984 the International Court of Justice (ICJ, created by the UN Charter at The Hague and in operation since 1946) ruled against the United States for salting mines in Nicaraguan harbors, a violation of international law. In 1986, the UN Security Council echoed the court's resolution, asking the United States to abide by it and cease supporting the Contras. Neither the ICJ nor the Security Council had the means to force compliance by the United States, but the official international pressure helped to raise the costs for acts of aggression that, until then, had been regarded as part and parcel of the Cold War and its logic of containment and suppression.[12]

ORGANIZATIONS

The development of international organizations was not linear and unidirectional after the end of the Second World War. Although the most important diplomatic forums, such as the UN General Assembly and the OAS General Assembly, time and again condemned the return of military rule to South America in the 1960s and early to mid-1970s, the Bretton Woods institutions—the International Monetary Fund and the World Bank—helped to prop up authoritarian regimes in times of acute financial crisis, as was the case with Chile under Pinochet in the early 1980s.

The lending policy of international financial institutions (IFIs) was not just subject to a number of technical criteria; its enactment also required voting by its funders, a process dominated by the United States in both the IMF and the WB. This meant that the positions taken by the US representatives on the boards of the IFIs depended to a significant degree on whether a Democratic or a Republican president occupied the White House. For example, President Jimmy Carter and the US Congress used threats to cut multilateral and bilateral resources to the Chilean military government and implemented trade, cooperation, and aid sanctions against it.[13] In contrast, President Ronald Reagan "lifted the prohibition imposed by Carter's government on credits from the Ex-Im Bank to finance US exports to Chile, and the White House convinced Congress to suspend the weapons embargo to that country."[14]

The main issue for our comparison is that, unlike General Ibáñez in 1930–31, after the 1982 bust the Chilean military junta had access to an international lender-of-last-resort through the IFIs. This was due to strong US government support for the neoliberal economic policy that the Chilean military regime had adopted. Once the Chilean government committed to implementing orthodox stabilization measures, the IMF gave its stamp of approval, and new international credit lines were reopened, which helped to renegotiate Chile's external debt.[15] For example, between 1985 and 1987 Chile received around 30% of the total annual financing that the IADB and the WB allotted to Latin America, even though the Chilean economy only represented about 3% of the region's GDP (in 1986 purchasing power parity dollars).[16] As scholars have noted, "the international organizations of the Bretton Woods system (IMF and World Bank) actually helped to keep [the] Pinochet [regime] alive during the 1982–83 crisis by bailing out the country."[17]

We can only speculate on whether the existence of an international lender-of-last-resort might have helped General Ibáñez's rule endure beyond July 1931. What can be reasonably said is that the existence of a type of international insurance system against financial shocks (like the IMF), and financing from other multilateral financial institutions in general, raises the likelihood that both democratic and non-democratic regime incumbents whose countries are members of these institutions and pay their assigned contributions can get an extra lease on life by drawing on fresh resources in the face of international and/or domestic financial shocks and economic crises. This was not the case before the creation of the IFIs in 1945–46.

All in all, international organizations had a mixed impact on the costs of exercising pressures in favor of and against democracy. While the diplomatic multilateral organizations consistently opposed military regimes and raised their costs of applying pressure against democracy through public condemnation, the multilateral IFIs actually helped prop up a military regime like Chile's by supplying it with fresh credit lines and renegotiating the country's foreign debt at a time when popular protests, including by the middle- and upper-middle-class sectors, threatened to confront the regime and topple it from power.

NON-STATE ACTORS

International non-state actors also contributed to raising the costs for pressures against democracy and lowering the costs for those in favor of it in Chile after the 1982 economic collapse. First, the Catholic Church, in the person of the Archbishop of Santiago, Cardinal Raúl Silva Henríquez, offered an invaluable source of resistance after General Pinochet's military coup on September 11, 1973. The top military brass issued threats and opposed the Church's embrace of political refugees, as well as its policy of documenting and voicing all the human rights violations that came to its attention. Cardinal Silva then asked Pope Paul VI to create a papal organization in Santiago; the military would think twice before harassing it. The pope agreed and created the Vicaría de la Solidaridad in 1976 to protect the politically persecuted and to monitor, document, and give a voice internationally to the way the military imposed order in Chile. The Vicaría's fierce resistance raised the costs for pressures against democracy by publicizing human rights abuses in Chile.

In addition, after Cardinal Silva retired in 1983 (due to his age, as mandated by the Church, not for a politically motivated reason), Pope John Paul II chose Archbishop Juan Fresno to replace Silva in Santiago (Fresno became a cardinal in 1985). Archbishop/Cardinal Fresno was instrumental in mediating between the leaders of the main parties (including the left, the center, and the right) after the post-1982 economic bust, which helped revive them as principal factors in the mass, multiclass mobilization against the military regime's mismanagement of the economy. Cardinal Fresno also played a significant role in forging the Acuerdo Nacional para la Transición a la Plena Democracia (1985), which established the mutual trust between pro- and anti-military regime supporters that allowed both groups to abide by the transition calendar. This engagement was instrumental in helping the opposition seek an electoral means—the 1988 plebiscite—for the demise of military rule and the return of democracy.[18] Thus the mediating and trust-building role that the head of the Catholic Church in Chile gave to the multiple segments of the opposition helped to lower the costs for their organization and exercise pressures in favor of the return of democracy.

Aside from the Catholic Church, a transnational human rights network—which had grown internationally in the late 1960s and early 1970s around issues such as the Vietnam War, nuclear energy, human rights, environmental sustainability, and a general questioning of authority—became very active in the late 1970s and early 1980s. These groups, based in the United States, Canada, and Western Europe, had substantial leverage, because they were made up of individual citizens who could put electoral or public opinion pressure on their national governments by exposing them whenever their policies resulted in human rights violations in developing countries.[19] For example, many of these groups became advocates of election monitoring as a way to find rules-based exits from authoritarian rule, and to put pressure on and raise the costs for anyone wanting to exert pressures against free and fair elections, one of the cornerstones of an electoral democracy. This activity was not novel; the OAS had engaged in monitoring elections in Western Hemisphere countries since 1962.[20] What the transnational human rights network brought to this arena was its commitment to advocacy—to gathering, processing, and spreading information—thus ramping up the costs for any regime or government that wanted to cheat in elections.

Although costs against pro-democratic organization and action remained high in 1980s Chile, given the military regime's willingness to use coercion, both domestic and international institutions like the UN General Assembly, the OAS, the Catholic Church, and nongovernmental organizations (NGOs) concerned with human rights helped to raise the costs for the exercise of anti-democratic action by the military. Neither of the two camps was able to fully impose its will on the other, and the end result was a highly structured process of transition to democracy, regulated by the military's 1980 constitution.

1997–2002 EMERGING MARKETS CRISES: PERSISTENCE OF DEMOCRACY IN ARGENTINA AND URUGUAY

Following the process used in my baseline comparison of the 1930s in the Southern Cone countries, Argentina and Uruguay are useful cases to examine in this later set of crises, given that they were under democratic rule both in the run up to the Great Depression and in the late 1990s and early 2000s. The key question here is, Why did democracy survive in both Argentina and Uruguay in 2001–3, given that it collapsed in 1930 and 1933, respectively?

Even though democracy survived in both countries during the emerging markets crises of 1997–2002, there was also an important difference in their outcomes, in terms of the continuation or interruption of the constitutional process. On the one hand, Argentina has suffered interrupted presidencies twice since the return of democracy in 1983. The first time was when President Raúl Alfonsín (1983–89) had to step down six month before his term was due to finish, given that Carlos Menem (1989–99) had already won the presidential elections, the country was suffering from hyperinflation, and mass protests had turned into anarchy (such as looting supermarkets). Exactly the same thing happened twelve years later, when President Fernando de la Rúa (1999–2001) was forced to resign the presidency less than two years after he assumed office in the face of mass, multiclass protests—with broad middle-class participation in big cities like Buenos Aires and Rosario—that led to violence, looting, and the death of several dozen protesters in clashes with police forces. Such pressures from below were multitudinous. Some of them started as spontaneous acts of defiance by the *piqueteros*, who blocked the free passage of cars and trucks in major arteries in cities as well as on highways, forcing authorities to negotiate before the blockages were lifted. Others were more organized: "the Peronist leaders (first and foremost future president Duhalde) and unions were instrumental in busing thousands of people on daily bases to participate in mass demonstrations to topple the government."[21]

President de la Rúa's evacuation by helicopter from the rooftop of the Casa Rosada (the presidential palace) on December 21, 2001, was said to resemble another interrupted presidency, namely, Isabel Perón's, and her similar evacuation from this seat of power in the early hours of March 24, 1976.[22] Still, a key difference between these two events was that the 1976 helicopter rescue announced the rise of the most brutal military regime in twentieth-century Argentina, while the later one led to a chaotic period of government: five presidents—all Peronists—between late December 2001 and January 2, 2002, when Eduardo Duhalde, Menem's vice president in 1989–91 and two-time governor of Buenos Aires province, was sworn in. President Duhalde stabilized public order and the economy by resorting to traditional machine politics, populism (through ample patronage and clientelism), and personalist leadership (typical of the Peronist movement), which saved the day again. In marked contrast to 1976 (or, for that matter, 1930), in 2001–2 there was no regime change, and thus no ascension of military rule.

On the other hand Uruguay, albeit hit like never before in terms of the financial shock and economic crisis it experienced in 2002–3—in large measure courtesy of Argentina's collapse—was able to engage in effective crisis management. Both the government and the opposition cooperated, so that, despite the deep short- and medium-term social costs, the economy was stabilized and resumed growth in such a way that the legitimacy and credibility of Uruguay's democracy was solidified. The situation was diametrically different in Argentina, where Peronist control of the masses in 2001–2 strengthened the country's dominant political party, rather than Argentina's democratic regime.

Domestic Institutions-as-Rules

Regarding institutions-as-rules in Argentina and Uruguay, I again turn to the role of constitutions and electoral laws.

ARGENTINA

Constitution and Electoral Laws. By the time Argentina's economy collapsed at the end of 2001, its constitution operated under a system that was revised in 1994, under the Pacto de Olivos (Olivos Pact), and is still being used today.

Because the 1994 constitutional reforms involved substantial changes in Argentina's electoral laws, I will treat both together.

President Carlos Menem (1989–99) set these constitutional reforms in motion in 1993. His goal was to promote his reelection, which the constitution did not allow. Menem could not pass the reforms relying only on his Peronist party, the Partido Justicialista (PJ), so he reached out to the opposition radicals, the Unión Cívica Radica (UCR), and their leader, ex-president Raúl Alfonsín (1983–89). The radicals in the UCR were deeply divided at first. While the party convention refused to support the constitutional reforms, Alfonsín's side thought it was better to negotiate, so that they could insert their own demands (weakening the federal executive) as well as avoid electoral confrontation with the PJ, which had strengthened considerably after Menem and his third Minister of Economy, Domingo Cavallo, successfully stabilized the Argentine economy in 1991.[23]

In the end, the 1994 constitutional reforms were unanimously approved. The changes established a direct presidential election (previously it was indirect, as it is in the United States). The Argentine indirect method had been based on an electoral college chosen by proportional representation in each of the provinces (the equivalent of US states). The reforms also reduced presidential terms from six to four years and created a second round of voting, or ballotage. The new rules required a presidential and vice presidential ticket to win at least 45% of the total vote, or at least 40% of the overall vote and more than 10% of the amount for the runner-up, to avoid a second-round election between the two tickets. The amended constitution introduced presidential reelection for a single consecutive term, in other words, a total of 8 years (as in the United States). The reforms created elections for the powerful office of mayor of Buenos Aires, who used to be appointed by the president. It also created a cabinet position, known as the Chief-of-the-Cabinet, with federal authority. This official reports directly to the National Congress, a measure intended to force legislative scrutiny and oversight of the federal executive. Moreover, the reforms gave the National Congress the faculty to ratify executive emergency decrees before they can come into operation, and these decrees can no longer be used for penal, tax, electoral, or legislative cases. Before the reforms took place, Argentine politics under Menem's first term were plagued by the use of executive decrees during the economic emergency.[24]

The constitutional reforms also changed the electoral rules for the legislative branch. In the upper chamber (the Senate), they established the direct election of senators. Previously, senators were elected through an electoral college, where the electors were chosen directly by their provincial constituents. The reforms increased the number of senators from two per province to three. Thus the party in each province that received the most votes would send two senators to the Senate, and the party that came in second would get one. The reforms called for biannual renewal of one-third of the Senate at a time. They also gave senatorial representation to the city of Buenos Aires. Therefore, the total number of Senate seats increased from forty-six (two for each of the twenty-three provinces) to seventy-two (three for each province and three for the city of Buenos Aires). This was a vital element in the Olivos Pact, which benefited Alfonsín and the URC because it expanded the size of the Senate; the second-party candidates (the radicals) were likely to take the third seats in the upper chamber. Senate terms were also reduced from nine to six years. The lower chamber (the Chamber of Deputies), however, was not changed. The election of deputies remained based on proportional representation. Following the Bigone Law, there was one deputy for every 161,000 people per province, and then three more deputies were added to that final number. However, no province could have less than five representatives. The 256 deputies of the lower house served four-year terms, and elections occurred every two years for one-half of the members from each district.

In sharp contrast to 1930, when fear of the elimination of veto points (which allowed the legislature to check the power of the federal executive) contributed decidedly to the conservative military-civilian coalition that deposed President Yrigoyen and broke down democracy, the 1994 constitutional reforms created more executive-legislative checks and balances, and a greater scope for multiparty coalitions and plural representation, so any fear of winner-take-all governance was much less of a concern in the late 1990s and early 2000s. Trepidation about potential radical policy outcomes did not become a driving force encouraging pressures against democracy, like those that led to its collapse in 1930. The major concern in 2001 was the opposite: a weak, fractious, multiparty coalition government in the midst of harsh financial shocks and an unraveling economy.

If anything, the danger, given President Menem's successful 1991 economic stabilization by using emergency decrees and packing the Supreme Court, was that whoever came to power in the wake of the 2001–2 collapse would resort to the same means. The Peronists duly followed this route; after five interim presidents between late December 2001 and January 2002, they eventually succeeded. The traditional, conservative boss of Buenos Aires province became President Eduardo Duhalde, who inadvertently passed the baton on to the then unknown governor of Santa Cruz province, Néstor Kirchner. This latter change signified an important shift within Peronism, which went from a traditional wheeling-and-dealing *caudillo*, dominant in the richest and politically most important province in the country, Buenos Aires, to the rise to power of a radical Peronist left-winger who, as a youth, supported the return of Perón to power in 1973–74, and who then went underground and fought in what is known as the dirty war against the military regime that ruled between 1976 and 1983 (which its leaders called the *Proceso de reorganización nacional*, or *Proceso* for short).[25] The main point, though, is that for the second time after major economic shocks, as well as the worst financial crisis since the early 1930s, democracy survived in Argentina—even if two presidents had to resign before their constitutional terms expired in 1989 and in 2001. In other words, in the face of these economic shocks and crises, Argentina experienced extraconstitutional changes of government rather than changes of political regime. This was in stark contrast to the years 1930–83, when civilian-military alternations in power were carried out through political regime changes.

Convertibility Plan. The reason for including this radical economic policy rule change here is that it was added to Argentina's constitution in 1991. This made it much more difficult to alter or overturn the plan, because this would require the supermajorities associated with changing the constitution, rather than the simple majorities needed to pass regular legislation. The Convertibility Plan was created on April 1, 1991, by Domingo Cavallo, the technocratic, Harvard-trained economist who was President Menem's third Minister of the Economy. Its aim was to stifle the dizzying episodes of hyperinflation that Argentina suffered between 1987 and early 1991. It was also the key economic institution-as-rule that, in retrospect, helps explain Argentina's economic performance between its adoption in 1991 and its demise in December 2001. The plan had excellent anti-inflationary credentials, but its monetary rigidity made the country's economy deeply uncompetitive and prone to balance-of-payments crises, culminating with the dramatic 2001–2 bust. It pegged the local currency (the austral became the peso again) to the dollar and was very successful initially at killing hyperinflation through its currency board. The board tied up the central bank's ability to issue money by linking it to foreign reserves; each peso in circulation had to be backed by a dollar equivalent in the reserves, which radically cut the money supply.

The main point for our analysis of relative costs is that early on, the Convertibility Plan raised the costs for exercising pressures against democracy. As the economy stabilized in 1991, anti-systemic calls by the elites and the middle and working classes died out, and democracy during the early Menem years recovered some of the credibility for effective economic management that it had lost in the Alfonsín years. Later, however, the plan's rigidity and the ultimately unsustainable problem that it created for Argentina's external accounts emboldened a mass, multiclass protest movement that, in late 2001, ended up repudiating democracy with a very telling rally slogan, "*Que se vayan todos!*" (Out with all politicians!). That the Argentine democratic regime managed to survive was probably more a function of the absence of political regime alternatives than of what popular sentiments expressed back then.

URUGUAY

Constitution. The return to democracy in Uruguay was negotiated in the 1984 Naval Club Pact, in which the 1967 constitution was restored, the military agreed to accept civilian rule and take only a minor advisory role in security matters, and several controversial political leaders were barred from participating in the presidential election for the following year. For the most part, the rules formulated in 1984 were the same as the ones in place before, and the resurrection of an institutional framework that had succumbed to deadlock and collapse over a decade earlier led analysts to label Uruguayan democracy as risk prone.[26]

Surprisingly, the incumbents and the opposition cooperated more, particularly in the face of an economic crisis. This was exactly the opposite of what had happened in the 1930s, when the bloc of more progressive *colorados* and *nacionales* confronted their more conservative peers, leading to executive-legislative deadlock and a zero-sum battle over the power of patronage, which was central to the Uruguayan system since the creation of the welfare state under President Batlle y Ordóñez.

Several constitutional changes between the return of democracy in 1984–85 and its subsequent reinstatement in 1996 partly explain the improvements in executive-legislative cooperation, which allowed effective crisis management. The costs for the organization and exercise of pressures in favor of working within the institutions of Uruguay's restored democracy were lowered considerably, compared with the same country during the Great Depression years. Unlike the Chilean case, Uruguay's and Argentina's regime trajectories conform to the general argument put forward in this book: democracy collapsed in the early 1930s, while it was restored in the early to mid-1980s.

Uruguay's original 1967 constitution abolished the *colegiado*, which strengthened the executive branch by making it a unitary rather than a collective office.

That constitution further enhanced the powers of the presidency by awarding him total and line-item vetoes, control over ministerial appointments, and exclusive authority in introducing budget and tax policy legislation. A 1986 amendment returned command of the armed forces to the president and, notably, gave the president emergency powers to bypass the legislature and implement policy in extraordinary circumstances involving internal disorder, although it required him to explain such actions to the legislature within 24 hours. A 1996 constitutional reform gave the president additional powers, shortening the time frame required for the General Assembly to vote on measures the president designated as urgent, and raising the bar for an override of a presidential veto by requiring a three-fifths vote in both the Chamber of Senators and the Chamber of Deputies (previously, a veto could be overridden by a three-fifths majority in the Chamber of Deputies alone). Such reforms boosted executive power not by guaranteeing legislative support, but by limiting legislative veto points for presidential programs, most significantly in cases of emergency. Another reason cited for this executive-legislative cooperation is the pressure arising from the constitution's mixed survival provisions—specifically, the ability of the legislature to censure and remove cabinet ministers, and the power of the president to dissolve the parliament. According to one author, "by raising the costs of interbranch conflict, Uruguay's mixed survival provisions enhance cooperation in governing, facilitating constitutionalism and democratic institutionalization."[27]

In the years before the 1973 Uruguayan coup, the executive bypassed the legislature in ruling by executive decree (as happened in Argentina during the economic emergencies of post-1989 and post-2001), but when democracy returned in 1984–85, the leaders of the historical parties accepted a tacit rule that "emergency measures are no longer included in the president's tool kit." Presidents Julio M. Sanguinetti (1985–90) and Luis Alberto Lacalle (1990–95) stressed cooperation over confrontation, taking "special care to avoid conflicts among the different branches of government and to negotiate parliamentary support."[28]

Electoral Law Change. The other major change to basic political rules in Uruguay was the replacement of the double-simultaneous electoral system—which led to the proliferation of intraparty factions (see chapter 3)—with a system mandating only one presidential candidate per party (internal primaries) and a second round of voting (ballotage) if no candidate received an absolute majority in the first round. The Colorado Party introduced this change in 1996, in large part as a means to prevent the left-wing Frente Amplio from winning the 1999 election. The reform package also proposed an important change to the parliamentary election procedures, ending the provision that allowed party lists to form electoral alliances (*sublemas*) and accumulate their respective votes to boost their electoral chances in the lower house in the General Assembly (the Chamber of Deputies). This provision had enabled parties to run hundreds of lists in a single election and gave voters broad electoral choices, but it created a confusing, cluttered electoral landscape and led to frustration on the part of some voters, who did not know whom their votes would benefit in the end.[29]

The 1996 electoral reform strengthened the position of the executive within his party as well as within the broader party system. Although some observers, such as Daniel Buquet, had predicted that this could have the opposite of its intended effect, leading to "extreme conflict" and "obstruction" between the legislative body and a less conciliatory president who felt empowered with a greater intraparty and interparty mandate,[30] executive-legislative standoffs have not ensued, even during the critical period of the 2002–3 economic crisis.

Domestic Institutions-as-Organizations

The armed forces, as well as political parties and party systems, are central domestic institutions-as-organizations in Argentina and Uruguay.

ARGENTINA

Armed Forces. The absence of military intervention was a surprise during the 2001–2 economic crises, because the return to democracy in 1983 had not been enough to firmly secure it in place. By the early 1980s the reputation and the credibility of Argentina's armed forces were in tatters—both in domestic public opinion as well as internationally—in the face of their reckless economic policy mismanagement and overweening corruption; the indiscriminate dirty war, in which close to thirty thousand individuals either were killed or "disappeared"; and the nationalist excuse to go to war with Great Britain over the Falkland/Malvinas Islands.[31] They could still mount credible threats to the civilian democratic regime, however, as confirmed by the three military rebellions that Presidents Alfonsín and Menem had to confront.

Aside from the irreparable loss of reputation, there were at least three other factors that help to account for why the armed forces were not a governing option in the late 1990s and early 2000s. First, the economic chaos of the 1980s destroyed much of the country's domestic-based, inward-looking industry. Argentina's military-industrial complex was second in size only to Brazil's in

Latin America, and the armed forces during that period were left without a material base to sustain autonomous political activity. Second, President Menem defused their capacity to act domestically in several ways, such as repeatedly cutting their budgets and deploying them for international peacekeeping operations (keep them active overseas, not at home). Third, in the international sphere the costs for the military to exercise pressures against democracy increased substantially.

Political Parties and Party Systems. The key difference, party-wise, between the economic busts of the late 1920s–early 1930s and the late 1990s–early 2000s was that the Peronist party—the Partido Justicialista—did not exist in the earlier years; since its creation in 1947, however, it has maintained almost uninterrupted electoral dominance (at least when allowed to compete, given its proscription by the military between 1955 and 1973). The 1994 reforms, which introduced a second round of voting in presidential elections, created incentives for second and third parties—or groups of parties—to forge multiparty coalitions. This, however, was still not enough to transform Argentina's party system. In fact, such coalitions have proven to be fickle and incapable of creating a cohesive government or an opposition bloc to the PJ, which has remained dominant, although internally divided between left-wing and market-friendly currents. Some traditional, conservative, provincial, *caudillo*-type leaderships, like Duhalde's in Buenos Aires province, operate within the broad Peronist movement.

The only serious attempt at multiparty government sank with the fall of President de la Rúa's multiparty coalition government, the Alianza para el Trabajo, la Justicia y la Educación, in late 2001. The Alianza was an ideologically incongruent political grouping (see chapter 9) that had come together because of the incentive (winning the presidency) for the second (the radical UCR) and third (the Frente por un País Solidario [FrePaSo]) forces to run together. The FrePaSo was a collection of small progressive parties and movements, created in 1994, that had at its core discontented Peronist leaders who criticized President Menem's embrace of neoliberal economic policies and defected from the party, such as José Octavio Bordón and Carlos "Chacho" Álvarez. Most FrePaSo members returned to the Peronist fold after the election of President Néstor Kirchner in 2003, which sparked a swing of the pendulum to the left in Argentina. Back in the 1990s, however, the progressive FrePaSo multiparty coalition formed a single legislative bloc during Menem's second presidency (1995–99), and it stood out as a bastion against the president's neoliberal revolution.

The Alianza won the 1999 elections by enough votes to avoid a second-round election, but the de la Rúa–Álvarez partnership never worked comfortably together. As Steven Levitsky notes, the beginning of the end for de la Rúa's presidency came with the resignation of Vice President Álvarez in October 2000, in protest over the government bribing opposition senators to pass a reform that would lower labor costs by weakening generous workers' rights. President de la Rúa's government was further undermined when all FrePaSo cabinet ministers resigned in March 2001, and his supporters suffered defeat at the hands of the Peronists in the October 2001 midterm elections. Facing a crumbling presidency and legislative support that had dwindled to a minority, President de la Rúa—who, on top of this political management crisis, also had to deal with the unenviable task of meeting regular interest payments on an external debt of 129 billion USD and an economy that, by late 2001, had been in recession for more than two years in a row—became a lame duck while still in the first half of his presidential term. The main point here is that without a viable alternative, the Peronist party movement has remained the key to governability in Argentina since the fall of President de la Rúa on December 21, 2001.[32]

From the perspective of relative costs for democracy, the greatest indictment that can be made against Argentina's political parties and party system is their inability to contribute to keeping the costs of organizing and exercising pressures against democracy high. The absence of a second-party-in-government alternative creates excuses for various factions to organize politically to destroy an electoral democratic regime, and the internal party dynamics of the dominant party movement have traditionally been characterized by a personalist, populist, authoritarian, and fractious culture. Infighting is the norm for Peronism, while no Radical president since 1928 has finished his constitutionally prescribed term. As Levitsky concludes, recurrent politicoeconomic crises in Argentina (during the rule of dictatorial as well as democratic regimes) have led to a long-term weakening of political and economic institutions; the actors always have short-term horizons, given the prevalent uncertainty in both of these spheres.[33]

URUGUAY

Armed Forces. In sharp contrast to the experience in Chile, after Uruguay's return to democracy, the military virtually disappeared as an institution with significant political weight. In the country's1984 Naval Club Pact, the military gave up its goal of maintaining veto power over certain civilian government decisions through the Consejo de Seguridad Nacional del Uruguay (Cosena).

Cosena had served as a council of military leaders that made final decisions in matters broadly related to national security, but the Naval Club Pact turned Cosena into a joint military-civilian council with advisory but not decision-making power, and it was formally derogated only two years later by an act passed by the General Assembly. The same act established a military amnesty for officials in the armed forces, barring their prosecution for human rights violations committed during the dictatorship period. The amnesty was supported by President Julio Sanguinetti as a measure to try to deal fairly with the human rights abuses of both the military and the urban guerrilla fighters in the tense period of the early 1970s. The amnesty was upheld in a 1989 referendum by a margin of 57% to 43%, and by a smaller margin of 52% to 48% in 2009. However, the issue of the prosecution of members of the military involved in human rights abuses during the dictatorship remains very much alive, in large part due to a 2009 ruling by the country's Supreme Court declaring the amnesty unconstitutional.

Since 1986, the armed forces have maintained a low profile. Uruguayans have a great sense of pride in their tradition of democratic civilian governance throughout most of the twentieth century, and they have sought to reclaim that legacy by relegating the military to a much smaller role in the past 25 years. Nevertheless, the Uruguayan military has redirected its focus to international peacekeeping. It has contributed almost 1,200 troops to the UN peacekeeping forces in Haiti (second only to Brazil, and by far the largest contributor per capita), and almost 1,400 to peacekeeping forces in the Congo (representing over 80% of the contingent of Latin American forces in that country).[34] Thus, while the Uruguayan military has ceased to be a domestic institution relevant to the issue of democratic pressures, it has maintained a raison d'être by becoming involved in the international security realm.

Political Parties and Party Systems. Since the nation's return to democracy, the political landscape in Uruguay has been profoundly changed by the emergence of a powerful third political force, the Frente Amplio, in a system that had been rigidly bipartisan since the mid-1800s. The Frente Amplio emerged in 1971 as a coalition of politicians who left the Colorado and Blanco parties—alarmed at the authoritarian tone and practice of Uruguayan politics back then—and forged an alliance with smaller parties on the left (Socialists, Communist, Christian Democrats, and other groups consisting of former Tupamaro guerrilla fighters). It was disbanded by the military after the 1973 coup, but in 1984 it reemerged and participated in the negotiations between the Colorado Party and military leaders that resulted in the Naval Club Pact and a return to democracy. (The Blanco Party boycotted the negotiations, adhering to a principled strategy by their leader, Wilson Ferreira Aldunate.) The Frente Amplio was home to the country's most radical political elements (including former guerrilla fighters), and its participation in the Naval Club negotiations gave the Left significant stakes in the new democratic order from the very beginning, although such involvement also committed it to act within the confines of the law. Between 1984 and 1999, support for the Frente Amplio grew from 21% to 40% of votes, culminating with the historic election of Tabaré Vázquez as president in 2004 with an outright majority of votes. The Frente retained the presidency after former guerrilla fighter José "El Pepe" Mujica won the 2009 presidential elections.

The emergence of the Frente Amplio as a powerful third electoral player meant that postmilitary presidents from the traditional parties could not rely on parliamentary majorities to advance their programs, prompting the traditional parties to turn to each other for support. The differences between the Blanco and Colorado parties were more historical than ideological in nature, and the growth of the more ideologically distinct Frente Amplio on the left led to the convergence of the traditional parties into a "political pole and an ideological family," although they still engaged in formal competition with each other.[35] As a result, the emergence of the Frente Amplio has led to a more clearly defined ideological division in the country's political landscape, with the Frente Amplio clearly representing the Left and the traditional parties representing the center-right (within which the Blanco Party is somewhat more conservative and free market, and the Colorado Party is known for its more statist and social democratic elements).

The 1996 reform did not end the factionalism that has long been the hallmark of Uruguayan politics. The number of formal factions within the Blanco Party has decreased, while factionalization within the Colorado Party has held steady and the Frente Amplio has became an even bigger tent and factionalized after the reform.[36] Nonetheless, the reform has greatly simplified the electoral offerings; the prohibition of vote accumulation among party lists for seats in the Chamber of Deputies led to a sharp decrease in the number of lists presented (the number in the 1999 election was less than half that in 1994), as the less competitive lists were dropped. A result of this consolidation of party lists has been "more disciplined legislative conduct from sector representatives."[37] And because the reforms did not give greater legislative weight to the party of the president-elect, the incentive for coalition building remained. Passing legislation is easier when coalition-driven voting discipline is added on top of greater intraparty voting discipline: "coalitions have not only served as binding conditions for enforcing party discipline, but they have also served to facilitate the policymaking process."[38]

In short, Uruguay's complex political party system seeks unity in diversity by aggregating interests into factionalized but disciplined partisan groupings. The rapid emergence of the Frente Amplio coalition on the left has meant that the traditional parties have had to work toward *inter*party unity in addition to *intra*party unity to ensure governability in the new multiparty context.

International Institutions-as-Rules

From the late 1990s on, institutions-as-rules affecting the Southern Cone countries featured developments in the realm of international law, as well as the adoption of democratic elements in the documents creating new international groups.

INTERNATIONAL CRIMINAL COURT AND UNIVERSAL JURISDICTION

The international juridical framework changed dramatically in the years following the end of the last military dictatorship in the Southern Cone, that of Chile in 1990. In 1998, the UN created the International Criminal Court (ICC) through the Rome Statute. It entered into force in 2002. The ICC serves as a permanent tribunal to prosecute individuals for egregious crimes against humanity. The ICC has jurisdiction over crimes that took place after July 1, 2000, in any one of its member countries (which include Chile, Argentina, and Uruguay), and it exercises its prosecutorial powers only when national judicial systems prove unable or unwilling to pursue these crimes.

The arrest of Augusto Pinochet in London in 1998, at the request of a Spanish magistrate, also marked a watershed in international law, due to its invocation of the principle of universal jurisdiction: the idea that certain crimes are so execrable that they can be prosecuted universally, should national courts not be able to address them. This principle had been enshrined in Belgium's 1993 law of universal jurisdiction. In Pinochet's case, he was ultimately set free on alleged grounds of poor health, but the British House of Lords had already ruled that the extradition could proceed, and the precedent stuck. Courts in other European countries, such as Spain and Belgium, have since invoked universal jurisdiction to prosecute human rights violators from Argentina, Chad, and Guatemala.

The creation of an International Criminal Court and the invocation of universal jurisdiction have raised the costs of flagrant anti-democratic activities by challenging the doctrine of sovereign immunity. In the past, repressive leaders had little fear of international legal reprisal for their domestic programs because they were protected from prosecution under the customary international legal tenet of sovereign immunity. Leaders still faced the threat of future prosecution within their own countries, but manipulation from within the system (amnesty laws and patronage) allowed them to avoid such situations. But by expanding the jurisdiction of a multilateral court (the ICC) as well as that of foreign courts over the most heinous activities, these laws and institutions have raised the costs of such actions. The true capacity of the ICC and universal jurisdiction to deter crimes against humanity is a matter of ongoing debate, but the dramatic shift in the international law that these institutions represent is undeniable.

In the case of Argentina, a Spanish court requested the extradition of a former naval officer, Ricardo Miguel Cavallo, from Mexico in June 2003. This was the first time that universal jurisdiction was invoked to arrest an Argentine citizen residing in a third country to face charges of crimes against humanity for his role in Argentina's dirty war. Emboldened by this case, in August 2003 the Argentine National Congress voted to annul the laws against prosecution that Presidents Alfonsín and Menem had been forced to pass to appease the military in the late 1980s and early 1990s.[39] The country's Supreme Court followed suit and overruled the amnesty laws in June 2005, and two months later the Chamber of Deputies nullified a nonextradition treaty so that officers could be sent overseas to be tried if this was requested by other governments.[40] Since then, several officers have been convicted, not only in overseas courts but also in Argentine ones. While retribution led to a military backlash against Argentina's young democracy during the 1980s, the contemporary weakness of the country's armed forces has allowed the legal process to run its course, raising the costs for future pressures against democracy.

In Uruguay, members of its military dictatorship were granted amnesty for human rights violations through the 1986 Expiry Law, which was proposed by Colorado President Julio María Sanguinetti, approved by the General Assembly, and upheld by public referendum in 1989. The Sanguinetti government proposed the law as a means for the fragile country to "close a painful chapter in its history," rebuild democracy unhindered by legal recrimination, and create "juridical symmetry" in the treatment of acts of violence committed by leftist guerrillas and the military.[41] As a result of this law, Uruguay has been the Southern Cone country least active in prosecuting members of its military junta. The tide shifted somewhat with the electoral win of the Frente Amplio in 2004, which brought to power the first government opposed to the amnesty. At the behest of President Vázquez, the national courts have used loopholes in the amnesty law to move forward with many prosecutions (47 total in 2008),[42] most notably that of ex-president Pedro Bordaberry for the assassination of political dissidents outside of Uruguay (the wording of the Expiry Law only protects those whose crimes were committed within Uruguay). Although the Expiry Law was upheld again by public referendum in 2009—albeit by the small margin of 52% to 48%—the Uruguayan Supreme Court declared the law to be unconstitutional in the same month, marking an important step forward in prosecution of the military. One author credits the sidelining of the amnesty law and the acceleration of prosecutions against human rights abuses to the Pinochet effect.[43]

OAS DEMOCRATIC CHARTER

The Inter-American Democratic Charter, adopted by the thirty-four member countries of the Organization of American States in 2001, provided a forceful commitment to democracy and against anti-democratic developments in the Americas.[44] The Charter has been invoked on two occasions: once in 2002 after the coup against the Chávez government in Venezuela, and again in 2009 after President Manuel Zelaya of Honduras was deposed by the military. The Charter states that "no State or group of States has the right to intervene, directly or indirectly, for any reason whatever, in the internal or external affairs of any other State."[45] In theory, the Democratic Charter raises the costs of anti-democratic pressures by committing governments throughout the Western Hemisphere to formalize their opposition to the exercise of pressures against democracy with the threat of diplomatic and economic sanctions.

However, the impact of the Democratic Charter on the ground has been negligible. The OAS has been sidelined by the United States during specific instances of governance crises, as happened most recently regarding Honduras, where—despite the country being suspended from OAS, and even though a majority of OAS's member nations expressed and then voted their opposition to the presidential elections in that country in November 2009—the United States and countries like Colombia and Peru recognized the electoral process and helped to legitimize the new conservative government under President Lobo.

While not invoking the Democratic Charter, other OAS organizations could, in theory, also contribute to raising the costs for perpetrators of pressures against democracy. Thus, in 1992, the OAS Inter-American Commission on Human Rights declared Uruguay's amnesty law (the 1986 Expiry Law) incompatible with the country's commitment to human rights, as expressed in the OAS

Charter and the 1969 American Convention of Human Rights.[46] The legal pronouncements of the OAS were said to have had "little or no legal impact on the country" at the time.[47] However, in the long run they provided legal and moral backing in the efforts to repeal the amnesty law. The Uruguayan Supreme Court eventually declared the amnesty law unconstitutional, both as a violation of the separation of powers and on the grounds that it was a violation of the supranational norms accepted by Uruguay as a member of the OAS and as a signatory to its human rights declarations. In a 2009 ruling, the Uruguayan Supreme Court invoked the opinion of the OAS High Court of Human Rights, which declared the Expiry Law to be incompatible with the country's international obligations.[48]

MERCOSUR

The Mercado Común del Sur, or Mercosur, is the regional common market of the southern half of South America. It came into being in 1991 with the signing of the Asunción Treaty by Brazil, Argentina, Uruguay, and Paraguay. While primarily known as an economic arrangement, Mercosur is also a political construct that formalized its defense of democracy after the adoption of a democracy clause (the Ushuaia Protocol) in 1998. Like the European Union, this clause makes membership in the bloc conditional on the existence and regular functioning of democratic regimes in member countries. The addition of this clause was prompted by an attempted coup in 1996 in Paraguay, during which time the regional community made it clear that such anti-democratic activity would come with substantial diplomatic and economic costs. Arturo Valenzuela called the restoration of President Juan Carlos Wasmosy and the resolution of the conflict with the military leadership in Paraguay "a triumph for the international community."[49] By adding the democratic clause, Mercosur institutionalized raising the costs of unconstitutional activity, threatening any such behavior with expulsion from the economic block.

International Institutions-as-Organizations

The two categories of institutions-as-organizations relevant to my analysis of the Southern Cone countries during the 1997–2002 period are (1) the multilateral international financial institutions and the dominant role of the United States government in them, and (2) international civil society groups who continued to rally against globalization (as represented by the IFIs and the neoliberal economic policy paradigm).

FINANCIAL INSTITUTIONS

Argentina and Uruguay reflect a marked contrast in their relationships with multilateral lending institutions during the emerging markets crises of the late 1990s and early 2000s. Although Argentina had a very public, stormy relationship with international lenders, Uruguay had been profiled as a major success story of the IMF and an "untold story of cooperation at work."[50]

Argentina. Given the recurrence of hyperinflation in the late 1980s and until 1991, convertibility was a blessing but also a curse for the competitiveness of Argentina's economy. After the emerging markets crises started in Southeast Asian countries in the summer of 1997 and later spread to Russia and Brazil in 1998–99, Argentina had no leverage to adjust its exchange rate in the face of the macrodevaluation of its main trading partner, Brazil, in January 1999 (just after President Fernando H. Cardoso had been reelected to a second term).

According to close observers of the implosion in 2001–2, the initial culprit was the IMF, whose officials were convinced that the Argentine economy was in an unsustainable trajectory since about 1998, particularly given its 1991 Convertibility Plan. Menem's Argentina was a poster child for the IFIs, however, so they kept rolling over and extending credit, and it was not until the second half of 2001, by which time the Argentine government was up against the wall, that they pulled the plug and froze any further credit lines.[51] Facing capital flight and the IMF's refusal to keep financing what was widely perceived to be a lost cause, President de la Rúa brought back Domingo Cavallo as Minister of Finance in November 2001, in the hope that he could once again create the magic of economic stabilization that he had achieved successfully in 1991. To stem mass financial outflows, Cavallo imposed capital controls on the banking system by creating what came to be popularly known as a *corralito* (playpen or animal pen), which initially limited and eventually banned Argentine depositors from having access to the assets they had deposited in banks. This move sparked the rioting, looting, violence, and breakdown of public order that ended in the resignation of the president and led to five interim presidents, one of whom, Adolfo Rodriguez Saá, stepped in and enacted the debt default on nearly 100 billion USD in Argentine external debt (to date, the largest sovereign default in history). Eduardo Duhalde was appointed interim president on January 2, 2002, and one of his first measures was to abolish the fixed peso–US dollar exchange rate. The peso's relative value plummeted, losing more than 70% of its value in the next four months.

While Argentineans continue to think that the major culprit of the 2001–2 collapse was the IMF, President Néstor Kirchner, who rode a strong populist tailwind and was elected in 2003, eventually emulated his neighbor, President Lula da Silva of Brazil, and paid off the balances owed by his country to the IMF at the end of 2005.[52] One of the reasons why Argentina has remained excluded from international markets (at least through 2011) is its $7 billion USD debt with the Paris Club (which defines itself as "an informal group of official creditors [from 19 member countries] whose role is to find coordinated and sustainable solutions to the payment difficulties experienced by debtor countries").[53] Negotiations over this debt require the IMF's seal of approval, which the Argentine government has remained reluctant to seek, even though the 2008–9 global financial and economic busts strained its fiscal capacity.

Uruguay. In stark contrast, Uruguay has had a friendly and productive relationship with the IMF and international lending institutions. This stems in large part from the fact that as a small country, Uruguay has never been in a strong position to take unilateral action in economic or geopolitical issues, and its domestic actors have come to agree that their country's size influences the policy directions it can take. As Mario Bergara and colleagues observe, "most of the actors are convinced that a small country like Uruguay has to be open to international financial markets, since it needs loans and foreign direct investment in the development process." Unable to go it alone like its larger neighbors, Uruguay has been more receptive to multilateralism and cooperation with international actors in pursuit of its domestic interests. Moreover, when Argentina and Brazil formed Mercosur, Uruguay had "no choice but to join them," given that they dominate the country's financial, tourism, and exports sectors.[54]

In the 1990s, Uruguay signed on to the policy of economic and financial openness advocated by the IMF. This reform was facilitated in large part by the emergence of a political consensus within Uruguay that the country had to be more open financially, and the positions of international lending organizations put additional weight behind this argument. For example, Bergara and his colleagues affirm that "The I[A]DB's conditionality plays a role when aligned with the government's goals, by providing ammunition for the government to weaken those who oppose reform," and "external enforcement mechanisms" are identified as a key factor in this nation's liberalization of its trade policy and financial openness.[55] In other, more controversial, deadlock-prone policy areas, the position of international lending organizations has carried political weight, but the powerful veto point of the public referendum, contained in the Uruguayan constitution, has stymied reform. Even the IMF's and the World Bank's backing of pension reform bills could not overcome the powerful veto gate of the public referendum: pension reform legislation presented by Presidents San-guinetti in 1989 and Lacalle in 1992 was overturned in public referenda by crushing margins. Ultimately, a moderate pension reform was passed in 1995, with the political as well as financial backing of the IADB and the WB, which agreed to pay for the transition costs.[56]

The close, collaborative relationship between the IMF and Uruguay became apparent during the 2002 economic crisis, and the degree of trust that Uruguay had built with multilateral lending institutions enabled it to convince the IMF to greatly increase its financial assistance to the country. IMF officials were hesitant about providing a large amount of liquidity to Uruguay and, at the height of the crisis, even suggested default on the country's sovereign debt. The government resisted and made a convincing case that sovereign default was off the table, because the country's reputation for financial stability was too im-portant: "any shift away from compliance with existing contracts would, in the Uruguayan context, be tantamount to institutional weakening, with adverse spillovers to the entire economy and the social fabric."[57] Uruguay is one of the few Latin American countries that, in its entire history, had never defaulted on its debt, and it wanted to preserve its "historically excellent standing in inter-national capital markets."[58] In the end, backed by the US Treasury, Uruguay was able to convince the IMF to provide emergency liquidity for a bailout of its banks in what became "one of the largest ever IMF lending operations."[59] This was an expensive course of action to preserve the nation's commitment to its contractual obligations, but in the end Uruguay lived up to its promise and repaid its 1 billion USD in debt to the IMF ahead of time, in late 2006.

CIVIL SOCIETY GROUPS

The continued strengthening of international civil society is another im-portant factor to consider in my analysis of the effects of institutions-as-organizations on democracy in the Southern Cone countries. Even compared with the early 1980s, when Amnesty International, Human Rights Watch, and the Washington Office for Latin America (WOLA) already had visibility on the ground throughout Latin America, particularly where dictatorships were still in power, the information revolution in the second half of the 1990s trans-formed possibilities for an international civil society. Mass access to the Inter-net, laptop computers, and cellular telephony made the globalization of politi-cal conflicts possible, such as the Zapatista rebellion in Chiapas, Mexico (1994). This technology also enabled the mass anti-globalization movement to bird-dog the senior-level meetings of the IFIs, the World Trade Organization, and the top private business forums to protest neoliberal globalization in cities like Seattle (1999), Genoa (2001), and Cancún (2003).

Thanks to the information revolution, civil society organizations from advanced capitalist countries consolidated their growing presence in Latin American and other developing countries around the world. But they also did more. By mobilizing domestic support, exerting leverage over their own countries' governments, and gathering information and sending it out to the world, these organizations have created an additional cost for anti-democratic activity, sometimes called a naming-and-shaming effect. The birth of the World Social Forum (WSF) in Porto Alegre, Brazil, was of particular importance in the aftermath of the emerging markets crises of the late 1990s and early 2000s. The WSF was an alternative to the free-market path of globalization supported by the IFIs, the WTO, and big-business forums, such as the World Economic Forum. In November 2005, many of the groups and movements that attend WSF meetings celebrated in a summit that paralleled the fourth Summit of the Americas in Mar del Plata, Argentina, where the US-driven hemispheric free trade project launched in 1994 finally sank. In short, by demanding public consultation and deliberation, the anti-globalization movement raised the costs for the technocratic, behind-doors decision-making style that characterized international discussions and support for Washington consensus policies (see chapter 9).

CONCLUSION

Compared with the 1930s, international institutions created in the aftermath of the Second World War evolved politically into a sector that rewards and promotes electoral democracy and, synchronically, attempts to raise the costs for anti-democracy organization and actions. Economically, these institutions have moved in a direction that, through the IMF as a lender-of-last-resort, has helped to put a floor on the extent to which financial shocks and economic crises reinforce each other and destroy productive activity.

The situation in Chile during the 1980s debt crisis, however, showed that the process of internationalizing rules and organizations was neither linear nor mechanical. In fact, different international organizations pulled in different directions, weakening the net potential result they could produce in the survival or breakdown of given political regimes. Thus, while the Chilean military regime was condemned and sanctioned in some forums (the UN system and the multiple NGOs that advocate for human rights), it received credit lines and guarantees from the IMF and other multilateral IFIs that helped it overcome its short-term financial and economic crises. The end result was that as macro-economic conditions improved for the military, the exact opposite happened to the likelihood of a full and immediate transition to democracy in the early and mid-1980s.

The evidence regarding Argentina's domestic institutions demonstrated, first and foremost, that chances for democracy increased in the 1980s, as compared with the 1930s, because the military-as-government option became morally, economically, and politically discredited—both domestically and internationally—in the wake of the human rights horrors and the economic mismanagement brought about by military rule in the 1970s–early 1980s. Since then, the conflicts and instability created by economic shocks/crises tended to lead to interrupted presidencies, that is, interruptions of the constitutional process rather than the breakdown of democratic regimes.

In terms of constitutions, electoral laws, parties, and party systems, the constitutional and electoral reforms in Chile (the 1980 constitution and the bi-nomial electoral system) and in Uruguay (reforms to the 1967 constitution between 1986 and 1996, which strengthened the national executive, and the 1996 electoral reform, which transformed political competition) helped to create relatively stable and successful (even if imperfect) processes of political competition, democratic representation, and governmental management capacity in the face of harsh financial shocks and economic crises.

As said, the opposite was true in Argentina. That country's 1994 constitutional and electoral reforms, while weakening the institutional powers of the presidency and enlarging the Senate, did not transform the party system, which continued to be dominated by the Peronist party. The Peronists, in turn, were internally divided into rivaling factions. A crucial difference from what happened in Chile and Uruguay is that there has not been a party alternative to Peronism that could govern Argentina effectively since the country's return to democracy in 1983. The two Radical governments that were elected since then had to step down, in the midst of economic chaos and social anarchy, before the end of their constitutionally prescribed terms. Argentina's democratic governance process has therefore been more unstable, and prone to high levels of risk and uncertainty, than Chile's or Uruguay's, particularly during harsh financial shocks and economic crises.

CHAPTER EIGHT

Interests

Capital Flight, Pressures from Below, and Democracy

In analyzing the relative costs of pressures in favor of and against democracy, a key change in international and domestic interests in the Southern Cone countries led to mixed outcomes, particularly given the different fate of pressures from below in Chile during the external debt crisis (1982–84), and in Argentina (2001–2) and Uruguay (2002–3) in the more recent emerging markets crises.

1982 CRISIS: BAILOUT AND TRIUMPH OF PRAGMATIC NEOLIBERALISM IN CHILE

The military regime under General Pinochet engineered a U-turn in terms of the growth in political weight of different economic interests in Chile. Between the start of the presidency of Eduardo Frei Montalva of the Partido Democracia Cristiana (PDC) in 1964 and the coup against President Salvador Allende of the Socialists and his multiparty left-wing coalition, the Unidad Popular (UP), on September 11, 1973, domestic interests decidedly took the upper hand over international ones. In Chile, as well as in Argentina and Uruguay, not only did the proportion of the agriculture labor force decrease significantly, but the total rural population also fell in absolute terms after 1960.[1] Partly as a consequence of the growth in political weight of urban, industrial, and service-based interests, particularly since the Second World War years, governments in these three countries privileged domestic industrial interests and those of the middle and working classes in urban settings, particularly in the big cities, which became the centers of gravity for modern mass politics. The losing interests were rural, particularly those of the traditional economic elites, focused around the major landowners who relied on strong export-led growth for their commodities. Between the Great Depression and the late 1960s, the increase in Chile's agricultural exports was below average, compared with the country's urban, industrial-based growth.[2]

In sharp contrast, the military regime under Pinochet restored primacy to the interests of the international and domestic elites after he implemented a free market revolution, starting in 1975, through his technocrat economists known as the Chicago Boys.[3] The military junta and its technocrats did not simply return economic power to the traditional elites, a small group with a long-standing reputation for exclusivism and a sense of entitlement over the country's fixed wealth.[4] Instead, the main pillars of early neoliberal policy, such as privatization and financial liberalization, benefited a small group of outward-oriented capitalists whose wealth was concentrated in liquid (financial) assets. These capitalists organized around the *conglomerados* (corporations) and *grupos económicos* (groups of firms)—which included banking, industrial, service, agricultural, and raw-material-exports firms—holding ownership of them under a single legal liability. Their owners and directors shared common social links with the Chicago boys, some of whom had employment and/or family histories that linked them to the *conglomerados*.[5] At a time when the military junta and its technocratic allies faced international condemnation and sanctions, an informal alliance with the country's most dynamic economic groups made sense. These groups were therefore allowed to engage in massive foreign borrowing to help prop up the economy. This process led, among other things, to a huge concentration of wealth. While twelve groups controlled around 52% of the assets of Chile's 250 largest firms and banks in 1970, by 1978 three *conglomerados* controlled 40% of these assets.[6] Still, economic recuperation between 1976 and 1980 permitted the state-*conglomerados* alliance to claim a "Chilean economic miracle." As long as international credit remained cheap and was readily available, this alliance was mutually beneficial: "Pinochet's protection boosted the internationalists' economic power . . . and the dynamic economy created by them boosted Pinochet's political power."[7] As it turned out, access to low-interest international credit from the banks allowed the larger industrial firms within these conglomerates to inflate their reported profits, even if such loans were used for consumption rather than raising the rates of capital formation in the Chilean economy.

In addition to the Chicago boys and the *conglomerados*, the military junta led by General Pinochet consolidated the neoliberal refashioning of the economy and created the bases for a restricted democracy by prompting a group of conservative lawyers, known as the *gremialistas*, to draft what became the 1980 constitution. The *gremialistas* were the midwives for the birth as well as the backbone of the development of Chile's more conservative right-wing party, the UDI, since 1983 (see chapter 9).[8]

From the perspective of competing economic interests, the reason why Chile experienced different political regime outcomes in 1931–32 and post-1982 is connected with Pinochet's U-turn in economic policy. The interaction of domestic and international spheres after 1982 raised the costs for organizing and exercising pressures in favor of an immediate return to democracy—which social mobilization demanded after the economic busts—and lowered the costs for the regime incumbents, regime allies, and the opposition domestically, as well as for foreign interests, to continue to operate within the status quo. Politically, the calendar spelled out in the 1980 constitution allowed the Pinochet regime to establish institutional bases and consolidate its power. Economically, with IMF backing, the Chilean state could bail out the country's international and domestic business interests. Moreover, the Chilean government exhibited exemplary behavior as a sovereign debtor, continuing to meet its interest and principal payments on time—even when that meant incurring a huge social cost domestically.

Domestic Sphere

The 1982 collapse triggered the first mass protests against the Chilean military regime since it came to power in 1973. As in 1930–31, the working and middle classes sparked the nationwide protests against General Pinochet and his handling of the economy. Moreover, in a move that was more dangerous for the military regime under Pinochet, the traditional, domestic-oriented Chilean private business community also joined the chorus of criticism against the radical application of neoliberalism since 1975. The regime answered predictably, brutally clamping down on dissent from the left while bailing out the Chilean private sector (and its international creditors). Pinochet switched the country's economic policy from radical to pragmatic neoliberalism (see chapter 9) to reinflate the economy and appease middle-class and elite discontent, damping down their participation in the mass demonstrations.

PRESSURES FROM BELOW

The clashes between the authorities and the protestors were so fierce that twenty-six individuals were killed and scores injured during one of the largest protests, in August 1983.[9] The regime carried out periodic sweeps in shanty-towns, arresting all males 15 years of age and older who were suspected of political activism, and arrest rates increased by more than 300% between 1982 and 1984, compared with 1976–82.[10] In addition, the regime targeted trade union leaders who called for protest and resistance, such as the leader of the public employees' union, Tucapel Jiménez, brutally murdered by the secret police (the Centro Nacional de Información, or CNI) in February 1982. Other labor leaders, like Manuel Bustos, leader of the textile workers, were exiled.[11] A key problem for Pinochet was that the well-heeled middle classes, particularly housewives, joined the protests by banging pots and pans (*cacerolazos*, which also became the main form of protest in Argentina during the 2001–2 bust), which raised the costs of all-out repression. In the end, the regime's uncompromising repression early on (in 1982–83), plus the radicalization of working-class protestors and terrorist acts carried out by communist organizations (such as the Frente Patriótico Manuel Rodríguez [FPMR], the Movimiento de Izquierda Revolucionaria [MIR], and the Grupo Lautaro), scared off the middle class and the elites, reducing their participation in further mass pressures against the military regime.

The final result was that pressures from below were unable to bring down the military regime in the 1980s, in contrast to what they had done in 1931. Costs for organizing and exercising pressures for democracy remained high, from violence by both the political regime's forces and extremists in civil society. The incumbents and the mainstream opposition decided instead to continue to engage by reviving Chile's traditionally strong political parties (see chapter 7) and adhering to the transition calendar contained in the 1980 constitution.[12]

PRESSURES FROM ABOVE

In stark contrast to the clampdown it carried out against mass protests, the military regime felt vulnerable in the face of a potentially serious rift with the country's business class—including not only big business, but also medium- and small-sized entrepreneurs in the agricultural, commercial, and transportation sectors—that was the backbone of the military's social base of support. The regime decided to compromise, spurred on by the effective organization of, among others, the main employers' associations, which came together in an umbrellalike platform called the *multigremio*, from which they coordinated public criticism of the regime's radical neoliberal experiment. Some observers saw this as an entrepreneurial revolt that forced the regime to respond with carrots (engineering a substantial economic policy switch that socialized private losses and supported private business through public subsidies for export activity) and sticks (intimidating the business sector by, for example, exiling the leader of the wheat producers' association).[13]

The main creditors of the highly indebted *conglomerados* were American and European private banks, which brought the dominant domestic and foreign interests together to put pressure on the military regime to assume their losses. Around two-thirds of the foreign indebtedness contracted by the private sector in the second half of the 1970s was not guaranteed by the Chilean state, and this precarious situation for creditors could have been a decisive factor in the debt restructuring that followed.[14] Faced with a potential massive debt default, creditors accepted a haircut (a discount on the original value of loans) of around 40%, and the IFIs supplied emergency financing in exchange for the Chilean state's assumption of the privately incurred external debts.[15] To secure this emergency financing from the IMF, the military regime also committed itself to restoring macroeconomic equilibrium through a drastic contraction in demand, which hurt the poor and middle classes disproportionately. In contrast, due to the regime's fear of losing support among the affluent, it extended fiscal benefits to private business activity: temporary tariffs; preferential exchange rate for firms' imports; tax exemptions for exporters; subsidized credit and collateral; and an undervalued exchange rate, which made the external sector more competitive.

In addition, the state did not completely divest itself of what it considered strategic areas (as Argentina under Menem or Peru under Fujimori did through wholesale privatization), retaining public corporations such as CODELCO, the public mammoth copper producer.[16] The nationalization of CODELCO by Socialist President Salvador Allende in 1971 was unanimously approved in Congress; in other words, the opposition Christian Democrats and, crucially, the traditional Right under the Partido Nacional both voted for outright nationalization of foreign—mainly American—mining investments in the country. The state copper monopoly under CODELCO became by far the most important foreign exchange earner in the 1970s, although it did go through significant oscillations, such as the global collapse of commodity prices in 1975, which (for a short time) put the military regime up against the wall. Nonetheless, this is the reason why—when the military took over after the September 11, 1973, coup—they never contemplated privatizing the copper industry. Foreign exchange earnings from copper exports became a particularly important lifeline for the military regime, particularly given the international financial and trade restrictions enacted by the United States during the Carter administration in 1977–80.[17] In sum, the combination of forces resulting from pressures from below and above, and the military regime's repressive response to the former and compromise with the latter, meant that the costs for pressures in favor of an immediate restoration of full democracy remained high. The revival of the opposition (through Chile's political parties and their permanent pressure on the military regime), however, forced General Pinochet to stick to the calendar his supporters had outlined for him in the 1980 constitution.

International Sphere

The likelihood that foreign business interests could lose everything, as would have been the case in the 1932 drive toward a nationalization of assets during the short-lived Socialist Republic—when the bulk of foreign interests were tied to the land and were therefore illiquid—was absent in the early 1980s. Instead, the 1982 bust was first and foremost a financial bust, based on the euphoria of international credit expansion that followed the two oil shocks of the 1970s (1973–74 and 1979–81). The gains/losses at stake were not rights over basic access to and exploitation of land, mineral, or energy resources. Rather, they were debts, that is, promises to pay interest and principal on monetary loans.

Two factors lowered the stakes for capitalists and the authoritarian Chilean regime incumbents in the 1980s, compared with the 1930s, and therefore helped to reduce the costs of engagement by going through the status quo, rather than by seeking a regime change. First, greater asset liquidity (financial rather than land based) was concentrated in fewer, larger investors (unlike the abundance of retail bond investors that dominated in the 1930s).[18] Institutional investors, such as big US and European private banks, dominated in the 1980s. Thanks to their concentration and clout, they found it easier both to lobby their national governments and to agree among themselves on a common strategy toward debtors. Second, Chile's activist trade policy and the international shift toward freer trade were in marked contrast to the protectionist move in the advanced capitalist countries in the 1930s, which accentuated the fall in global economic activity.

ASSET SPECIFICITY

As opposed to the preponderance of illiquid assets during the 1920s–1930s, assets since the 1970s have been highly liquid. This transformation was a consequence of the rise first of the Eurodollar market in the 1960s and then the petrodollar market in the 1970s. These two markets have recycled liquidity through European and American private banks since the late 1960s and since the 1973–74 international oil shocks, respectively. These private banks channeled close to 10 billion USD to Chile in 1976–81. The country's total external debt jumped threefold, from 5.4 billion USD in 1976 to 17.2 billion in 1982. The ratio of annual serviced debt to exports jumped from a manageable 25.4% in 1973 and 53% in 1976 to an unsustainable 71% in 1981 and 88% in 1982.[19] The bulk of the debt was incurred by the outward-oriented Chilean private sector; in 1976 only 21% of total external debt was owed by the country's private sector (the rest was public), while by 1981 it had exploded to 84%. Likewise, the participation of US and European private banks, compared with the multilateral financial institutions, zoomed from 28% in 1976 to 87% in 1982.[20]

In short, the bulk of the steep growth of Chile's external debt involved private creditors (mainly Anglo-American banks) and debtors (mainly the big *grupos económicos*, or conglomerates). The former were backed up by their countries' national governments—primarily by the US government under President Reagan—and by international organizations such as the Paris Club. The *grupos económicos*, in turn, had the support of the Chilean military regime, which socialized the losses these businesses had incurred in the credit binge of soft loans that the regime had allowed in the first place. The fiscal cost of the Chilean state's bailout of the country's private sector was around 41% of annual GDP, which compares very unfavorably with most other recent public bailouts in Latin America.[21] What was bad for Chilean taxpayers—a public bailout—was nonetheless good for the dominant international and domestic interests, who refrained from calling for or otherwise pushing regime change and instead supported the option of following the transition calendar that was part of the 1980 constitution.

TRADE POLICY

The 1982 economic bust forced the Chilean military regime to turn its back on its indiscriminate implementation of free market reforms. It adopted countercyclical fiscal policies (export tax exemptions, subsidized prices for imports, and subsidized credit for new investments that were used in export-related activity), which created a " 'new style' natural resource–based exports" model that, aside from mining, created growth engines in sectors such as forestry and fishing.[22] Protection and support for exports initiated a new type of industrial policy that was very effective at promoting growth, but was also very different from the early indiscriminate trade liberalization of the radical phase of neoliberalism in 1975–82. Instead, the military regime returned to Chile's long tradition of assigning a developmental role to the state.[23]

In addition to state support of domestic economic activity in Chile, particularly in the externally oriented sector, in the 1980s Chilean and other export-dependent economies also benefited from international support for trade liberalization, which received a huge boost after the end of the Cold War. World economic growth resumed in the second half of the 1980s, and "Chile's turn toward exports paid off in the 1990s, as the economy doubled in size; in 2000 it was the richest country in Latin America."[24] Had the world reverted instead to 1930s-style nationalism and protectionism, Chile's strong economic recovery in the second half of the 1980s might not have happened. This, in turn, would have fueled pressures from below and above to demand a regime change that returned to a full rather than a restricted democracy. As things turned out, however, economic improvement and the best growth rates in Latin America in the second half of the 1980s gave the military regime breathing space and helped it to impose its own terms on its withdrawal from power, through the 1980 constitution and its market-oriented and restricted-democracy rules.

The case of Chile in the 1980s highlights the fact that a coalition of interests—including foreign and domestic capitalists, the military regime and its civilian allies, and the US government and its influence with multilateral financial institutions—managed to prevail in the wake of the country's worst economic crisis since the Great Depression. The internationally sponsored bailout and injection of resources helped to establish a floor on financial outflows and economic decline. Successful stabilization strengthened the hand of the regime and contributed (along with the brutal deployment of coercion) to sapping the momentum of the multiclass pressures from below that called for an immediate return to democracy.

1997–2002 EMERGING MARKETS CRISES: SURVIVAL OF DEMOCRACY IN ARGENTINA AND URUGUAY
Domestic Sphere
ARGENTINA

The beginning of the end for Argentina's version of neoliberalism—and the start of a series of events that rocked the country's democratic regime, culminating in an interrupted presidency and several weeks of great uncertainty amid social and political instability—started on December 1, 2001, when Argentina's Minister of the Economy, Domingo Cavallo, issued a restriction on the withdrawal of bank deposits, known popularly (and infamously) as the *corralito*. Prescribed correctly as a means to stop the bleeding of Argentina's foreign exchange—which, from a trickle in 1997–98, became a crippling hemorrhage in the second half of 2001—it nonetheless triggered a massive social and political backlash. The reaction was largely instigated by the urban middle classes and Peronist-led clientele networks, and joined by more spontaneous popular organizations, among them the mobilized unemployed (the *piqueteros*) who had become prominent since the late 1990s, when they organized to block roads in protest against high unemployment.[25]

The buildup to the social explosion gained momentum on December 5, when the IMF formally declared that it would not disburse a 1.3 billion USD aid package because of Argentina's unsustainable fiscal outlays. Two days later, on December 7, the Argentine government announced that it could not meet its debt obligations. With unemployment at 18%, social protest widened and deepened at the behest of national union leaders, who were calling for strikes. Unrest spiraled into chaos as rioting and the looting of supermarkets signaled the potential onset of anarchy. Ominously, the fall of de la Rúa's fellow Radical president (Alfonsín) in 1989 was also preceded by the outbreak of rioting and looting amid crisis conditions. Further, distraught by the lack of access to their rapidly depleting life savings, the citizenry at large took to the streets in an unorganized, massive protest on December 19, stretching into the wee hours of the next day. Cavallo was forced to resign, and the protests became violent, with renewed rioting and looting, which led the government to impose a state of siege. Nearly thirty people died in these protests, and President de la Rúa was forced to resign on December 20, famously departing the Casa Rosada by helicopter.

The Argentine National Congress appointed the sitting President of the Senate, Ramón Puerta, as temporary president until a proper replacement was voted in. On December 23, the National Congress appointed Adolfo Rodríguez Saá as interim president until elections could be held in 2002. President Rodríguez Saá announced a new economic plan on December 26, one that formally defaulted on all outstanding public debt, which was nearly 100 billion USD. As liquidity dried up, Argentine citizens continued to riot and loot. Public order broke down again in some cities, and President Rodríguez Saá, trying to extend his hold on power for longer than had been agreed on with leading Peronists, was forced to resign on December 30. Immediately afterward, Ramón Puerta (who had already been interim president) resigned as head of the Senate. The next in line was Eduardo Camaño, leader of the majority in the Chamber of Deputies, who became interim president until the National Congress chose and swore in sitting senator Eduardo Duhalde as president on January 1, 2002. President Duhalde, boss of the powerful Peronist party machine in Buenos Aires province, stabilized conditions in the short term by relaxing the *corralito* after January 6.[26] President Duhalde also put an end to the fixed peso-dollar parity. The day before the *corralito* was imposed, November 30, 2001, the Argentine peso was trading at 1.0005 pesos/USD. After the peso was depegged on February 11, 2002, the exchange rate fell to 2.30 pesos/USD and would eventually bottom out at 3.74 in September 2002.

In all, this was an extremely volatile period in Argentina, characterized by mass protests, some spontaneous, others organized by Peronist leaders through their patronage and clientistic-based control of many popular movements. A whirlwind of anarchy engulfed the country between December 18 and 21, 2001, when rioting, looting, and confrontations between protestors and police forces led to more than two dozen people being killed.

Pressures from Below. The massive anarchic social protests of 2001–2 contrasted sharply with previous pressures from below in Argentina. Whatever resistance there was to the 1930 military coup came from union workers and, as it turned out, was very weak. The leftist guerrilla movements that fought a succession of military regimes between the late 1960s and the mid-1970s—resulting in the dirty war, which has haunted Argentine society ever since—pursued explicit political aims: the construction of different versions of utopian regimes, and, at the extreme end, the pursuit of nihilism through violence and destruction for their own sakes.

Protests and mayhem against the government in the light of the December 2001 economic shock and collapse did not come from guerrillas or a well-organized communist or other far-left organization. The December 2001 social protests that toppled President de la Rúa came in the form of massive marches, with a large portion of the middle class banging pots and pans (the *cacerolazo*) as a form of protest, a phenomenon that had been seen in previous financial collapses, such as the one in Chile in 1982–83. The *cacerolazo* expressed the public's anger and fear regarding present and future economic conditions in the face of financial collapse and a severe economic crisis. The 2001–2 events went on to be Argentina's worst economic collapse in modern history.

A second source of mobilization and capacity for sustained collective action during the 2001–2 financial and economic meltdowns came from popular organizations linked to Peronist leaders and from the *piqueteros*, many of whose organizations ended up being absorbed by the patronage and clientelist-driven Peronist machine. The *piquetero* movement began in the 1990s as a result of sharply rising unemployment as President Menem's neoliberal agenda was implemented. A *piquetero* group started operating formally on June 21, 1996, in Neuquén province, after the state owned-oil company, Yacimientos Petrolíferos Fiscales (YPF), was privatized and workers lost their jobs.[27] The newly displaced workers joined together to block a national highway in protest, and they only lifted the barricades after the authorities bargained with them and promised new jobs or lower living costs (for utilities and food). The success of the fired workers in extracting money and concessions from the authorities caught the nation's attention, and sooner, rather than later, groups of unemployed around the country organized and applied the same method to force authorities to engage with them and negotiate side payments.

Piquetero groups grew strongly in and around the major roads and highways of Buenos Aires. Early success led *piquetero* leaders to affiliate with each other to gain clout, and they organized into large movements, such as the Movimientos de Trabajadores Desocupados (MDT). Once the *piquetero* groups organized, their role in Argentine politics became harder to disregard. At its apex, total membership in *piquetero* organizations reached 300,000, a vast increase from the few dozen adherents at the YPF protests. There were 140 road blockages in Argentina in 1997. By 2002, in the midst of the crisis, that number exploded, to 2,236.[28] The *piquetero* leaders looked to the marginal and poor members of society to support their groups, often drawing them from sectors such as the disabled, women, and youth. This was very different from when the *piquetero* movement began; then it consisted solely of the unemployed.

The increased importance of the *piqueteros* and their ability to literally shut down traffic in major urban areas made the government highly susceptible to their demands, which, according to some authors, considerably weakened the strength of government institutions. As Edward Epstein noted, the *piqueteros* focused on clientelism. At first they participated in demonstrations for fear of being "ousted from the work programs controlled by group leaders, and thereby losing their monthly income."[29] These work programs were originally created and funded by the national government as a form of relief for poor and unemployed workers. Leaders of various *piquetero* movements then saw gaining access to these programs for others "as something central to their new organizations' survival and possible numerical expansion."[30] Politicians handled the *piqueteros* differently during the acute phase of the crisis than after the economic woes began to abate in 2003. According to Isabella Alcañiz and Melissa Scheier, "during the Menem administration approximately 100,000 government subsidies (*planes trabajar*) were distributed to key [electoral] areas of counties. . . . Beginning with the Duhalde administration (2002–3), these subsidies increased to 2,000,000, covering close to 15% of the economically active population. President Néstor Kirchner distributed approximately 1,700,000 in his first year in office."[31] The governments of Presidents de la Rúa and Duhalde were forced to bargain with *piquetero* leaders and provide places in official aid programs for their members. President Kirchner permitted the *piqueteros* to retain their right to demonstrate. He stipulated, however, that a large police force would be present, a move considered by some to have been intimidating.[32] A tougher stance by President Kirchner, plus a dramatic turnaround between 2003 and 2008 that saw Argentina's economy growing at its highest rates since before the Great Depression, helped to defuse and drain the strength of and public sympathy for the *piqueteros*.

In sum, two main sources underpinned the explosion of collective action against the government's handling of the economy. On the one hand, the *cacerolazos* were mass marches and gatherings in plazas, with participants coming from multiclass backgrounds; middle-class individuals and groups were prominent among them. These protests were reactive, without a political program. On the other hand, Peronist clientele networks and the *piqueteros*, who (in many cases) came to be controlled by Peronist party bosses, blocked roads as a way of ensuring government concessions by paralyzing the country. These groups had a clear purpose: gaining access to public benefits for their members in exchange for allowing freedom of movement to the citizenry. Their methods were similar to extortion, and it was through mafialike cooptation and the use of force that Presidents Duhalde and Kirchner and the traditional Peronist party machine managed to bring them under control by institutionalizing handouts, the Peronists' time-honored way of establishing control of the masses.

These two very different sources of collective action nonetheless produced similar effects in terms of the mass disruption, violence, and chaos that overtook the streets of Argentina in December 2001. The end result was that the descent into anarchy forced the resignation of President de la Rúa and his government and opened the door to more than ten days of acute instability, dire uncertainty, and, finally, the return to power of a traditional *jefe*, the political boss of none other than what was by far the most important political and economic subunit of Argentina's federal structure, the province of Buenos Aires. De la Rúa had bested Duhalde in the 1999 polls, but Duhalde beat de la Rúa and his ill-fated multiparty coalition government experiment in the streets. President Duhalde restored order and stability by means of cooptation and coercion, methods traditionally associated with Peronism's political machines.

The main point here is that democracy did not fall—unlike what happened in 1930. But what saved it were the personalist, boss-led politics of mainstream Peronism that, without an effective opposition counterweight to check it, weakened the chances for democratic institutions and practices to become institutionalized in Argentina.[33]

Pressures from Above. As generally happens, the financial crisis of 2001–2 disproportionately hit the middle classes and the lower working and unemployed classes; unlike the upper classes, they could not transfer their wealth abroad, so they bore the bulk of the cost of the peso's macrodevaluation. In fact, after the crisis the middle classes shrank considerably, thrusting many people below the poverty line and giving way to the phenomenon of *cartoneros,* displaced members of the lower middle and upper lower classes who collected rubbish for recycling around the posh Buenos Aires neighborhoods of La Recoleta and Barrio Norte.

The financial crisis affected the interests of the upper class differently, according to whether they formed part of the urban or rural economies. Upper-class Argentines were concerned with ensuring ample returns on their wealth and, as it turned out, the rural elite enjoyed increases in their exports with the devaluation of the peso. Domestic corporations and industrialists were able to wipe their debts off their books after the massive debt default decreed by the state, although this was at the expense of Argentina's credibility and creditworthiness in the international capital markets; the country has been excluded from these markets since then. The main role of the elite in response to the crisis actually contributed to deepening it. Capital flight, in the face of mounting public debt and the overvaluation of the peso through the Convertibility Plan, grew as the signs of instability became more apparent. Estimates suggest that around 18.7 billion USD fled Argentina in 2001–2002.[34] The ratio of capital accounts to GDP showed inflows equivalent to 6.3% in 1998 and 5% in 1999, which reversed to −5.5% in 2001 and −7.5% in 2002.[35]

In short, although very different from one another, pressures from below and above (mass multiclass mobilization and capital flight) fatally weakened the de la Rúa government's authority and capacity to maneuver in the run up to and aftermath of Argentina's economic and political explosions in December 2001–January 2002. Still, after Eduardo Duhalde assumed the presidency on January 1, 2002, order was gradually restored and democratic rule did not collapse, as opposed to the breakdown of democracy in September 1930.

URUGUAY

Pressures from Below. After the spectacular violence preceding the 1973 coup and the repressive military dictatorship that followed, Uruguayan society embraced peaceful means of resolving disputes when democracy was restored in 1984–85. The Tupamaro guerrilla movement (the Movimiento de Liberación Nacional-Tupamaros [MLN-T]) left its violent tactics of social protest behind and joined the political system as the Movimiento de Participación Popular, which would become a powerful faction of the left-wing multiparty coalition under the Frente Amplio that came to power in 2005. It is the political base of "Pepe" Mujica, the ex-guerrilla fighter who became president of Uruguay after winning the 2009 elections.

On only one occasion did social protest result in major violence, when members of the radical Left staged a huge protest in 1994 at the Hospital Filtro in Montevideo, in support of several Basque militants from the ETA (Euskadi Ta Askatasuna) terrorist organization after Spain's request for their extradition had been approved by the Uruguayan court system. One person died and many were injured when the police used repressive means to control protesters as the latter tried to prevent the transport of the Basque militants to the international airport. Former Tupamaros defended the protesters and the national labor union (PIT-CNT) staged a general strike. Nevertheless, the collective shame induced by the Hospital Filtro incident reaffirmed Uruguay's postauthoritarian commitment to peaceful protest and the condemnation of violence: "the fear and grave concern following these incidents offered certain guarantees that the chain of events that led to the breakdown of democracy in 1973 would not reoccur."[36]

Interests that support the Left have used elections and public debate as a means of advocating their primary concerns: the continuation of Uruguay's highly statist, interventionist economic model and the prevention of neoliberal reforms such as privatization. These groups represent a substantial proportion of the Uruguayan population, which has consistently been one of the societies least supportive of the free market paradigm in Latin America.[37] The most powerful interest groups have been labor unions (represented by the PIT-CNT), the student union (the Federación de Estudiantes Universitarios del Uruguay, or FEUU), and the pensioners' organization (the Organización Nacional de Asociaciones de Jubilados y Pensionistas del Uruguay, or ONAPJU). These interest groups have been more reactive than proactive with regard to policy. According to Bergara and colleagues, "interest groups have limited influence as agenda setters. However, they have important veto power."[38]

Labor unions have been the most successful in using referenda to reverse privatization efforts. In 1992, the unions gathered enough support to overturn the Law of Public Enterprises, which would have privatized the state telephone company (ANTEL) and the country's flagship airline (Pluna). They did so again in 2002 to block an effort to allow the state oil company (ANCAP) to affiliate with private enterprises. Pensioners also represent a powerful group, due in large part to the relatively high proportion of elderly people in Uruguay.[39] In 1989, pensioner groups were able to use a plebiscite to index pension payments to past rates of inflation, and in 1994 they employed a referendum to block a reform of the pension system. These interest groups have proven to be powerful veto players in postauthoritarian Uruguay.[40]

The presidency of Jorge Batlle Ibáñez (2000–2005) was marked by the emerging markets bust that engulfed Argentina, and later Uruguay, in 2001–3. This Batlle—whose granduncle was President Batlle y Ordóñez, the father of statism and creator of a robust welfare state in Uruguay—found himself having to push for austerity, cuts in public expenditures, and fiscal sustainability, causing him to lose the support of the working class that *batllismo* had historically championed. The economic chaos of July and August 2002 marked a low point in Jorge Batlle's presidency and in Uruguay's postauthoritarian period. The chaos was triggered by nervous Argentine depositors who withdrew their savings from the Uruguayan banking system. Around one-third of the deposits were withdrawn within a few days, and this led to the insolvency of five national banks. After the runs on the banks began, the government declared a five-day bank holiday, which led to panic in a society that had prided itself in its strong, reliable banking sector.

As the economy deteriorated, the ratio of fiscal deficit to GDP burgeoned (reaching 4% by May 2002). To maintain state solvency and the nation's good standing in credit markets, the government raised taxes in February and May of 2002 and cut spending.[41] This ran directly counter to the interests of workers and the middle and lower classes, who demanded state intervention to shore up wages and protect jobs in a time of uncertainty. These groups expressed their disaffection in a series of general strikes organized by the PIT-CNT, starting in June 2000, with demands for "full employment, fair wages, rights to collective bargaining, respect of labor unions, and rejection of privatization."[42] Employees of banks and hospitals supported the strikes, demonstrating widespread popular disapproval of the state's actions.[43] In late June the government decided to allow the peso to float, which led to a 50% devaluation of the currency, causing the dollar-denominated debt to increase dramatically. This move prompted further unrest in society, as well as within the political system, enough to cause embattled Minister of Finance Alberto Bensión to announce his resignation on July 15. When a bank holiday was declared in late July 2002, social unrest reached a peak, and several incidents of looting occurred at supermarkets.

President Jorge Batlle and the General Assembly approved bills in May and August of 2002 to support solvency, rather than catering to popular demands for wage and job security. By choosing the path of a state bailout for banking losses and fiscal retrenchment—in other words, socialization of private losses—Batlle and the Colorado Party saw their electoral support collapse. Nevertheless, "there was not significant pressure for the President to resign or for the scheduling of early elections,"[44] as had occurred in Argentina. In response to the social unrest, Minister of the Interior Guillermo Sterling alleged that acts of looting at the height of the crisis had been organized, memorably claiming that a "little Bin Laden" was behind them. Notably, Sterling didn't rule out the possibility of a suspension of constitutional guarantees, saying such a decision depended on the president.[45] In the end this drastic measure was not necessary, and the government did not resort to any form of repression.

Several more movements arising from social unrest emerged in the year following the bank bailout of 2002, but they never presented a real threat to Jorge Batlle's presidency. Two more general strikes were staged by the PIT-CNT against the bank bailout, the high rate of unemployment (which hovered around 17% through 2003), and the significant decline in real wages.[46] The unemployed attempted to exert pressure from the grassroots level by forming the Unión de Trabajadores Desocupados del Uruguay, staging protests and road blockages that were disbanded by government officials, but its membership quickly dwindled. In 2004, an Argentine *piquetero* leader, Néstor Pitrolo, traveled to Montevideo to establish a Uruguayan affiliate of his confrontational and violent protest movement, but he did not receive a warm welcome, even from the Left. Minister Sterling urged Uruguayans to resist the *piquetero* mentality, and the leader of the national union claimed that he did not consider the methodology of the *piqueteros* appropriate for Uruguay.[47]

In short, the 2002 crisis saw the interests of state solvency trump the popular interests of job and wage security. The bailout implemented by the government ultimately saved the Uruguayan economy, but it came at the cost of a dramatic collapse in support for the traditionally dominant Colorado Party and a steep social cost.

Pressures from Above. The interests of the economic elites have had a more ambiguous role in Uruguay since the country's return to democracy than well-organized pressures from below. Álvaro Forteza has observed that although the interests of unions and pensioners are largely singular and cohesive (preventing neoliberal reform), entrepreneurial groups such as banks have divergent positions and interests, which have prevented them from being important actors in the reform process.[48]

The policy area that experienced the most progress in the 1990s—trade policy—did so not due to lobbying by business interests, but by an emerging consensus that a small country like Uruguay could not afford to be protectionist. A 1994 World Bank study showed that the country's trade barriers had led to highly inefficient production, a diversion of income from rural to urban sectors, and overall welfare loss; rent-seeking behavior by the industrial sectors, mostly concentrated in Montevideo, were what sustained them.[49] While these industries' interests in trade protection remained, the need for liberalization was too difficult to ignore. Politicians therefore moved forward with trade liberalization reforms, but they adopted a regional instead of a multilateral approach by integrating into South America's Mercosur trade bloc.

Similarly, banking interests were not the driving force behind the laws that liberalized Uruguay's financial sector in the 1990s: permitting foreign agents to transfer capital and profits into and out of the country freely, allowing commercial banks to accept foreign credit, and lifting controls on interest rates. The managers of retirement savings funds were the only ones who took an active role in advancing these reforms. Uruguayan banks were ambiguous, because more open capital markets would mean their banking credit would face stronger competition.[50] Thanks to capital liberalization and lax banking regulations, Uruguay became an important offshore banking center for Argentine and Brazilian depositors and businesses in the 1990s. Uruguay increased its capital inflows, but it also became more vulnerable to bank runs if economic crises in Argentina or Brazil led to sudden, mass capital withdrawals from Uruguayan banks, which is exactly what happened after Argentina's implosion at the end of 2001.

Business interests were also important in the passage of the 1992 Ports Law, which granted participation in port operations to private enterprises and overcome opposition from the union groups and the Frente Amplio. For the most part, however, the liberal reforms of the 1990s were not driven by business lobbying, but by a hands-on political leadership that recognized the problematic nature of the bloated Uruguayan state.

The economic elites and business interests do not appear to have played a major role either in the economic reforms of the 1990s or during the 2002 crisis. Remarkably, the crisis did not significantly undermine the progress the country had made in liberalizing the financial sector during the prior fifteen years. As Bergara and colleagues note, "even during the recent financial crisis in 2002, there were no calls to control capital movements, showing a high level of consensus on preferences."[51]

$\_\_\odot\ \odot\_\_$

In sum, pressures from below and above were much less disruptive in Uruguay than in Argentina during the 2001–2 economic shocks and subsequent crises. Bipartisan support for President Jorge Batlle's crisis management, coupled with the substantial social base of support for the two traditional parties, meant that, paradoxically, the political impact of this economic meltdown was less disruptive in Uruguay, a much smaller and therefore more vulnerable and dependent country, than in its neighboring giant.

International Sphere

Between 2001 and 2003, Argentina and Uruguay were hit with brutal financial shocks and economic crises. Both countries faced capital flight on a large scale, leading to runs on banks and the imposition of bank holidays to stop reserves from bleeding away. The governments of both countries were forced to float their respective currencies, which prompted rapid currency devaluations that caused their debt burdens to soar. But the crisis management by their respective governments produced very different results. Argentina declared sovereign default and was excluded from international capital markets, but the Uruguayan state, backed up by multilateral and US government emergency financing, bailed out the banks, managed to work with creditors to avoid default, and ultimately gained international praise as a model for future debt workouts. Nonetheless, Uruguay's social costs were high.

ASSET SPECIFICITY

Argentina. International assets in Argentina in 2001 were more liquid, and therefore movable, than they were in the 1920s–30s. The international investment community and domestic capitalists had the ability to withdraw at least part of their investments (those stored in financial wealth) as Argentina's economic horizon deteriorated gradually between 1998 and 2001 and close to 20 billion USD was pulled out of the economy in 2001–2 as the public debt soared. According to the World Bank, Argentina's total public debt in 2001 was 148.58 billion USD.[52] Of that amount, the government defaulted on around 100 billion USD in debt to foreign creditors, including the IMF. Although it seemed as though Argentina defaulted on its debt overnight, there were actually two debt operations conducted by the IMF in 2001 to prevent this collapse. These attempted bailouts were unsustainable, however, leading the Argentine government to default on its debt to international creditors.

In June 2001, Argentina completed a voluntary market-based debt exchange through the IMF to help provide some breathing room in meeting its external obligations. It succeeded in scaling back payments due in 2001–6. However, the interest rate on these swapped bonds was a staggering 17%, which made their eventual repayment unlikely when compared with Argentina's limited growth projections.[53] The country's economy had been in recession since 1999, and the economy had to grow at 8% to service its huge debt obligations. In July 2001, the Argentine National Congress had passed a zero-deficit law aimed at reining in the public debt, but this was too little too late. A massive withdrawal of between 700 million and 2 billion USD on November 30, 2001, broke the back of the system and signaled its eminent collapse. The IMF again stepped in, this time with an immediate 5 billion USD disbursement to stabilize the economy, but this did little to boost confidence in Argentina's government. There was also a political component to the loss of confidence in President de la Rúa. The midterm elections of October 2001 led to a defeat of the executive's support in the National Congress, making him an isolated lame duck. Thus, when the IMF's second attempt at economic stabilization at the end of 2001 failed, it refused to intervene for a third time, leading to the largest sovereign default in history, macrodevaluation, a fall in GDP of more than 11% in 2002, and 20% unemployment before the pieces could be put back together. The devaluation of the peso meant that while the ratio of public debt to GDP was already high at 65% in October 2001, by the end of 2002 it had more than doubled, to 135%.

After Argentina formally defaulted on its debt, its creditors organized to push for debt repayment. The global commodity boom between 2003 and the first half of 2008 rescued Néstor Kirchner's government, and big windfalls from taxes on Argentina's expanding agricultural exports helped the government assume a tough stance toward creditors, 75% of whom accepted conditions that amounted to haircuts of 65%–75%, which meant a repayment of only 25%–35% of the value of their original investment. Nonetheless, Argentina was left owing around 10 billion USD to American private investors and around

6.5 billion to the Paris Club. Moreover, even though the commodity boom strengthened the Argentine government's position, the post-2008 global bust revived concerns about the country's macroeconomic fundamentals, particularly its inflation rate, as well as its fiscal sustainability, given the country's exclusion from international capital markets since the December 2001 debt default.

More recently, President Cristina Fernández de Kirchner's Minister of the Economy, Amado Boudou, presided over a successful debt swap with outstanding creditors in June 2010. This offer was taken up by many of Argentina's creditors, whose claims amounted to more than two-thirds of the 18.3 billion USD still in default. Thus by mid-2010, despite Argentina's continued exclusion from international capital markets, the country had successfully restructured more than 90% of the nearly 100 billion USD it defaulted on at the end of 2001.[54] Still, Argentina's return to international capital markets will need to surmount several other challenges, such as the Kirchner government's reluctance to submit to a routine IMF Article IV evaluation, a prerequisite to negotiations with Paris Club investors. This remains problematic, given the acrimonious relationship and persistence of bad feelings between Argentina and the IMF.

Uruguay. The troubles in the Argentine economy spread to Uruguay in early 2002. What struck Uruguay in 2002 was primarily a liquidity crisis, rather than a solvency crisis,[55] and it is this feature that distinguishes it from past situations. In the 1930s, foreign assets were tied to the land, impeding a quick exit and preventing them from becoming a powerful source of leverage against the state, while in the 1990s and 2000s foreign assets existed primarily in the form of liquid financial instruments. Through the ratification of strict banking secrecy laws after the nation's return to democracy, Uruguay had developed into an important banking center for the Mercosur bloc and for international private banks, and liquid foreign savings represented 43% of the deposits in Uruguayan banks. Debt issuance to foreign bondholders also became an important source of finance for the state. The bond market gave foreign investors significant leverage, because the Uruguayan government's failure to repay bonds could restrict its ability to issue debt in the short-term future. Disregarding the interests of foreign investors could trigger capital flight, which was a principal cause of the emerging markets crises of the 1990s.

As a result of this new economic reality, maintaining the country's good standing with the international investment community was paramount to the Uruguayan government. This gave foreign interests a degree of leverage in Uruguay that they did not enjoy in Argentina when the two countries' respective crises developed. Default appeared to be a very real possibility in Uruguay as well as Argentina, but in the end the Uruguayan government was able to chart an exit from the crisis that satisfied foreign interests and, importantly, its own, given the economy's growing reliance on banking and financial services since the 1990s.

In 2001, bank deposits represented an imposing 83% of Uruguay's GDP, and almost half of all deposits were held by foreigners (primarily Argentines). When the Argentine government imposed the *corralito* on December 1, 2001, and froze bank deposits, nervous Argentines quickly withdrew their savings from banks in Uruguay, and total nonresident deposits plummeted from 6.5 billion USD in December 2001 to 2.2 billion in September of the following year, a decline of 66%. Eventually, uneasy Uruguayans began to withdraw their savings, which fell from 7.4 billion USD to 5.3 billion between December 2001 and September 2002, a decline of 29%.[56] The unprecedented drying up of liquidity left five banks insolvent and the government negotiated a massive bailout with the IMF and other IFIs that amounted to 20% of the country's annual GDP.

Throughout the crisis, Jorge Batlle's government made it clear that its prevailing interest was to maintain Uruguay's good standing in credit markets and avoid any freezes on deposits. In May 2002, President Batlle promised that "there will be no *corralito* in Uruguay."[57] In spite of this resolve, he had little choice but to declare a five-day bank holiday in late June 2002, in order to address the intractable liquidity crisis facing the nation's banks. While the liquidity of financial assets was a major aspect of the nation's 2002 crisis, Uruguayan officials were very resistant to hindering it in any way. They argued that banking security was a cornerstone of the country's economic model, and even claimed that deposits were "covered by a guarantee embedded in the constitution."[58]

Representatives of the Uruguayan government convinced the US Treasury, the World Bank, the IADB, and eventually the IMF to front the liquidity needed to back all deposits by 100%, resulting in the 1.5 billion USD Fund for the Stabilization of the Banking System. In designing the bailout bill, lawmakers were careful to accede to the interests of both domestic deposit holders and foreign banks (notably the Banco Santander of Spain and the Banco Itaú of Brazil). The bill emphasized that there would be no restrictions on bank deposits and that the government would not impose any restrictions on foreign banks. After the bank holiday ended, deposit withdrawals were less than originally feared, and the liquidity crisis was stabilized by October 2002 as deposits began to return to the banking system.

The government's parallel interest in preserving Uruguay's impeccable track record of public debt repayment was the main factor that led to a successful debt workout. Uruguay was the only Latin American country that had never defaulted on its foreign debt, including during the crucial Brady Plan bond-debt restructuring of 1989–90.[59] The closest Uruguay came to restricting its external debt obligations was in the early 1930s, when it declared that it would only make payments in domestic currency rather than in gold, but it did not default. Still, Uruguay's sovereign debt faced a precarious situation in 2002, when a weakening peso and declining GDP caused the mostly dollar-denominated public debt to rise to over 100% of GDP, up from 53% the previous year. The skyrocketing debt-to-GDP ratio led some observers to speculate that debt default was only a matter of time.[60] In February 2002, Uruguay lost its investment-grade status, a major blow to the confidence of the country that prided itself as a reliable place for investment.

But in April 2003, Uruguayan officials designed a debt-exchange offer that replaced old bonds with newer ones that had longer maturities but no reduction in the principal of the loans, and a remarkable 93% of the bondholders agreed. The debt restructuring was driven by the convergent interests of foreign bondholders and the Uruguayan government: the former were eager to avoid any haircut on the principal of their loans, and the government was eager to maintain its reputation as a reliable debtor by making the terms of the new bonds as favorable as possible to creditors. This ingenious workout received praise from international investors: "Uruguay's rescue was handled so efficiently that many of the deans of global finance are holding it up as a model for defusing future sovereign debt bombs."[61]

In the end, the intervention of the IMF and other IFIs enabled Uruguay to restore creditor and depositor confidence in the system, while such intervention failed in Argentina. Uruguay's successful bailout can be attributed to a convergence of priorities of the various stakeholders in Uruguay's financial system. In the 1930s, foreign economic interests were at odds with government interests over the nationalization of foreign holdings (especially in the energy industry) in both Argentina and Uruguay, while in 2002 the two sets of interests converged, due to the much greater liquidity of foreign investments in the 1990s. The specter of capital flight convinced government officials that maintaining a reputation as a safe and reliable debtor was essential to the country's economic future. Its best course lay in appeasing bondholders and maintaining financial confidence in the Uruguayan state.

—⟋ ⟍—

In both Argentina and Uruguay, asset specificity changed significantly, becoming more liquid and therefore more mobile in the last third of the twentieth century than it had in the 1920s and 1930s. This similarity notwithstanding, the two countries experienced opposite outcomes in terms of how their affected interests fared, with Argentina's massive sovereign default on one side and, on the other, the bailout of the Uruguayan economy, backed by the US Treasury and the IFIs. The result was that Argentina cut its losses but excluded itself from international capital markets, while Uruguay, rescued by the international financial system led by the United States, remained in them. Inasmuch as access to international credit can buy governments time in the face of economic shocks/crises, Argentina's default removed this tool, while Uruguay still held on to it, giving the country more room to maneuver in the aftermath of the more recent 2008–9 global busts.

TRADE POLICY

Argentina. Argentina embraced trade liberalization under President Menem. With a strong currency from the Convertibility Plan, Argentina was able to import goods cheaply, although its exports were negatively affected in a deteriorating and self-reinforcing situation, since the economy did not grow between 1999 and 2001. Its current account–to–GDP deficit was −4.8% at the end of 1998, mostly explained by appreciation in the relative exchange rate. In the context of the emerging markets crises that started in East Asia in the summer of 1997, and particularly in light of Brazil's crisis and macrodevaluation in January 1999, the Argentine government chose to defend its national accounts, partially turning its back on the early Menem years of euphoria and an apparently strong commitment in favor of economic liberalization. It now raised tariffs on imports from non-Mercosur countries for final consumption goods. It imposed higher anti-dumping duties on its Mercosur partner Brazil and its other major trade partners. It also increased export reimbursements in order to raise the profitability of the tradable sector, given the straitjacket of a fixed exchange under the Convertibility Plan.[62]

An interesting paradox is that the 2001–2 Argentine economic implosion caused President Duhalde, who had resigned as President Menem's vice president in 1991 in protest against the neoliberal direction the executive branch pursued, to reverse protectionist trade measures. The intent was to increase fiscal revenues, first by allowing the external sector to grow, and then by taxing such activity. Argentina's return to taxing its exports put the government on a collision course with powerful rural interests engaged in agricultural, livestock-based, and related activities.[63] This change was nonetheless effective in fiscal terms, and it sustained the high level of public expenditures made during both President Néstor Kirchner's term in office (2003–7) and the first year of that of his wife and successor, President Cristina Fernández de Kirchner. In addition, the 2003–7 economic expansion saw Argentina's trade with Asian countries, particularly China, growing at the expense of Mercosur.

Uruguay. In contrast to Argentina, Uruguay has continued with a gradual process of trade liberalization that begun in the late 1980s. Surprisingly, the 2002 crisis did not prompt Uruguay to adopt restrictive trade measures to protect its domestic business interests, as the WTO noted in its 2006 "Trade Policy Review,"[64] although, according to Forteza, it may have contributed to some protectionist sentiment.[65] In 2005, the PIT-CNT came out as a staunch opponent of a potential Free Trade Agreement (FTA) with the United States, saying that such an agreement would "jeopardize the sovereignty of the country."[66] However, 57% of Uruguayans were in support of the FTA, and even a large number of moderate members of the Frente Amplio (including Minister of Finance Danilo Astori) considered an FTA to be an important opportunity to achieve economic growth. This pro-FTA sentiment came at a time when support for Mercosur had soured, as Uruguayans did not believe that this regional trade bloc was delivering proportionate benefits to its smaller partners. President Vázquez took an ambiguous stance on the issue, and he ultimately chose to sign a Trade and Investment Framework Agreement instead of an FTA, a move that Jasmin Kossman describes as a conciliatory measure that allowed opposing interests to each claim victory.[67]

_⚬ ⚬_

In sum, in trade as in finance, the two Southern Cone countries responded differently to the 2001–2 busts. Trade policy manifested continuity in Uruguay (moving in an increasingly open direction) and change in Argentina (from early enthusiasm for trade liberalization, to renewed protectionism under a fixed and overvalued exchange rate, followed by regained competitiveness after a financial crisis forced a macrodevaluation and pragmatic concentration on taxing exports rather than imports). The Argentine government's decision to

reverse some of its trade protectionism and concentrate on raising public revenue through export taxes, initiated by Duhalde and continued under the Kirchners, led to a growing confrontation and then a showdown between the government and the traditionally powerful rural interests. The government was
ultimately defeated in its attempts to raise revenue through higher export tax
rates. The end result was the politicization of a conflict that, while not seriously
destabilizing the democratic regime, raised uncertainty and worsened short-
term prospects, as the clash between landowning interests and the Argentine
state has always done.

In contrast, the bailout of Uruguay's economy, orchestrated by the United
States and IFIs, and the consensual management of the 2001–2 economic
shocks and crises meant that its economic policy changes were gradual and not
nearly as dramatic as in Argentina. A more internationally integrated, small,
dependent economy, coupled with a political system that earned international
and domestic kudos for its economic crisis management, resulted in less uncertainty, improvements in short- and medium-term prospects, and a credible,
reliable electoral democratic regime.

CONCLUSION

The relative rise in liquid, financial-based assets (and their options for capital
flight) in the Southern Cone countries—particularly compared with the dominance of fixed assets in the 1930s—could be one influence that led to lower relative risk adversity for foreign and domestic capitalists since the 1980s. This is
especially the case when worsening conflicts over redistribution are combined
with harsh financial shocks and economic crises. These lower stakes for foreign
and domestic capitalists might also have contributed to reducing the likelihood
that their top preference would be to support military rule—which in any case
had became totally discredited by then—in the face of threats to their wealth.
Foreign investors in Latin America since the 1980s have been more inclined to
seek redress in a New York City court than to side with an anti-democratic coalition of interests in a given country where they operated, as foreign energy
companies did in 1930 in Argentina and in 1933 in Uruguay.

Pressures from below were ferociously repressed during the 1982–83 economic collapse in Chile, helping the military regime regain the upper hand and
then dictate the terms of its withdrawal. Although civilian rule returned in
1990, it was still a restricted democracy until 2005. In Argentina and Uruguay
during the years 2001–3, pressures from below helped to create very different

outcomes. In Argentina, some of these pressures were provoked by Peronist clientele network groups; others by huge multiclass, reactive protests against the system itself (the *cacerolazos* and *"Que se vayan todos!"*); and still others by the rise of the Argentine-specific *piquetero* movement. The conflict spilled over from basic public institutions into the streets to an extent and with an intensity that led to the breakdown of order, rioting, looting, and police crackdowns that left more than two dozen dead in Argentina in late December 2001. The end result was the fall of President de la Rúa, and then of three other presidents, between December 21, 2001, and January 1, 2002. In Uruguay, despite strong opposition by trade unions and the leftist Frente Amplio, President Jorge Batlle's signed off on an orthodox macroeconomic adjustment (with its resultant horrific recession). Pressures from below remained alive and well organized in the wake of Uruguay's 2002 financial collapse, but a significant proportion of this country's population found an institutional outlet for their fear and anger by voting out the long-lived, dominant party duopoly and electing the Frente Amplio, a left-wing coalition, and its presidential candidate, Tabaré Vázquez, in 2004.

As for how various interests were affected by and reacted to changes in trade policy, events between 1982 and 2002 could not have been more different from what happened during the Great Depression years. In the early 1930s there was a wholesale move toward protectionism in the aftermath of the 1929–31 financial shocks. Started by the advanced core capitalist countries and then copied throughout the periphery, such moves led to no more than a weak trade channel as a source for recovery, particularly in countries whose economies were as significantly dependent on commodities exports as our three Southern Cone nations. In sharp contrast, most of the world jumped on the bandwagon of a trade liberalization process that gathered momentum during the final multilateral GATT round in the 1980s and culminated in the establishment of the World Trade Organization in 1994. As a consequence, harsh economic shocks and crises between the 1980s and 2011 have occurred against the background of a growing, opening world trade system. Now there are more international sources for economic recovery after a bust, particularly when compared with the trade-destroying, market-shrinking protectionism of the 1930s.

CHAPTER NINE

Ideas

———

Cold War Endgame, Unipolar Moment, and Neoliberalism

Just as the rise in liquid-based wealth since the 1970s–80s has helped to lower the pressure against democracy by foreign and domestic capitalists, changes in the realm of ideas—political ideologies, and economic ideas and policy—since the Cold War ended have reduced the stakes for dominant foreign and domestic actors, at least in the Western Hemisphere.

1982 CRISIS: COLD WAR ENDGAME AND REDISCOVERY OF THE ROLE OF THE STATE IN CHILE

Similar to the 1930s, the international sphere during the early 1980s affected events and trends in periphery countries, such as those in Latin America. More often than not, dominant political ideologies and economic ideas in the international sphere produced a magnifying glass effect in domestic spheres, in the sense that the main issues of the day internationally—politically, the last years and the endgame of the Cold War; economically, the Volcker effect, felt through the recessionary monetary policy of 1979–81, the debt crisis, and the turn to neoliberalism—were amplified and stoked the fire of domestic conflicts in the Southern Cone countries and, more generally, throughout Latin America.

International Sphere
POLITICAL IDEOLOGIES

The 1980s were the endgame decade of the Cold War, although the leading actors did not know this at the time. To President Reagan and his top advisers, communism was still a menacing force at the gates of the free world; moreover, it had gained a foothold in the Western Hemisphere after the victory of the Sandinista revolution in Nicaragua in 1979. Reagan launched a major counteroffensive, training and supplying mercenaries (the Contras) against Nicaragua's leadership. The US government also expanded its aid and training to neighboring military regimes in El Salvador and Guatemala, which were fighting left-wing insurgencies. Honduras served as the US hub for arming and training the Contras. The end results were appallingly violent and destructive: civil wars that killed more than three hundred thousand and displaced more than two million people.

The Reagan administration's financial and military involvement in the Central American civil wars came under growing pressure from international and domestic public opinion. As a consequence, President Reagan's advisers convinced him to modify US foreign policy toward South America in 1982. Initially, Reagan subscribed to the Kirkpatrick doctrine, where the United States would continue denouncing and condemning human rights abuses that took place in countries under totalitarian communist rule, but would refrain from doing so in the case of anti-communist, authoritarian regimes (like the bureaucratic-authoritarian military regimes in South America), who were America's allies in the Cold War.[1]

Several factors explain the policy switch that happened during Reagan's presidency, according to Kathryn Sikkink. First, both houses in the US Congress remained under Democratic majorities, and they fought against the Reagan administration's early attempts to dismantle the robust framework of human rights policy that President Jimmy Carter had put in place as a guiding principle of US foreign policy. Second, the Argentine military junta's decision to invade the Islas Malvinas (Falkland Islands) and push for war with Great Britain in April 1982 called into question some of the core beliefs of Reagan's advisers regarding the predictability of military allies' actions and their potential regional security implications. In the case of Chile, the issue of predictability meant that Washington was concerned about the insurgency launched by left-wing guerrillas in the mid-1980s, as well as about General Pinochet's recalcitrance and his upping the stakes by responding in the form of violence. The Reagan administration wanted to help avoid what it saw in this trend: the potential for a spiral of violence and disruption in the run up to the October 1988 plebiscite.

Third, given the direct military involvement of the United States in propping up the Contras to bring down the Sandinista regime in Nicaragua, and military and financial assistance to the armed forces of El Salvador to continue waging what by 1983–84 were horrific counterinsurgency wars, Reagan came under growing pressure domestically and internationally. Civil society organizations, the Catholic Church, and what in effect became a transnational network of governmental and nongovernmental organizations fighting for the respect of individuals' human rights worldwide all called for the United States to get out of Central America.[2] Therefore, a key change in US foreign policy was the replacement of hawk Alexander Haig by George Shultz as Secretary of State in July 1982. Secretary Shultz worked with Elliott Abrams, Assistant Secretary of State for Human Rights since November 1981, on the place human rights should have in President Reagan's foreign policy. As a member of the neoconservatives, Abrams believed in using human rights to fight the Cold War. Once given the green light by the president, the administration tried "to appropriate the banner of human rights for itself—to use it in the battle not only against communist regimes but also, in a more defensive way, against domestic opponents of its human rights policy. It was a brilliant strategy, no more than half cynical, and it almost worked."[3] In other words, the administration needed examples of instances where it promoted democracy that could counter allegations about its complete disrespect for human rights in Central America. President Reagan made this policy switch official in December 1984, when, during a Human Rights Day speech, he singled out Generals Pinochet and Stroessner by declaring that "the lack of progress toward democracy in Chile and Paraguay" was "an affront to human consciences."[4]

Thereafter, the Reagan administration offered the Chilean military regime sticks and carrots to try to steer it in the direction of embracing the transition calendar spelled out in the 1980 constitution. Two measures sponsored by the US government were particularly important in strengthening the opposition to the military regime in the run up to the October 5, 1988, plebiscite that would ratify or reject Pinochet remaining in power. First, a professional, conciliatory foreign service individual, Harry Barnes, was made US Ambassador to Chile in 1985, and he reached out to the opposition: political parties (Socialists included), human rights groups, and the Catholic Church. Second, the US government (through USAID) made a grant of 1.2 million USD to help the Cruzada Cívica organize a massive voter registration process in the run up to the plebiscite.[5] In addition, through the National Endowment for Democracy, or NED (a private, nonprofit, grantmaking organization created by the US Congress with bipartisan support in 1983), the US government financially supported efforts to give more visibility to opposition media, increase voter registration, and monitor the polls on election day itself, including a quick count.[6]

That President Reagan had been willing to turn against such reliable US military allies and Cold War friends in South America lent some support to the view that the administration had taken a strong stance (although a selective one) on human rights and democracy. The evidence for such a serious change was provided by none other than General Pinochet himself. In one of the many delicious ironies of Cold War incidents in the Western Hemisphere, Pinochet—who was keenly aware of Washington's desertion—declared to the French newspaper *Le Monde* that the first thing that had come to his mind during the failed assassination attempt against him in September 1986 was that the Central Intelligence Agency (CIA) had hatched the plot to get rid of him.[7] (In fact the far-left FPMR, the armed branch of the Chilean Communist Party, was behind this operation.)

The end result was that an unforeseen change in the sphere of political ideologies (the United States turning against Cold War military allies and rulers in South America) raised the costs for those who wanted to or could exercise pressures against democracy. At the same time, the US foreign policy switch lowered the costs for those pushing for a return to democracy in Chile during the second half of the 1980s.

ECONOMIC IDEAS AND POLICY

These years also saw the growing importance and spread of free market economics, ideas that were fostered and promoted by the IFIs and successive US governments. Toward the end of the 1980s, the neoliberal paradigm had crystallized into an identifiable basket of pro-market policies and reforms that came to be known as the Washington Consensus, due to the geographic location of some of its main backers (the US federal government, the IMF, the WB, the IADB, and think tanks like the Institute for International Economics, the Cato Institute, the American Enterprise Institute, and the Heritage Foundation).[8]

Emerging democracies in Latin America, Central and Eastern Europe, the Far East, and Africa were pushed to adopt these policies. Under IFIs' conditionality, after member countries suffered from a financial shock, they could have access to fresh credit lines in exchange for orthodox stabilization and the implementation of structural reforms that strengthened market-based economic discipline. The mantra of economic liberalization continued to gain force internationally, in spite of the financial shocks that emerging markets countries underwent after liberalizing both their capital and trade accounts, as Chile had done in the second half of the 1970s. Even after Mexico's financial collapse (starting at the end of 1994) strengthened the evidence for those making the case that the combination of opening up capital and trade accounts resulted in financial volatility, which then tended toward recurrent balance-of-payments crises, and finally culminated in disorderly macrodevaluations and harsh economic crises, the World Bank's chief economist for Latin America, Sebastian Edwards, saw the Mexican crisis as a nasty hiccup, but one going in the right direction. This meant that there was continued official international support for further implementation of the Washington consensus policies as the best way to move forward in the second half of the 1990s.[9] It was not until after the East Asian financial and economic collapse, which started in the summer of 1997, that the IFIs changed their tune and admitted that free capital markets had tended to produce dramatic short-term financial fluctuations that led to spectacular booms and busts.[10]

Chile's place during the international strengthening of neoliberalism in the 1980s was quite distinctive. Although this country had been a pioneer in the radical implementation of pro-market policies since 1975—the military dictatorships in Argentina and Uruguay had also implemented economic liberalization in the second half of the 1970s, but without the breadth and depth of the Chilean embrace of neoliberalism[11]—after the 1982–83 bust Chile was also a forerunner in the subsequent partial rollback of free markets across the board in Latin America.

Domestic Sphere

POLITICAL IDEOLOGIES

The rhetoric and actions of the Cold War were still in full swing in Chile's domestic political sphere in the 1980s. The key difference with the Great Depression was that the 1930s were years with a three-way, irreconcilable ideological conflict between communism, liberal democracy, and fascism, while bipolar conflict dominated the Cold War during the1980s. The three-way type of ideological conflict in the 1930s produced more instability—and therefore created greater uncertainty for international as well as domestic actors—than bipolar conflict of the Cold War–type, which led to long periods of defensive containment and stability.

In Chile, a small but potentially highly disruptive contingent of insurrectionary left-wing groups was willing to bring the system down through violence in the mid-1980s. The exiled leaders of the Communist and Socialist parties,

Luis Corvalán and Clodomiro Almeyda, had endorsed the insurrectionary path ever since the military regime enacted the 1980 constitution.[12] In fact, the presence of the left-wing guerrilla groups and their highly visible actions—the MIR's assassination of Santiago's military chief in 1983; smuggled weapons cargoes coming from Cuba for the FPMR, and their discovery by regime officials in the northern region's desert coast on August 11, 1986; and the same group's assassination attempt against General Pinochet on September 7, less than a month after the discovery of the weapons—weakened the mainstream Left. In contrast, the hand of the military regime and its civilian allies was strengthened in the run up to the October 5, 1988, plebiscite.

Although the middle classes and some among the private-business elites had protested against the military regime in the wake of the 1982–83 financial and economic bust, the in-your-face acts of violence that the insurrectionary Left carried out scared these groups away from continuing to oppose Pinochet's rule. At the same time, the violence gave him the perfect excuse to impose a state of emergency and rule through it. As a prominent opposition member put it, "the retreat of the middle classes thwarted the viability of social mobilization as a tool to topple the military regime."[13]

The end result was that the costs for pressures in favor of the restoration of full democracy remained relatively high after the targeted but nonetheless highly visible escalation of conflict between the left-wing guerrilla groups and the military regime led to both a strengthening of authoritarian rule and more constraints for those who supported the return of civilian rule through legal means. The repeated flare-up of radical bipolar conflict (guerrilla insurrection versus military clampdown) instead strengthened the hand of those among the incumbents and the opposition who wanted to stick to the calendar and the procedures for a transition to democracy spelled out in the 1980 constitution. In short, the irreconcilable conflict between contending political ideologies, still locked in the logic of the Cold War during the second half of the 1980s, gave additional support to those in favor of democracy (albeit of a restricted kind, as specified in the constitution) while raising the costs for the more extreme positions (a left-wing insurrection and revolution, or the continuation of military rule after 1988).

ECONOMIC IDEAS AND POLICY

In contrast to political ideologies, international economic policy ideas did not have much of an effect in Chile in the second half of the 1980s. While the free market, Washington consensus paradigm gathered steam and extended its influence geographically, the radical version implemented by the Chilean military regime between 1975 and 1982 was partially rolled back after the country's 1981–83 financial and economic bust. Pinochet changed his economic teams several times between 1982 and 1985, leading to an economic policy switch in a countercyclical and state-interventionist direction. His new economic policy, which turned its back on the indiscriminate liberalization of all prices and protections promoted by radical neoliberalism, enshrined a pragmatic approach that did not balk at providing subsidies or temporary tariffs to protect domestic production and demand. This idea did not originate with the military regime. Rather, the top domestic business associations were able to force it on the government when the latter found itself weakened and against the ropes in the aftermath of the 1981–83 meltdown.[14]

This new, pragmatic economic policy implemented aggressive countercyclical crisis management in the short term, and selective state intervention and protection of domestic economic activity over the medium and long terms. This approach supported a public bailout of private debt (close to 90% of the dollar-denominated credit borrowed since the late 1970s); reflationary policies, such as subsidized new credit, increased public spending (on public works and housing construction), and lower interest rates; a tolerance for fiscal deficits and annual inflation rates of up to 30%; and an active industrial policy that used tariffs and export incentives (such as tax cuts), and gave exporters greater access to the policymaking process.[15] It is not an exaggeration to say that with a massive state bailout, and the broader adoption of a mixed economy with a center of gravity that shifted from radical neoliberalism to a market-oriented economy underpinned by strategic state intervention and growth promotion, Chile's notable economic success since the mid-1980s has been a function of state strategy/intervention and a private business sector that is subject to international competition.

Even after the economy was successfully stabilized and growth resumed in 1985, which allowed Pinochet to dismiss his expansionist economic policy team and reappoint technocrats of the neoliberal persuasion (led by Hernán Büchi), Chile's economic policy retained such objectives as strengthening export capacity, investment, and domestic savings; reorienting the private sector; effectively managing external debt; and stimulating employment.[16] The return of career bureaucrats also gave the military regime the autonomy to arbitrate conflicts among different interest groups.[17] The end result was that successful economic stabilization and resumption of growth strengthened General Pinochet's hand in the run up to the October 5, 1988, plebiscite. This particular outcome illustrates a more general point in this book: successful stabilization of unstable economies has strengthened incumbents since countercyclical economic policy started being implemented in the 1930s (in the case of Chile back then, it added to the credibility of democracy during Arturo Alessandri's second presidency).

Successful countercyclical economic policy stabilization during the 1980s in Chile was in stark contrast to the pro-cyclical economic policy and steadily worsening conditions in the economic crises during General Ibáñez's failed attempt to stabilize the Chilean economy in 1930–31. These worsening conditions decisively contributed to the mass protests that toppled Ibáñez's authoritarian regime in July 1931, while stabilization and the resumption of growth in 1984–85 meant that economic success bred political success. It did not hurt that the run up to the 1988 plebiscite was underpinned by rapid growth and relative price stability. It allowed Pinochet's regime to regain strength and control the process for a transition to democracy. Hence the military regime did not collapse (as it did in 1931), but instead was able to impose its politicoeconomic model, enshrined in the 1980 constitution—a restricted democracy and a market-oriented economy with room for strategic state intervention and the promotion of growth—on the incoming civilian government.

1997–2002 EMERGING MARKETS CRISES: DOMINANCE OF DEMOCRACY IN ARGENTINA AND URUGUAY

The world of the late 1990s and the early 2000s was very different from the early 1980s. To start with, the Cold War had come to an end. The United States enjoyed monopoly superpower status during the unipolar moment, and it promoted electoral democracy and free markets wherever it could. The Washington consensus basket of free market policies ruled and went almost unquestioned until Mexico's 1994–95 financial and economic implosion started what became an all-too-frequent phenomenon of financial shocks and economic crises that rocked emerging market countries in Southeast and East Asia in 1997, Russia in 1998, Brazil in 1998–99, and culminated with the implosion of Argentina's economy at the end of 2001 and Uruguay's in 2002.

As a consequence, the pendulum of ideas swung back. In the realm of political ideologies, its arc was against the US model of liberal democracy—that is, a political system that controls government action with strong checks and balances, thus strengthening the status quo and forcing policies aimed at changing it to proceed in a gradual, piecemeal way. In the realm of economic ideas, the momentum was against the Washington consensus policies and their foreign and domestic supporters. The backlash against the US version of economic and political globalization was not uniform, but several countries in Latin America experienced the return of nationalist populist leaders, such as Venezuela, Argentina, Ecuador, and Bolivia. Once in power, they exalted the primacy of domestic popular interests over those of foreign investors and governments, whose joint influence in these countries had grown during the years when Washington consensus policies were implemented.

International Sphere
POLITICAL IDEOLOGIES

The main difference between the turn of the twenty-first century and the previous periods analyzed in this work was that, while an irreconcilable, tripolar ideological conflict dominated in the 1930s and a bipolar one held sway in the 1980s, the United States and its version of liberal democracy and free markets prevailed after the end of the Cold War, during the unipolar moment. The primary effect of these ideological changes has been to lower the stakes for the dominant foreign and domestic political and economic actors. Lower stakes mean a narrower range of potential gains and losses by allowing electoral democracy to rule uninterruptedly, compared with more cutthroat periods in the past, such as the Cold War years or the fight to the death of liberal democracy, communism, and fascism during the interwar years. This does not mean that ideological conflict has waned or that liberal democracy has reigned unchallenged since the end of the Cold War. In Peter Smith's telling words, "democracy has become more widespread (and to some extent more durable) throughout Latin America because it has been tamed. From the 1940s to the 1970s, democracy was seen as 'dangerous.' It amounted to a social provocation. From the 1980s to the end of the century, that was no longer the case."[18]

In the aftermaths of the 2001–2 crises, there was no credible appeal that could be translated into a non-democratic civilian or (even less so) a military government alternative in Argentina and Uruguay. This was in sharp contrast to the years 1930–33, when many among the ranching elites and their foreign business partners, and some among the urban middle classes, supported a military coup in Argentina and a presidential *autogolpe* that then created a civilian dictatorship in Uruguay. The lack of a credible non-democratic governing alternative since the return of democracy in these countries in 1983 and 1984–85, respectively, owes much to three sets of circumstances: the collapse of a radical left-wing ideological alternative, more liquid (and thus more mobile) wealth for capitalists, and the utter discredit the armed forces brought upon themselves during the years of bureaucratic-authoritarian regime rule (1976–83 in Argentina and 1973–84 in Uruguay). Military rule (especially in Argentina) led to widespread international and domestic condemnation on grounds as diverse as mass human rights violations, unpredictability in international politics, and management incompetence. The latter, as it turned out, produced disastrous economic outcomes in the wake of the 1980–82 financial and economic busts.

Lower stakes for dominant players and the absence of a military-as-government alternative meant that despite the worst economic collapse in their modern histories in 2001–2, democracy survived in Argentina and in Uruguay (unlike in the 1930s, when it broke down). One reason for the greater likelihood of democratic survival more recently could be the absence of irreconcilable international ideological conflict (and the high politicoeconomic stakes that have gone with it) in the Western Hemisphere, compared with its growing presence during the 1930s.

ECONOMIC IDEAS AND POLICY

The recurrence of financial shocks and economic crises in emerging market countries in the 1990s and early 2000s led to a growing and more widespread questioning of the Washington consensus and its neoliberal economic policy prescriptions. Populist leaders used the tide of growing opposition to the neoliberal paradigm, whose aims were internationalist, to revive nationalist themes in the political sphere and activist policies in the economic sphere. The goal was to roll back the flagship policies promoted by the Washington consensus.

Diehards for and against neoliberalism usually miss the mixed results that the implementation of this economic policy produced in the Latin American countries. On the plus side, capital and trade liberalization, accompanied by orthodox monetary policy, brought prices under control and killed inflation in a part of the world where several nations had experienced chronically high inflation and hyperinflationary episodes since the 1970s. Orthodox economic policy also managed to turn around the traditional fiscal profligacy associated with the state in Latin America. Fiscal strengthening put a majority of Latin American economies in a much more solid position after the 2007–9 global financial busts than had been the case during any of the major shocks analyzed in this book: the Great Depression, the 1982 external debt crisis, and the 1997–2002 emerging markets crises.

On the downside, the way neoliberal policies were implemented promoted a type of growth—characterized by booms and busts—where the end result was to reward disproportionately the few who were already rich and to displace and marginalize the majority of the populace. In Latin America this meant multiplying the wealth and income of the elites in the most economically unequal region of the world.[19] The growth of inequality, coupled with a very meager capacity for job creation in the formal sector of national economies, were specific points that became easily politicized.[20]

The seeds of disenchantment with neoliberalism in Latin America were sown during 1997–2002. This period was known as the half-lost decade of socioeconomic development, because of both the concentration of wealth and the weakness and erratic character of wealth trickling down from the few to the many, which had been one of the key legitimating arguments behind the revival of free market economics in Latin America in the 1980s. The process of disillusionment culminated with a backlash against Washington consensus policies in general, and US and other foreign interests in particular, after the implosion of the Argentine economy in late 2001.

Domestic Sphere

The main effects of disenchantment with the Washington consensus model of globalization in the domestic sphere were varying degrees of politicoeconomic polarization and mobilization throughout Latin America, and the return to power of nationalist populist leaders in some countries.

POLITICAL IDEOLOGIES

The shift to the left in Latin America in the second half of the 2000s has been partly the result of an ideas-based questioning of globalization (the embrace of American-style liberal democracy and free markets).[21] The growth and diffusion of a new internationalist versus nationalist populist cleavage took off more or less throughout Latin America during the 2000s, although its politicoeconomic outcomes varied significantly, given the diversity of local conditions in the subcontinent. The cases of Argentina and Uruguay, although generically similar—democratic regime rule and relatively open economies survived the 2001–2 financial and economic implosions in both countries—led to relatively different politicoeconomic outcomes. Argentina experienced its second interrupted presidency since the return of democracy in 1983. Uruguay was able to manage the crisis effectively, and it emerged from the bust with stronger credibility among both Uruguayans and foreigners.

Argentina. In Argentina, strongman Peronism emerged triumphant from the ashes of economic collapse under the presidency of Eduardo Duhalde in 2002–3. The left-wing generation that came of age during the late 1960s and early 1970s took over during the presidencies of Néstor Kirchner and Cristina Fernández de Kirchner, which meant the return of traditional Peronist beliefs and actions, nested in nationalist populism. This spelled trouble for those who had supported and done extremely well from President Menem's neoliberal turn in the 1990s, because nationalist populism remains at heart a combative type of political practice, with roots in the critique of foreign economic interests and its domestic elite allies.

The presidencies of Néstor Kirchner (2003–7) and Cristina Fernández de Kirchner (2007–11 and reelected for 2011–15) saw the growth and strengthening of nationalist populism. Aside from using interests-based methods (such as substantial public expenditures), President Néstor Kirchner also mobilized mass support through ideational means, such as reviving prosecutions against military officers accused of human rights violations during the dirty war by annulling the military amnesty laws, the Leyes de Punto Final.[22] Third, President Kirchner highlighted the excess greed that had led to foreign capitalists' crass behavior, dominated by fickle investment stratagems that only sought to use Argentina and other emerging markets as casinos, where get-rich-quick schemes proliferated. Finally, Kirchner cast blame on the IFIs for "having driven [Argentina] into the abyss through the [forced] adoption of faulty policies."[23] In short, an ideational mechanism—President Néstor Kirchner's ability to provide a narrative about how Argentina had been wronged (once again) by greedy foreign capitalists—hit the right note, and his popularity as president remained high when he stepped down. He was the undisputed *jefe del peronismo*, which helped ensure the subsequent presidential victories of his wife, Cristina Fernández de Kirchner, in 2007 and 2011.

Although ideological directions changed, democracy survived in Argentina during the 2001–2 busts. This was no mean feat in a country where the military brought down civilian governments six times between 1930 and 1976. A return to military rule is almost undreamt of in Argentina today—or in the foreseeable future—because of the total destruction of the armed forces' moral, political, and economic credibility during the *Proceso* years (1976–83), and their weakening and marginalization, purposefully carried about by President Menem and his successors. The main issue in the second decade of the twenty-first century is Argentina's unbalanced and weakly institutionalized democratic regime, given the dominance of Peronism and the lack of a second-party alternative to govern the country.

Uruguay. In contrast to the situation in Argentina—where the traditional Peronist machine restored order in the aftermath of the country's 2001–2 bust, thereby reinforcing its dominance of Argentina's democratic process—liberal democracy in Uruguay emerged as more pluralist and with greater credibility, due to that country's multiparty approach to crisis management in the aftermath of its 2002 financial and economic busts. Satisfaction with democracy in Uruguay is the highest in the Latin American region, with almost 80% saying they are satisfied or very satisfied in 2009 (followed by 63% of Costa Ricans), representing an increase from a percentage in the mid-50s in 1996 and 2001.[24]

Two ideological changes permitted democracy to become more pluralist yet still govern effectively: the ideological convergence of the Colorado and Blanco parties, and the moderation of the Left. Yet some observers, such as Luis Costa Bonino, think that the "Uruguayan political stage has been sawed off at its ends. A growing centrism of political discourse has contributed to democratic stability while diluting the debate over ideas."[25]

Historically, there has been greater ideological variation within Uruguay's traditional parties than between them. While the Colorados have tended to be the more progressive party (representing the interests of urban workers), and the Blancos the more conservative one (representing the interests of the rural interior of the country), the parties have switched positions on the ideological spectrum several times. For example, in the run up to the 1973 coup, the Blanco Party became more progressive under the liberal, populist platform of Wilson Ferreira Aldunate, and the Colorado Party veered to the right under the more authoritarian platform of President Jorge Pacheco Areco (1967–72).

The Blanco Party chose not to participate in the 1985 Naval Club Pact, but Ferreira called for his party to respect the agreement and the new Colorado President Julio Sanguinetti in the interest of governability, marking an important reconciliation between these two traditional parties.[26] Subsequently, the Colorado and Blanco parties began to converge under the same ideological umbrella by forming electoral alliances, adopting more liberal positions on economic issues, and supporting the 1986 military amnesty bill. As Bergara and colleagues explain, "even when they are still competing, [the traditional parties] reach compromises and form coalitions, thus creating a political pole and an ideological family."[27]

The 1980s and 1990s were also marked by the moderation of the leftist Frente Amplio coalition. After the restoration of democracy, the Frente Amplio incorporated radical factions of the Far Left, namely the Tupamaro guerrilla movement (the MLN-T) and the Movimiento Revolucionario Oriental (MRO), which joined together as the Movimiento de la Participación Popular (MPP) to become the largest contingent of the Frente Amplio. But the radicalism of the Frente Amplio as a whole was tempered by a number of factors after the return to democracy.

First and foremost, there was a desire on the part of the Left—and society overall—to move away from violence: "the signs are that the experience of authoritarianism led to a revalorization of democracy by almost all of the Left."[28] This coincided with a departure from the hard-left ideology of violent social revolution in the past, prompted by communism's global decline and the death of Tupamaro leader Raul Sendic in 1989. In the words of one Tupamaro, the death of Sendic meant that "his colleagues felt free to enter the muddy, postmodern waters" of liberal democracy.[29] As revolutionary leftism lost credibility, the Left began a process of gradual moderation. Nonetheless, the tempering of the Frente Amplio led to the alienation of some of its most radical elements: in 1993 the MRO broke from the Frente Amplio because the coalition had deviated too far from Sendic's militant position.[30]

Electoral pressures also explain the toning down of the Left. Since the return of democracy in 1984–85, the Frente Amplio realized that the victorious candidates were the ones with the most moderate platforms.[31] By modifying its stance, the Frente Amplio was able to appeal to broader and then even broader groups of voters in subsequent elections, expanding its representation from 21% in 1984 to 40% in 1999. One Frente Amplio senator characterized the motivations behind the Left's moderation: "I believe the Left has reconsidered the importance of the mechanisms of formal democracies, in the sense that the functioning of democratic institutions in and of itself is extremely important because these institutions are the only instruments available to the marginalized sectors of society for solving their problems."[32]

In the end, the 2002 economic crisis strengthened democracy in Uruguay by demonstrating the commitment of civil society and political leaders to the rules of the democratic system, even in times of extreme hardship. The decision of the Colorado government of Jorge Batlle to respect civil liberties set an important precedent and represented a fundamental departure from, say, the form of democracy back in the late 1960s, when President Pacheco Areco went along with the tide to implement increasingly authoritarian practices during a time of extreme ideological and political confrontation between left-wing guerrillas and a bloated, paralyzed democratic regime under strain.

Uruguay in the early 2000s was very different from Argentina in those same years. In the latter, civil society challenged the entire democratic system ("*Que se vayan todos!*"), while in the former, civil society found a political alternative to express its frustration, leading to the 2004 election of Frente Amplio candidate Tabaré Vázquez in the first round of voting. For the first time in that country's history, a third party (of the Left, no less) had won the presidency and a parliamentary majority. There is no doubt that Uruguay's democracy became stronger and more pluralist through the emergence of the Frente Amplio as a competitive and responsible ideological alternative to the traditional parties.

ECONOMIC IDEAS AND POLICY

In addition to their political ideologies, Argentina's and Uruguay's economic policy trajectories also diverged after the 2001–2 financial and economic busts.

Argentina. From 2002 on, Presidents Eduardo Duhalde, Néstor Kirchner, and Cristina Fernández de Kirchner turned decidedly against Menem-style neoliberalism. Instead, they implemented heterodox, nationalist populist policies that were an anathema to the supporters of neoliberalism. Interestingly, these presidents otherwise came from two sides of the ideological fence: Duhalde was a traditional, conservative, Peronist strongman; the Kirchners were members of the left-wing Peronist youth generation that came of age during the ideological as well as armed confrontations with the military regimes that ruled Argentina between 1966–73 and 1976–83.

The anti-Menem, anti-neoliberal Peronist governments that took over from 2002 on made a U-turn in Argentina's economic policy. They violated the neoliberals' main commandment—free prices—by establishing price controls through legally mandated price freezes as well as by manipulating the consumer price index to underreport inflation. They disregarded another neoliberal commandment—if not a conservative, at least a prudent fiscal policy—by ratcheting up public spending and rolling back some of the privatizations that took place during the Menem years. President Néstor Kirchner was lucky, because the great international boom in commodity prices in 2003–8 allowed his government to get away with breaking these commandments. Politically, the economic rebound and subsequent years of expansive growth gave President Kirchner a substantial political dividend, making him the undisputed *jefe del peronismo*. For example, Levitsky notes that "Kirchner was the first Argentine president in more than a decade to actively push wages upward, both by promoting corporatist wage bargaining and by increasing the minimum wage."[33] It should be no surprise that Peronism went on to gain a majority in both chambers of the National Congress, which helped consolidate the nationalist populists in power, or that Kirchner's wife, Cristina Fernández de Kirchner, was elected president by a large majority in 2007 and 2011.

Of the three Southern Cone countries, economic policy turned furthest against neoliberalism in Argentina. The first President Kirchner strengthened the moral, political, and economic standing of nationalist populism by his explanation—which became the perception of a substantial majority in Argentina—of why the 2001–2 busts occurred. According to Kirchner, Menem's neoliberal policies were responsible for the economic collapse. Moreover, Kirchner claimed that the country's neoliberal turn had been orchestrated and promoted by international bank investors; pension fund and hedge funds managers in New York, London, and other Western European capitals; and international organizations (such as the IMF), based in Washington, DC, that were dominated by the advanced economies of the West. It is therefore unsurprising that the backlash against the Washington consensus and neoliberal policies was particularly strong during the 2000s in Argentina.

Uruguay. Unlike Argentina, Uruguay did not go through a radical embrace of neoliberalism in the 1990s. On the contrary, free market reforms in Uruguay have been slow, such that it has been called a "reluctant reformer" and an "egalitarian but slow-moving social democracy."[34] Bergara and colleagues note that "Uruguay's endorsement of the free market economy is by far the lowest in Latin America."[35] Central to this deep-seated culture of statism are the legacies of *batllismo*, the ideology pioneered by President José Batlle y Ordóñez (1903–7, 1911–15) and deepened under his nephew Luis Batlle Berres (1947–51, 1955–56). *Batllismo* is centered on the idea of a strong national state that respects property rights and civil liberties but actively intervenes in the economy to redistribute income, protect national industry, and provide a comprehensive welfare system (see chapters 3 and 5).

The economic prosperity achieved under *batllismo* in the 1940s undergirds the strong preference for the state that has continued in postauthoritarian Uruguay and has slowed the pace of neoliberal reform. After the return to democracy, both traditional parties shifted in the direction of neoliberalism and internationalism. Ironically, the leading figure in the Colorado Party when it advocated neoliberal reform and a movement away from the *batllista* model was a Batlle himself—Jorge Batlle Ibáñez, grandnephew of President Batlle y Ordóñez, who served as an influential Colorado senator before winning the presidential election in 1999. Demonstrating a more internationalist, neoliberal economic policy orientation than his *batllista* forbearers, on one occasion he asked, "Who could be opposed to free trade? Free trade generates prosperity."[36] The Blanco Party returned to the center-right of the political spectrum following the death of Ferreira in 1989. After visiting Chile in the early 1990s, Blanco President Lacalle (1990–95) expressed his admiration of Chile's neoliberal reform and economic success, exclaiming, "I've just returned from the future."[37] As the traditional parties have moved to the right, the Frente Amplio has become the standard-bearer of the *batllista* legacy. It now occupies "an extensive ideological space from the left to the center," while the Blancos and Colorados "share the space from the center to the right."[38]

Politicians across the political spectrum have recognized that a small country like Uruguay cannot afford economic nationalism, since the country has a negligible domestic market on which to base a globally competitive economy, so the reform agenda in Uruguay has been increasingly internationalist, that is, seeking development through greater integration into the world economy. With unanimous parliamentary approval, Uruguay joined the Mercosur trade bloc in 1992 and adopted its common external tariff in 1995, which greatly reduced the number of industries protected by the state and neutralized domestic opposition by "tying the government hand in terms of granting sectoral privileges."[39] A marked shift toward internationalism in financial markets occurred when the movement of capital was liberalized, leading to a large increase in capital inflows in the 1990s. Uruguay has made heroic efforts to consistently honor its debt obligations, earning a reputation as a reliable debtor on international markets.

While the Frente Amplio served as the principal institutional channel for opposition to many of these neoliberal reforms, it has distanced itself from the populist, nationalist policies of the past: "Not only had agrarian reform fallen by the wayside, but left-wing activists also were compelled to accept the ideas that foreign debt could and should be paid, and that privatization was no longer an abomination."[40] Still, in the wake of the great financial bust of May 2002, the Frente Amplio voted against the August 2002 bill that bailed out the banking system with international funds, and it opposed the 2003 bond restructuring as well, claiming default on foreign debt was inevitable.[41] But by the 2004 elections, the economy was recovering and radical deviations from the orthodox policy of the outgoing government's economic agenda would have been too costly. Thus incoming President Tabaré Vázquez pledged to honor all foreign debt; maintain orthodox monetary policy, including a floating exchange regime; and reform the tax system to encourage foreign investment. As one observer commented, "any illusions that the FA's political program will spell a return to the early twentieth-century Uruguayan model of state welfarism will be quickly dispelled by the incoming government's economic policies."[42]

President Vázquez's selection of moderate Frente Amplio economist Danilo Astori as Minister of Finance was a clear sign of his economic pragmatism. In one interview, Astori said that "in today's world, to break with the IMF and repudiate the [foreign] debt would mean self-isolation and going toward some sort of Africanization." President Vázquez fulfilled campaign promises to increase social spending in the areas of health, education, infrastructure, and security. His administration quickly passed the Emergency Social Plan (Plan de Atención Nacional a la Emergencia Social, or PANES) and created the Ministry of Social Development (Ministerio de Desarrollo Social, or MIDES) to combat rising poverty, malnutrition, and substandard housing conditions stemming from the 2002 crisis. However, this spending did not come at the expense of financial discipline, and the fiscal deficit was reduced to 0.8% in 2006.

As a result of his economic prudence, Vázquez received criticism from the Left for being too similar to his predecessors. In August of 2008, the first general strike during his presidency was organized by labor unions to protest his economic policies, specifically with regard to salary increases.[43] One journalist described the frustration with President Vázquez by members of the radical Left, saying they "hoped for more from a government of the left, and they don't forgive it for its 'aggiornamento' that has involved a shift to the center."[44] Nevertheless, Uruguayans as a whole generally approved of President Vázquez's moderate approach. The president remained popular throughout his tenure. His successor, President "Pepe" Mujica, a radical leftist in the past, did not make any substantial changes in the new framework of prudent macroeconomic management and an open economy. In short, the harsh 2002–3 financial shocks and economic crisis did not alter Uruguay's idiosyncratic but highly effective approach to economic policy: combining a liberalized external sector—open capital and trade flows—with extensive state involvement in production and substantial public transfers that have created the least unequal society in Latin America.

CONCLUSION

Compared with the interwar years (1920s–30s), when three ideologies fought irreconcilable battles that culminated in the Second World War, international ideological conflict during the bipolarity of the Cold War period opened up opportunities for both pro- and anti-democrats to steer US foreign policy, depending on the stakes on the ground and risk perception about the likelihood of any given Latin American country turning communist. Thus the case of Chile during the 1980s showed how a US foreign policy change by President Reagan's administration, used as a means to keep fighting the Cold War—the United States fed civil wars in Central America, while it criticized the last two military regimes in South America, Chile and Paraguay—raised the costs for those who wanted to or could exercise pressures against democracy, particularly in the context of the October 1988 plebiscite, in which Pinochet was defeated.

In the late 1990s and early 2000s, the international ideological sphere was dominated by the United States and its version of liberal democracy and free markets. This unipolar moment has more or less prevailed since the end of the Cold War (1989–91), although with an important adjustment— the rise of regional powers, such as the BRICs (Brazil, Russia, India, China), in the 2000s. The dominance of liberal democracy as a political regime option, at least in most of the Western Hemisphere, meant that there was no political regime alternative for would-be supporters of anti-democracy during the financial shocks and economic crises in Argentina and Uruguay between 2001 and 2003.

In terms of economic ideas and policy in the international sphere, the Washington consensus basket of economic liberalization policies gathered steam and spread as a consequence of the 1982 debt crisis in Latin America. In contrast, by the time Argentina's and Uruguay's economies imploded in 2001–2, there had been a string of financial crises in emerging markets (Mexico in 1994–95, East Asia in 1997, Russia in 1998, Brazil in 1998–99) that had sapped the support of both leaders and the public for what was perceived as the Washington consensus idea of globalization (free markets with no strings attached). The backlash against neoliberalism saw the return of nationalist populist leaders in countries such as Venezuela, Argentina, Ecuador, and Bolivia. Once in power, these leaders exalted the primacy of domestic popular interests over those of foreign investors and governments whose influence in these countries had grown during the years when Washington consensus policies were implemented.

In the domestic sphere, political ideologies in Chile during the early and mid-1980s continued to be propelled by the Cold War. Small but extremist and well-armed left-wing guerrillas in Chile tried to bring down the military regime by force, which gave General Pinochet and his close advisers a justification for declaring states of siege, clamping down on all forms of dissent, and reminding the Chilean middle classes that the communists were still knocking at the door, even if the threat was overblown. The end result was that the costs for pressures in favor of the restoration of full democracy remained relatively high, and the military regime and its civilian allies were able to force the opposition to accede to the rules and timetable for transitioning to a restricted democracy contained in the 1980 constitution. Domestic political ideologies also had an important impact during the 2001–2 financial and economic meltdowns in Argentina and Uruguay. Argentina saw the return of nationalist populism under the Peronists, while the traditional political establishment under the Colorado and Blanco parties paid the price for Uruguay's highly unpopular though effective orthodox economic stabilization. For the first time in that country's history, the modern Left (under the Frente Amplio) won a presidential election (in 2004). The main difference between the two countries was that ideological conflict was channeled in a highly institutionalized direction in Uruguay, through the country's deeply rooted party system, while it remained personalized, embodied in the *jefe en turno* (current boss) of the Peronist movement, in Argentina.

As for economic ideas and policy, Chile, the pioneer of free market reforms in the post–Second World War years, moved in a heterodox economic policy direction after the 1982 debt crisis. The military regime under General Pinochet turned against the pure version of a free market economy it had embraced and implemented between 1975 and 1982. Instead, the regime brought on board economists who pursued pragmatic programs, such as aggressive short-term countercyclical monetary and fiscal policies, and, over the medium and long terms, a strategy of combining selective state intervention, protection, and promotion of domestic economic activities destined for export with a private business sector that was subject to international competition. The end result was a highly successful, market-oriented economy. In contrast, Argentina declared the largest sovereign default in history. Once its economy was stabilized, however, successive Peronist governments adopted selective intervention to prop up the economy, spearheaded by increasing public spending, maintaining an undervalued exchange rate, and taxing exports in order to subsidize the growth of state intervention. Uruguay did not default. Instead, it implemented unpopular IMF-led economic policies of orthodox stabilization and adjustment, and continued with cautious macroeconomic management.

Implications for Democracy after the 2008–9 Financial Meltdown

When the music stops, in terms of liquidity, things will be complicated. But as long as the music is playing, you've got to get up and dance. We're still dancing.

—*Chuck Prince, then CEO of Citigroup, interviewed in Tokyo*

Those of us who have looked to the self-interest of lending institutions to protect shareholders' equity, myself included, are in a state of shocked disbelief.

—*Alan Greenspan, ex-chairman of the Federal Reserve Board,
in a hearing before the House Committee on Oversight
and Reform, US Congress*

The proliferation of analyses, speeches, and news reports using the Great Depression as a point of reference in understanding the magnitude and potential destruction that the financial global busts of 2008–9 (the Great Recession) might have led to should not surprise anyone. As Carmen Reinhart and Ken Rogoff have observed, the 2008–9 financial busts were the first since the 1930s (excluding 1939–45) to be global in scope.[1] In contrast, financial busts—particularly between the end of the Second World War and 2008—happened in single countries or, at most, at a regional level, but not globally.[2] Very significantly, the 1929–31 and 2008–9 credit crunches that led to global financial busts shared the same epicenter, namely, the command center of mature financial capitalism and its key axis—Wall Street in New York City and the City of London.

Yet, despite the common origins and similar global scope of the Great Depression and the Great Recession, the growing consensus among scholars, policymakers, and analysts has pointed to quite different outcomes for these two economic crises. This conclusion is unremarkable, because historical events do not repeat themselves mechanically, but it is open to shadings. Pessimists will keep reminding us that stabilization and apparent recovery can be short lived—as the seesaw economic trajectory of the 1930s attests—and that optimists should therefore wait until at least 2020 to make a fair assessment of the similarities and differences between the 1930s and the 2010s. Optimists, however, will continue to cheer on short- or medium-length rallies, even if we end up going through a prolonged—say, a ten-year—bear market.

What *is* clear is that the massive monetary and fiscal countercyclical policies coordinated by the governments of the world's twenty-plus largest economies through the G-20 in 2008–9—something that had never been done before, and in part an action explicitly undertaken to avoid another Great Depression— were a powerful example of politicians and policymakers responding, economic policy-wise, differently than their peers in the 1930s.[3] Back then, monetary policy was ruled by the gold standard, which forced central bankers to raise interest rates to reverse gold outflows and keep meeting international payments regularly, even when their national economies were in recession. Such procyclical economic policy savaged the livelihoods of millions of households in the United States, Western Europe, and periphery countries. As Barry Eichengreen has observed, recovery after the worldwide Depression "proved possible . . . only after abandoning the gold standard."[4] Though not the sole factor, currency flexibility was a key step in economic adjustment and a return to growth. This has been the dilemma for countries in the periphery of the eurozone—like Greece, Portugal, and Ireland—stricken by the sovereign debt crisis since 2010. Membership in the euro area precludes adjustment via currency devaluation; therefore adjustment follows another route: the slashing of demand (cutting public spending, raising public service prices), deep recession, and incalculable social costs. Latin America's lost decade of growth and development (1982–90) is a mirror that the small European eurozone countries in crisis in the early 2010s can use to reflect on their own situation.

Back in the early 1930s, it took the worsening and lengthening of the Great Depression, however, to force a fundamental change. Advanced economies started using fiscal policy as a systematic, countercyclical tool to pump up demand— something Keynes had advocated for the British economy since 1924–25—a move that countries on the periphery then copied.

For all the vilification of economics as a science and as a business activity since the September 2008 global financial bust, the majority of policymakers in a position to steer the world economy in the second decade of the twenty-first century made the right (Keynesian) call in the winter–spring of 2008–9. As a result, the extraordinary expansionist monetary and fiscal policies that followed were a direct application of the policy lessons of the 1930s to combat debt deflation. That the chairman of the Federal Reserve at the time of the 2008–9 busts, Ben S. Bernanke, also happened to be the leading scholar on the role that credit destruction had in accelerating and amplifying the Great Depression, was a remarkable roll of the dice.[5]

The end result this time around was that the internationally coordinated stimulus short-circuited a spiral toward a second Great Depression: Economics is dead! Long live economics![6] Still, we should remain guarded and resist any triumphalism, because booms and busts are inherent in the workings of capitalist economies. A Minsky moment (a sudden turn in a process of credit expansion that triggers fire sales, which, like a whirlwind, become a self-reinforcing and accelerating course of credit contraction) is not an aberration. Rather, it is an integral part of the system of financial capitalism, inasmuch as the core of this system—that is, what allows it to grow and reproduce—is the expansion of credit. Shocks are therefore here to stay. The disease cannot be cured, only managed.

In light of this, let us return to the topic of this volume, the effects of financial shocks and economic crises on democracy. I divide the conclusion into three sections. The first recounts the structural changes in the institutional, interests-based, and ideas-based mechanisms that raised the likelihood of democratic regime survival. I note the significant differences among the three Southern Cone countries in their governments' effectiveness and ability to govern during the harshest economic shocks and crises, contrasting the situation during the Great Depression with what happened in the 1982 debt crisis and the emerging markets crises of the late 1990s–early 2000s.

The second section assesses the extent to which developments in the Southern Cone countries—the high probability of democratic regime survival or reinstatement, coupled with important variations in terms of the survival or breakdown of governments—might also apply in other Latin American countries (Brazil, Mexico, Colombia, Peru, Venezuela, Ecuador, and Bolivia). For example, ethnicity and its politicization in the Andean countries highlight a basic limitation of my analytical framework, which does not include this factor.

The third section identifies further limits to my framework by confronting it with comparable past events in other emerging market countries: East Asia and

Eastern Europe. Critically examining such basic constraints helps formulate new questions and further avenues of inquiry regarding the political impacts on regimes of major financial shocks and economic crises around the world and across time.

HARSHNESS OF THE GREAT DEPRESSION
AND PREVALENCE OF DEMOCRACY SINCE THE 1980S

Above all, I hope that my analysis has shown that we have been lucky not to go through what our forebears had to endure in the 1930s. The depth and duration of the Great Depression remain in a class of their own. For example, in 1933, the year of Franklin D. Roosevelt's first inauguration as president, unemployment in the United States affected close to 25% of the workforce, and average mortgage delinquency rates in American cities across the country were around 33%.[7] In sharp contrast, in 2009, when Barack H. Obama was inaugurated, unemployment broke the 10% mark, and circa 8% of mortgages around the country were in delinquency.[8] Also, the average fall of peak-to-trough real GDP per capita was close to 30% in the United States during the early years of the Depression (1929–33), while it was just 9.3% in the wake of the biggest financial busts between that time and 2001. In the 1997–99 bust, the average fall was 9%–14% in Korea, Thailand, and Indonesia, and, in the early 1990s, between 0%–8% during the banking crises in Sweden and Japan.[9] Moreover, the Depression was not only much deeper, but it also lasted much longer than subsequent harsh economic shocks and crises. While the average duration of economic crises in individual countries was 4.1 years during the Great Depression, it has been 1.7 years for post–Second World War crises (excluding the 2007–9 global busts).[10]

In fact, a concise general argument for the harsher conditions and lower likelihood of democratic survival or instatement in the 1930s, compared with later financial shocks and economic crises in the 1980s, 1990s, and 2000s, would be the depth and breadth of the Great Depression: more stringent economic circumstances led to rougher political ones. As the GDP annual growth figures for the three Southern Cone countries show (see chapters 2 and 6), the level of annual economic variation was significantly lower in the 1980s, 1990s, and 2000s than in the 1930s. Booms and busts were much more pronounced back then than they have been since the creation of the Bretton Woods international financial system at the end of the Second World War. The severity of the financial and economic collapses in the 1930s and the salutary absence of such crises since 2008–9 might be the main reason why democracy is expected to fare better in the present and the near future.[11]

The widespread economic decline of the early 1930s was a causative factor, but the high-stakes politics and the regime changes that occurred in our three Southern Cone countries during the Great Depression years were also due to the state of their basic institutional, interests-based, and ideas-based mechanisms, which informed the calculations and behavior of their main foreign and domestic political and economic actors.

Institutions. A thin and ineffective international legal and organizational system during that period was incapable of promoting democracy and sanctioning anti-democratic forces around the world, and there was no international financial architecture capable of helping to stabilize economies in crises. Domestically, the armed forces in Argentina, Chile, and Uruguay had strong organizational, resource, and ideological bases that helped them remain autonomous from civilian control and gave them the capacity to be decisive forces in the destruction and creation of political regimes (chapter 3).

Interests. In the sphere of wealth, the politicization of fixed assets, such as those in the energy industry, translated into foreign and domestic capitalists becoming highly risk adverse in the face of organized mass calls for redistribution in the aftermath of the 1929–33 international economic collapse. In the trade sector, a wholesale move toward protectionism by the world's advanced economies, either by enacting tariffs and/or devaluing national currencies, was copied by countries on the periphery. This reinforced the drastic fall of international economic activity (chapter 4).

Ideas. Political ideologies during the interwar years of the twentieth century were dominated by the irreconcilable, tripolar conflict between liberal democracy, communism, and fascism. This raised the stakes for all actors (political and economic, international and domestic), because their clashes reached the point where the main leaders and followers of these ideologies ended up seeing the advancement of their particular mode of thought as an all-or-nothing affair. The implication was that survival itself required destroying the others. As for economic ideas, the disastrous pro-cyclical macroeconomic policy responses in the world's leading economies after the 1929 US market bust were followed by the trial-and-error adoption of countercyclical measures, based on Keynes's fiscal and monetary policy prescriptions. The advanced economies began putting these in place after the global 1931 banking bust, and the periphery countries were not far behind. These measures helped establish a floor on the self-reinforcing process of debt deflation, and then revived economic activity by expanding private demand through public spending (chapter 5).

The subsequent structural changes to these institutional, interests-based, and ideas-based mechanisms raised the likelihood of democratic regime survival or reinstatement in the face of harsh economic shocks and crises since the 1980s in Argentina, Chile, and Uruguay. Democratic regime survival, however, has also been coupled with sizeable differences in the effectiveness of each county's government in tackling these harsh shocks/crises and their challenges to governability. In the post-1980s economic crises, Argentina's two interrupted presidencies are in contrast to relative governmental stability and effectiveness in Chile and Uruguay.

Institutions. A growing international legal and organizational architecture, with a wider and deeper reach, has developed since the establishment of the UN and the Bretton Woods systems in 1945–46. Politically, these two international factors have moved in a direction that rewards and promotes electoral democracy and, at the same time, tries to punish anti-democratic forces around the world. Such actions have had varying degrees of effectiveness and, usually, limited success. Nonetheless, the existence and application of an internationally sanctioned process is in sharp contrast to the Great Depression years, when there was nothing. Economically, the international economy has become less volatile, particularly in the financial sphere, through the creation of the IMF as a lender-of-last-resort to national economies in crises. The extension of credit guarantees and/or direct injections of liquidity have helped to put a floor on the precipitous fall in economic activity that is typical of harsh shocks and crises. Thus, even though the incidence of financial crises has remained relatively unchanged after 1945, compared with before, the level of destruction within economic activities has been considerably lower in the post–Second World War years.

An important caveat is that this process of internationalizing rules and organizations since the end of the Second World War has not been mechanical and unidirectional. Actions by different international organizations have pulled in different directions, weakening the net potential result they could produce regarding the survival or breakdown of given political regimes. The example of Chile in the early 1980s illustrates this tension between forces that could help and those that could hinder the cause of democracy. UN bodies (such as the General Assembly) and dozens of NGOs advocating human rights protested, condemned, and called for sanctions against the military repression unleashed by the regime led by General Augusto Pinochet during the 1970s and

1980s. After the country's economy imploded in 1981–83, however, the Chilean Finance Minister was able to negotiate credit lines and guarantees with the IMF, which strengthened the capacity of the military regime's response to the crisis. The end result was that improving conditions for the military regime was the exact opposite of what domestic and international actors were calling for, that is, the return of Chilean democracy.

In the realm of domestic institutions, the military-as-government option— which was endemic in fast-modernizing Latin America (with its expansive growth in urbanization, industrialization, and literacy) between the early years of the twentieth century and the early 1980s—collapsed amid the moral, economic, and political bankruptcy resulting from both left- and right-wing types of military regime rule. The 1982 regional financial and economic shocks and, later, the end of the Cold War, meant that the relative costs for the military to intervene and decide political regime outcomes escalated quite considerably. Since then, political instability and the general uncertainty produced by economic shocks/crises have been more likely to lead to interrupted presidencies— that is, interruptions in the constitutional process, but preservation of electoral democracy—than to the replacement of democratic regimes by military ones. The years since the return of democracy to each of our three countries, however, have evinced significant differences in their other domestic institutions: constitutions, electoral laws, and parties and party systems. Reforms in Chile and Uruguay have induced successful (if imperfect) processes for political competition, democratic representation, and governmental management capacity, particularly in the wake of harsh financial shocks and economic crises. In Argentina, however, constitutional and electoral reforms since 1994 have not altered the pattern of Peronist dominance, due to the absence of a viable second party as a governmental alternative (chapter 7).

Interests. In the sphere of wealth, the years since the Great Depression have seen a near-universal dominance of liquid, financial-based assets with easy exit options (capital flight) in the face of worsening conflicts over redistribution, due to harsh economic shocks and crises. Nonetheless, pressures from below in the Southern Cone countries, however, have produced different outcomes: Chile's protests and mobilizations were ferociously repressed, Argentina's explosion of social discontent toppled President de la Rúa and his government, and Uruguay's general discontent was channeled through the polls by electing members of the Frente Amplio. In terms of trade, most countries in the world, rather than making a wholesale move toward protectionism and inward-looking development (as they did in the aftermath of the 1929–31 financial busts), instead jumped on the bandwagon of a trade liberalization process that gathered momentum during the closing round of the multilateral GATT agreements in the 1980s and culminated in the establishment of the WTO in 1994. This has meant that harsh economic shocks and crises between the 1980s and 2011 have occurred within a growing, opening world trade system that offers more international sources for economic recovery after a bust, particularly when compared with the trade-destroying, market-shrinking protectionism of the 1930s (chapter 8).

A trade war that could emulate the global protectionist war of the early 1930s remains a low probability in the light of the 2007–9 global financial shocks and economic crises, although it cannot be ruled out, particularly in the context of the global imbalances of the 2000s, exemplified by diametrical opposites: growing Chinese trade surpluses, and increasing twin deficits (trade and fiscal) in the United States.[12]

Ideas. Bipolar competition between political ideologies during the Cold War led to a US foreign policy switch in South America in the 1980s, which translated into support for democratization to balance the US government's military involvement in the Central American civil wars. After the end of the Cold War, bipolarity gave way to the unipolar moment, in which the United States ruled the roost unchallenged. Its foreign policy approach in the Western Hemisphere more often than not has been to support electoral democracy, which was not necessarily the case during the Cold War years. In the sphere of economic ideas, the dominance of the free market basket of policies associated with the Washington consensus between the 1980s and the turn of the century has been followed by a backlash in some countries during the first decade of the twenty-first century. Regardless of the extent of either a backlash against neoliberalism or the preservation of an official commitment to free markets, the key difference with the 1930s has been the availability of countercyclical economic tools: some internationally based, such as IMF credit or US Treasury support, and others domestically based, like monetary easing and fiscal stimuli (chapter 9).

Structural changes in the realms of institutions, interests, and ideas have affected most of the world's countries since the Great Depression, but this does not mean that they have produced similar effects everywhere. This is—and will remain—highly unlikely. The identification of these structural changes does not imply that we have reached, or will reach, a destination point like the "End of History," where liberal democracy rules unchallenged. There is no historical law preventing some or all of these structural changes from continuing to morph, or barring shifts in directions that could lower the likelihood of democracy surviving or being reinstated during harsh economic shocks and crises in the future. Political regime outcomes remain contingent and are subject to changing probabilities rather than to any overall structural determination.

Nor has change been mechanical and linear, in the sense of a gradual move from less to more democracy. Argentina's and Uruguay's political regime trajectories conformed to the general thrust of this optimistic view of progress (the Whig interpretation of history), but not Chile's. The Chilean case was an outlier both in the 1930s, when it was the only country in Latin America that was able to install a democratic regime, and in the 1980s, when the military regime led by General Pinochet imposed its own terms on a return to democracy, one that was tightly regulated by constitutional rules and a transition calendar created by the military and its allies. In spite of adverse conditions, democracy was not impossible in Chile in the early 1930s, but neither was it a foregone conclusion in the 1980s.

These structural changes to institutional, interests-based and ideas-based mechanisms identified in this work raised the possibility of democratic regime survival or reinstatement in the Southern Cone countries, while preserving substantial variations in the effectiveness of each nation's government and its ability to govern during harsh shocks, but what should we expect in these countries after the 2007–9 global financial busts? And, more broadly, what is the likely range of outcomes for other emerging market countries?

ECONOMIC SHOCKS AND DEMOCRACY IN EMERGING ECONOMIES
Latin America

The most glaring difference between the Great Recession and any of the previous harsh financial shocks and economic crises studied in this work is that this time the Latin American countries did not experience shocks that led to deep, long-lasting crises. Anyone acquainted with the zigzagging politicoeconomic trajectories of Latin American countries between the second half of the nineteenth century and the 1980s would have been forgiven for thinking that a 2010 editorial in the *Financial Times* was an April Fools' Day joke: "Developed markets are a crash zone. Emerging Europe's fate is closely tied to the euro's [fate]. Africa is a possibility; although given the size of their economies, Asia and Latin America are probably the regions to beat. Furthermore, of this pair Latin America might even have the best prospects of all."[13]

Inasmuch as most of Latin America's major economies had solid foundations in their fiscal, trade, and balance-of-payments accounts in the run up to the 2008–9 global financial and economic busts, the region as a whole has experienced its best response to international shocks since the debacle of the Great Depression. This regional perspective, however, conceals significant variations among these countries. Thus, while Brazil faced only the slightest of recessions in 2009 and bounced back so rapidly that concerns about economic overheating became a serious consideration in 2010–11, Venezuela suffered a pronounced two-year recession, which hit President Chávez's popular-support base. Inflationary expectations have become ingrained in that country, leading to a price spiral that has hurt wage earners disproportionately.

The likelihood of democratic survival in the midst of harsh financial shocks and economic crises might be better in the 2010s than it was between the 1930s and the 1980s in most Latin American countries. Yet local context trumps any easy generalization, and the bottom line remains (1) that political regimes of all stripes around the world will continue to face pressures from above and from below, and (2) that such pressures will probably intensify in the face of harsh financial shocks and economic crisis. Democracy—or, for that matter, authoritarian or totalitarian regimes—will continue to be pressed by the type of antagonistic competition that arises in any society when resources and opportunities vanish in the face of financial shocks.

SOUTHERN CONE COUNTRIES

The good news for Argentina, Chile, and Uruguay is that democracy does not seem to be at serious risk of breaking down since the 2008–9 global financial and economic implosion. This is in marked contrast to the 1930s, when the prevailing institutional, interests-based, and ideas-based mechanisms undermined democracy through the proliferation of uncompromising ideological conflict; an escalating battle over the control of politicized, fixed-wealth assets (hydrocarbons); a pro-cyclical macroeconomic policy response to the 1929–31 international financial busts; a weak international system incapable of supporting democratic activities and punishing anti-democratic ones; and national militaries that remained a decisive force in establishing and terminating political regimes (by explicit actions in Argentina and Chile and acquiescence to the civilian *autogolpe* in Uruguay). In addition, these three countries have more or less repeated their successful crisis management performances since the 1980s. The national governments of Chile and Uruguay have been effective in tackling the latest crises; the national government of Argentina, while still surviving, has experienced more difficulties.

Argentina. A key problem for Argentina has been its exclusion from international capital markets since its 2001 debt default. The nationalist populist, Peronist governments in power between 2003 and 2011 used interests-based, ideational, and institutional mechanisms to mobilize their popular base and retain loyalty and mass support. Regarding interests, the Peronist governments have relied on the redistribution of resources and opportunities through clientelism and patronage. When it comes to ideas, they have emphasized their nationalist populist credentials, blaming foreign interests and their allies among the domestic elites. As for institutions, the government of President Néstor Kirchner reopened the process for trials against the military officers in the 1976–82 dictatorship, which cemented his support among progressive sectors.

Of the three mechanisms, the interests-based component was the one the most negatively affected after the 2008 global financial and economic implosion. The sudden onset of resource scarcity forced President Cristina Fernández de Kirchner into a series of high-stakes moves, such as the failed attempt to introduce a scaled tax for agricultural exports, where its level would rise and fall with the international price of these commodities; the nationalization of the pension systems; and the use of the central bank's foreign reserves to pay off debt and retain the capacity to engage in extensive public spending in the run up to the 2011 presidential elections. These actions resulted in higher stakes for both the government and its enemies. They were competing for scarce resources at the same time as ideological conflict became more polarized and uncompromising, factors that are potentially detrimental to or can completely undermine democracy, particularly in the context of a harsh economic crisis. Deteriorating conditions in a country that has experienced repeated episodes of interrupted presidencies (in 1989 and 2001) during severe economic crises since its return to democracy raised the risk and uncertainty that both foreign and domestic actors faced, although the economy bounced back strongly in 2010–11.

The bottom line for Argentina is that as long as the military-as-government is not an option, democracy can and should survive the ups and downs of the global business cycle, but democratic politics will remain a conflict-prone, high-stakes process. To be better prepared to respond to future economic shocks and crises, Argentine leaders need to be able to tap international capital markets, because the availability of resources to implement countercyclical macroeconomic policy is one of the main tools that policymakers have used effectively to stabilize declining economic activity during the past crises discussed in this volume.

Chile and Uruguay. The reason for considering these two countries together is that their national governments have been effective at tackling harsh economic shocks and crises since the return of democracy. In terms of ideas, ideological competition has been contained and channeled institutionally within the plural and vibrant parties and party systems in the two countries. Economically, the availability of international and domestic resources has enabled these nations to mount countercyclical responses to crises. Chile's and Uruguay's relationships and standing with successive US governments and with the IMF have been very positive, unlike Argentina's.

Regarding interests, in both countries the state has been an effective mediator in distributive conflicts, particularly in the institutionalization of moderate left-wing governments whose gradual, targeted redistribution has helped portray democracy as a form of government that delivers tangibles. A very important difference still remains, however: the levels of socioeconomic inequality in these countries. Uruguay is the only country in Latin America that can boast of a European-style welfare state, and it has the lowest levels of inequality in the region. Chile's prolific and almost uninterrupted growth since the mid-1980s has been coupled with a sharp rise in inequality, making it a country that has been among the best in the region at tackling poverty, but one where class disparities have soared.

The Concertación (Chile) and Frente Amplio (Uruguay) administrations have been multiparty governments that have brought together diverse political movements and parties of the center and the left, and the opposition in both countries has also gravitated toward one center-right pole, emphasizing that under these nations' current basic institutions, electoral democracy has aggregated interests and ideas into two broadly based camps. Relative stability and predictability among political and economic adversaries has lowered the stakes during periods of harsh economic crises. The end result has been that democratic regimes have not only survived in these countries, but have also emerged with stronger reputations and greater credibility as political systems whose governments are capable of effective crisis management, generating a positive feedback loop that has strengthened adherence to and support for democracy.

BRAZIL AND MEXICO

Economic shocks since the 1980s have had important political consequences in the two largest Latin American economies. As it did in the Southern Cone countries, the 1982 bust created widespread disaffection, mass mobilization, and protests that contributed to the military's willingness to relinquish power in Brazil in 1984–85, while in Mexico it emboldened the opposition to defy hegemonic rule by the Partido Revolucionario Institucional (PRI) from both the right (Partido Acción Nacional [PAN]) since the early 1980s, and from the left (Frente Democrático Nacional [FDN], which later became the Partido de la Revolución Democrática [PRD]) since the 1988 elections. Both countries continued to suffer financial shocks. Brazil went through a string of crises between 1990 (under President Fernando Collor de Melo) and 1993–94 (under President Itamar Franco). Mexico experienced one financial bust in 1987–88 and a far worse one in 1994–95. Factors that changed the crisis-inducing conditions in Brazil were the implementation of orthodox macroeconomic adjustments under the Plano Real, the rise of Fernando H. Cardoso to the presidency, and the partial adoption of Washington consensus policies. In the case of Mexico, President Ernesto Zedillo signed off on provisions to guarantee free and fair elections in 1996 in exchange for support from both the Left and the Right for a new round of orthodox adjustments and a continued adherence to free market policies. From the perspective of the mid-2000s, Brazil overcame the problems it had suffered in the 1990s, such as an interrupted presidency and repeated episodes of hyperinflation, while Mexico extricated itself from hegemonic party rule without experiencing a rupture and managed to avoid financial crises— endemic every six years between 1976 and 1994—during presidential election years in 2000 and 2006.

Despite their common gradual economic and political improvements, the two countries' trajectories became more divergent in the 2000s. Brazil's economy has grown increasingly dynamic. Long one of the most indebted countries in the world, it became a net foreign creditor in 2008, and it achieved energy self-sufficiency in 2006.[14] The country's politics also converged toward the pragmatic center. In contrast, Mexico's economy grew slowly and its politics became polarized, repeatedly leading to stalled legislative and policy processes. Moreover, the 2008 global financial and economic implosion hit these countries very differently. Brazil's diversified trade profile, and its growing exchange relationship with East Asia (particularly China), helped the country be one of the last to go into and one of the first to emerge from recession; it was virtually unscathed. Mexico's overwhelming dependence on the US economy, which was the epicenter of the 2008–9 global busts, meant that it suffered the worst economic downturn in Latin America in 2009. This decline (a fall of around 7% annual GDP) was more severe than the one produced by the country's great financial bust of 1994–95.

Despite these performance differences, democracy should prevail in both countries. In terms of institutions, both countries have remained active players in international organizations, supporting democratic clauses and multilateralism through the UN system. Domestically, the armed forces have continued to emphasize their institutional role, although Brazil has been more successful than Mexico at defusing the military's participation in domestic conflicts. The Brazilian armed forces have been assigned to foreign missions, such as the leadership of the UN-led MINUSTAH operations in Haiti, while Mexico's military acquired a highly visible public profile since President Felipe Calderón declared a war on drugs when he came to power at the end of 2006. By the end of 2010, more than 50,000 troops were mobilized and in operation around the country.[15] The Mexican armed forces' tradition of loyalty to institutions and to civilian supremacy since the 1940s has not changed substantially, but their protagonist role in the war on drugs, particularly if extended over several years, could alter their long-term relationship with the civilian political class and with Mexican society, laying the groundwork for a power-brokering role that could undermine democracy in that country.

Regarding interests, the two largest Latin American economies are diversified enough so that the bulk of their wealth-producing assets are not in a relatively fixed, illiquid form. This is not to say that dominant actors do not benefit from their control over fixed assets: giant state energy companies (such as Petrobras and Pemex), big mining corporations (like Vale or Grupo México), and major landowners who have made Brazilian agribusiness a world powerhouse will all continue to depend on them. Nonetheless, the Brazilian and Mexican economies also possess a substantial manufacturing base and growing, deepening financial systems that did not suffer devastating losses in 2008–9, like the American and European banks did.

The stakes will continue to be high for the dominant actors who enjoy monopoly rents from the extremely concentrated nature of economic activity in both countries, and democracy will face the challenge of promoting the redistribution of resources and opportunities in these two highly unequal societies by lowering barriers to access, which the monopolists will continue to fight against. Since the 1990s, the governments of both countries have implemented conditional cash transfer programs (CCTs)—Oportunidades in Mexico and

Bolsa Familia in Brazil—that have become the backbone of a social policy that has yielded significant improvements on the ground, prompting multilateral institutions like the World Bank and the IADB to adopt and recommend CCTs around the developing world. An editorial has called CCTs "some rare good news from the world's most unequal continent."[16] In addition, the implementation of CCTs has reaped substantial political dividends, as it was instrumental in the parties in power being reelected in 2006 (the left-wing Partido dos Trabalhadores [PT] in Brazil and the right-wing PAN in Mexico).

Both countries possess a broad and lively ideological spectrum, and the mediation of domestic institutions has been a key to this pluralism remaining functional to the democratic process. Thus, even though some factions in the main left- and right-wing parties of both countries (the PT and the PRD on the left, and the Partido da Frente Liberal [PFL]—known as Democratas since 2007—and the PAN on the right) will continue to pursue confrontational and uncompromising positions, the nexus of gravity for the political process lies in the center, and both extremes will continue to rely on the support of pragmatic, catchall parties like the Partido do Movimento Democrático Brasileiro (PMDB) and the PRI, which dominate the center. Without their support, it would be difficult to govern effectively. The type of governance that these pragmatic parties favor is based on patronage and clientelism, which undermines the idea of democracy as a government by laws. Still, this is a paradox that electorates have thus far continued to support. The main difference concerning future governability lies in Brazil's relatively cohesive though plural Left, which built the PT (the largest and most effective contemporary Progressive party in Latin America), versus Mexico's fractious PRD, whose lack of cohesion and discipline has made left-wing policy and political positions erratic and unpredictable. Thus, while President Lula da Silva of Brazil (2003–2010) was being praised internationally as the most influential leader of a moderate Latin American Left (which included Presidents Michelle Bachelet of Chile and Tabaré Vázquez of Uruguay), strongman and ex-PRD leader Andrés Manuel López Obrador in Mexico ended up dividing the Left and raising uncertainty about the capacity of its various factions to act together as a programmatic political force.

Lastly, US foreign policy during the unipolar moment has been supportive of both countries' political processes. The availability of lender-of-last-resource funds has been a key mechanism in helping to stabilize conditions during harsh economic shocks and crises by putting a backstop behind them. The US government has repeatedly employed this mechanism—both directly (through the Treasury and the Federal Reserve) and indirectly (through its dominant position in international financial institutions like the IMF, the WB, and the IADB)—to support the governments of Mexico (1995) and Brazil (1998–99 and 2001–2) during severe financial busts or situations that threatened to unravel in that direction. This commitment has continued unabated; it was very significant that in the wake of the 2008–9 global financial busts, the Federal Reserve extended a 30 billion USD swap line to the central banks of Brazil and Mexico (and also to South Korea and Singapore) to preempt the possibility of disorderly macrodevaluations. The inclusion of Latin America's two largest economies in the inner circle of emerging markets over which the US government spread its protective monetary wing in the wake of the 2008 global bust was not just a function of the size of those economies and the consequences that runs on their currencies—leading to crises—might have on the global system, but also a sign that Washington supported the politics and the policies pursued by a moderate left-wing government in Brazil and, less surprisingly, the pro-American, pro–Washington consensus direction of the PAN governments in Mexico in the 2000s.

ANDEAN COUNTRIES

Of the large Latin American countries, democracy faces its greatest challenges in the Andean subregion. These are the countries where political ideological conflict became more uncompromising and irreconcilable in the 2000s. In terms of interests, the economies of Venezuela, Bolivia, and Ecuador concentrate the bulk of their wealth-producing assets in the fixed hydrocarbons industry. While Colombia's and Peru's economies are more diversified, extraction activities related to energy and mining exports are similarly dominant sectors, also with fixed assets.[17] Indeed, scholars such as Kurt Weyland think that the rise of ideological polarization in the Andean countries, where their economies are based on the revenue from energy exports arising from fixed assets, is no coincidence.[18] Moreover, the armed forces in most of the countries in the region can tap into a tradition of left-wing social reformism, memorably dubbed by one author as a "revolution by the general staff."[19] The rise of nationalist populist leaders from among the military ranks—including President Hugo Chávez of Venezuela, ex-President Lucio Gutiérrez of Ecuador, and ex-Captain Ollanta Humala of Peru (a close runner-up in 2006 who was later elected president in 2011)—are only the latest episodes of the man-on-horseback tradition, whose contradictory promises of authority, prosperity, and justice go back to El Libertador, Simón Bolívar himself, and have remained a powerful font of inspiration for the military in the Andean countries.

Venezuela, Bolivia, and Ecuador. The global commodity price boom of 2003–8 was a godsend for heavy commodity exporters like the Andean countries and for South America more generally. They had not experienced such positive terms of trade since the energy shocks of the 1970s, which also produced a temporary boom in the price of commodities. This latest upsurge provided the material means for massive growth in the appeal of and support for nationalist populist leaders like Hugo Chávez, Evo Morales, and Rafael Correa, who called for redistribution on the basis of turning part of the windfall gains from burgeoning commodity-export prices into social policy.[20]

These leaders went on to win elections by significant margins and, once in power, engineered the most defiant U-turn yet against the US government (the administration of President George W. Bush), US foreign policy, and the Washington consensus basket of free market policies. Presidents Chávez, Morales, and Correa then used resources from hydrocarbon exports to raise public spending significantly, which cemented and broadened their social bases of support (although to varying degrees). To a greater extent than elsewhere in Latin America, the nationalist populist strategy followed by Venezuela, Bolivia, and Ecuador led to the escalation of clashes as business sectors (foreign and domestic) and the state (under the control of "socialists of the twenty-first century") fought increasingly hard-line battles that raised the risks and challenges for democratic regime rule.

Such higher risks and greater challenges for democracy cannot be blamed solely on the forces of the radical Left or the reactionary Right, but rather on the strengthening, self-reinforcing, irreconcilable conflict created by their repeated clashes. As the nationalist populist governments have gone in the direction of controlling more economic activity, and have rolled back some of the policy and resource privileges that business elites (foreigners and their domestic partners) enjoyed in the 1990s, the leaders of the deposed establishment have responded with more aggressive and uncompromising moves, and the nationalist populist governments have retaliated. This repeated dynamic has generated a spiral of conflict that fits poorly with the tolerance and compromise that democracy requires, so that politicoeconomic adversaries can realize mutual gains in the medium and long terms, and therefore come to see that the preservation of democracy is in their interest.

The harsh ideological conflict that erupted in the domestic spheres of the Andean countries worsened and became more inflexible through the US government's attempts to isolate and weaken their nationalist populist leaders. Evidence of American complicity, starting with the short-lived coup which removed President Chávez from power on April 11, 2002, remains contested: some sources claim that US agencies like the CIA and USAID had previous knowledge of the coup, while others deny any US government wrongdoing.[21] What is beyond question is that in the midst of international condemnation of the coup, the administration of President George W. Bush moved swiftly to recognize the *golpista* government under businessman Pedro Carmona, only to backtrack and condemn it when Carmona stepped down and Chávez returned. Elsewhere, the US embassy in Bolivia tracked and condemned the rise of Evo Morales since the early 2000s, calling him an "illegal coca agitator" and laying the groundwork for American agencies like USAID and NED to fund the regional opposition of the *media luna* (centered in Santa Cruz). This culminated with President Morales throwing out US ambassador Philip Goldberg and the US Drug Enforcement Administration's agents in Bolivia.[22] In Ecuador, the US government made no secret of its support for banana tycoon Alvaro Noboa, who ran against nationalist populist Rafael Correa in that country's 2006 elections. Noboa was defeated; since then, President Correa has had a rocky relationship with US agencies and US-influenced organizations, going so far as to expel American diplomats, including the US ambassador, and the World Bank envoy to Ecuador.[23] In contrast to the approach in countries like Chile, Uruguay, Brazil, Mexico, Colombia, and Peru, US foreign policy has alternated between being cautiously distant and sometimes openly belligerent in countries where nationalist populist governments are in power. The end result has been higher stakes and greater animosity between the contending sides in these countries, which has lowered the costs for their organizing and exercising anti-democratic actions against one another.

On top of effects from ideas-based and interests-based mechanisms, institutional ones also point to a conflict-prone ride for democracy in Venezuela, Bolivia, and Ecuador. In the domestic sphere, the basic rules and organizations of political engagement (constitutions, electoral laws, parties and party systems) have undergone substantial changes. The rise of their nationalist populist leaders was possible thanks to the creation of outsider movements, rather than coming through any of the establishment's political parties: in Venezuela these parties simply imploded, in Bolivia they were sidelined, and in Ecuador they have remained fickle. The crisis of the traditional party systems in the Andean countries—not only in these three countries, but also in Colombia and Peru—led to what some scholars have dubbed a crisis of representation. Though this interpretation has been criticized by other academics, the establishment was shoved aside in the sense that the masses' support for nationalist populist movements soared at the same time that the most venerable of the long-established parties fell into disrepute.[24] The ascendency of outsiders and the changes this rise triggered in the party systems of the Andean countries redrew the lines of the fierce traditional distributive clashes that these countries have historically experienced. High-intensity confrontations are not surprising, due to extreme inequality and an abundance of popular uprisings concerned with redistribution and grievances over issues of justice in a subregion of Latin America that is also characterized by deep ethnic cleavages and territorial conflicts.[25]

Presidents Chávez, Morales, and Correa refashioned their polities by creating new constitutions, which strengthened the executive branch of government, extended the protection of social rights, and added mechanisms for direct citizen participation, such as referenda and plebiscites. The major difficulty for the new constitutions is not so much the superabundance of aspirations they include that, if and when they are unmet, can lead to frustration and future opposition from the popular sectors whose livelihoods and opportunities they are meant to advance. Rather, the main problem is that the social groups that feel strongly either in favor of or against the new constitutions are locked into an irreconcilable ideological battle. The nationalist populists have been on top for some years. But what happens if and when the pro-US, Washington consensus types return to power? Having changed the constitution once, the precedent exists for changing it again, particularly if a given society is sharply divided into irreconcilable camps, as is the case in the Andean countries. Therefore, the principal challenge for the constitutions drafted and put in place by the nationalist populists in the 2000s is not just a potential need to tweak them here or there, but rather their future survival, if and when the Right returns to power.

Colombia and Peru. Colombia and Peru are clustered together here, and placed in a different group from Venezuela, Bolivia, and Ecuador, because in the 2000s Bogotá and Lima housed governments that were staunch US allies and supporters of the Washington consensus basket of free market policies. In Colombia, Presidents Andrés Pastrana (1998–2002) and Alvaro Uribe (2002–10) established and then managed the Plan Colombia, whereby the US government gave its Colombian counterpart more than 6 billion USD between 2000 and 2010 to fight drug trafficking. As a result, Colombia has become the hub for US influence in northern South America. Governments in Peru since Alberto Fujimori first assumed the presidency in 1990 have remained pro-American and pro–Washington consensus. Both Presidents Alejandro Toledo (2001–6) and Alan García (2006–11)—surprisingly for the latter, given his earlier populist presidency (1985–90)—remained committed to the optimistic 1990s view that liberal democracy and free markets provided the best avenues for growth and development. Peru's turn to the left after the presidential victory of Ollanta Humala in 2011 opened up a possibility for significant change regarding the general international and economic policy orientation of that country, but thus far he seems to want to maintain a moderate Lula profile rather than a radical Chávez one.

Another key difference that justifies dividing the Andean countries during the 2000s into the two groups is that while the governments of Venezuela, Bolivia, and Ecuador have sought to limit their dependence on foreign financial portfolio investments, Colombia and Peru have sought to make themselves more attractive to foreign investors. Regardless of this difference, all the Andean countries accumulated substantial foreign exchange reserves in the wake of the 2003–8 global commodity price booms, but similarities within the two groups then start breaking down. For example, Venezuela and Bolivia retained relatively large foreign exchange reserves; Ecuador did not, and in 2008 it defaulted on its debt obligations to external creditors.[26] In the other Andean subgroup, President Alvaro Uribe and his government remained very popular in Colombia, despite allegations of government-paramilitary cooperation against left-wing guerrillas (the Fuerzas Armadas Revolucionarias de Colombia [FARC] and the Ejército de Liberación Nacional [ELN]) that implicated many of Uribe's closest political followers in the executive and legislative branches of the government. Paradoxically, Alan García's government in Peru had little support beyond the Alianza Popular Revolucionaria Americana (APRA) voter base, so it was unable to reap electoral benefits from the financial upswing, despite its being Peru's longest-lasting economic boom in many decades.[27]

Another important difference is that while President Uribe's government built substantial support among the poor, thanks to a visible social policy and greater security in different parts of Colombia's territory, the opposite happened in Peru. Peru's significant historical social deficit, and popular awareness that the expansive growth of the 2000s went to the few—the rich and the small, professional, upper middle classes, who have been the main beneficiaries of the way neoliberalism has been implemented since the early 1990s in that country—has led to a lack of enthusiasm even for a traditionally nationalist populist party like APRA. Adding to the establishment's worries, this trend has been coupled with spectacular growth in political support for outsiders like

Ollanta Humala, who was elected to the presidency in 2011. Some redrawing of the social contract in Peru is very necessary if democracy is to retain the adherence of the masses. The question is the extent of this redrawing: to go along the radical path of Chávez in Venezuela, or in the more moderate direction pursued by Lula in Brazil?

Despite these differences, Colombia and Peru had many similarities in the 2000s. The Bretton Woods institutions have largely applauded and encouraged the neoliberal economic policies that both countries' governments have pursued, while the governments of Ecuador and Venezuela have had hostile relations with the WB and, especially, the IMF, largely shunning their advice and their funds. An interesting contrast is that the IADB has maintained smoother relations with the governments of Ecuador and Venezuela, as well as with Bolivia. Another similarity between Colombia and Peru is that in the 2000s their governments sought to cement their closeness with the United States through free trade agreements and greater cooperation on security issues. A trade agreement with Peru went into effect, and an agreement with Colombia, which stalled due to concerns in the US Congress about the targeting and killing of labor organizers by Colombian security forces, was finally enacted in 2011.

The Peruvian and Colombian economies were well prepared for the 2008 global financial bust and its aftermath, thanks to the countries' conservative fiscal and monetary policies during the boom years. Bolivia also followed this path, which helped strengthen President Morales's government and allowed the country to have a "good crisis" after 2008. In contrast, extensive, pro-cyclical public spending during the boom, followed by economic decline after the world economy fell off a cliff in September 2008, forced the governments in Ecuador and Venezuela to implement politically unpopular cuts in public spending and left them licking their wounds amid one of the worst recessions in Latin America. National governments' access to international and/or domestic resources is critically important during harsh economic shocks and crises, in order to put a floor on economic decline. This, in turn, can help lower the odds that the social and political fallout from economic collapse will also endanger a democratically elected government or, more fundamentally, a country's democratic political regime.

—◦ ◦—

In short, the rise of uncompromising ideological and distributional conflicts centered on fixed assets, a latently politicized military, and radical disagreement about the constitutional basis of the state have created more pressures and uncertainty for democracies in the Andean countries than in the Southern Cone nations (although Argentina's nationalist populist governments between 2002 and 2011 share some of the same challenges) or in Brazil and Mexico. A factor that my analysis did not include is the politicization of ethnicity, or ethnonationalism, and its effects on political regimes in the midst of harsh financial shocks and economic crises. My framework was built thinking about Argentina, Chile, and Uruguay, where, even though ethnonationalism has led to significant political conflict (as illustrated most poignantly by the Mapuches in Chile), it is hard to envisage it becoming an issue that could decide the fate of political regimes, as has been the case in Bolivia and potentially could be in neighboring Peru. Nor should it become a significant power factor, as it has in Ecuador and—to a lesser extent, but with arguably more potential—in Guatemala, as well as in small enclaves in Mexico.

Other Emerging Markets Regions

This first limitation on the extent to which my analytical framework can travel, even within Latin America, in light of the post–2008-9 global busts now leads me to identify other basic limits by observing two additional regions of the world with similar middle-income, emerging market countries: East Asia and Eastern Europe. These last comparative exercises, however, are very general and highly speculative. In brief, the larger countries in these two regions, along with those in Latin America, became an asset class—designated as emerging markets—in international capital markets in the early 1990s. Since then, competition for international capital flows and the unpredictable character of those flows have created similar constraints and opportunities for the governments and the publicly traded corporations of these countries. Aside from the disciplining effect of capital movements, most countries in Latin America and Eastern Europe, and several in East Asia, (re)adopted democracy as their form of political regime relatively recently, during the third wave of democratization in the 1970s–2000s.

EAST ASIA

East Asia had its day of reckoning with foreign-debt-fueled growth during its own 1997–98 regional financial and economic implosion. Events there paralleled what happened in Latin America after its 1982 financial and economic busts. In both situations, mass political protests, fueled by anger and desperation, helped force the incumbents in authoritarian regime to step down (Argentina, Brazil, Uruguay; Indonesia). Even where authoritarian regimes survived (Chile until 1990; Malaysia), or where young democracies had been in power for some years (Peru, Venezuela; South Korea, Taiwan), the regional economic implosions created mass anger and fear as entire populations suffered brutal shocks to their incomes, their consumption habits, and their personal opportunities. Most countries in the two regions appear to have learned from the lessons taught by the regional financial and economic collapses of the 1980s and 1990s. Since then, the majority of their governments have pursued cautious macroeconomic management, which meant that when the 2008–9 global financial and economic busts hit, they possessed solid fiscal and monetary fundamentals. Ever since economic recuperation started in 2009–10, Latin America and East Asia have been seen as the best bets to be regional engines for global growth. Nonetheless, they remain fundamentally different in many respects. At least three factors operant in East Asia were either absent or played a limited role in the Western Hemisphere: geopolitics, religious-fueled conflict, and the politicization of ethnicity.

First, geopolitical considerations in the early twenty-first century in East Asia are centered on the emergence of China as a major global player and a dominant economic force in the world. Even though China's rise has significant implications for the Western Hemisphere in general—and Latin America in particular[28]—its influence and dominance will be much more pronounced on the politics and economics of its Asian neighbors. Geopolitical considerations could not be more different in Latin America, where an undisputed sole hegemonic power, the United States, has had a decisive international influence and has been a factor in lowering the likelihood of international conflicts escalating into wars. This is not to say that the United States has not played a dominant role in East Asia since the end of the Second World War, but this influence is more limited and, in many instances, not decisive, unlike the situation in the Western Hemisphere.

Geopolitical conditions in East Asia can easily become more conflict-prone and uncertain, due to a plural distribution of power: a rising China; a still-prosperous Japan; other emerging midlevel players, such as South Korea; and big nation-states that still don't fight up to their weight, like Indonesia. Some observers think this is the black swan that could trip up East Asia's dominance of the global economy: "The clincher . . . is surely geopolitics. Latin America has no rogue nuclear powers, nothing like the China-Taiwan dispute, Indonesia's febrile religious atmosphere, let alone Thailand's coups."[29] The geopolitical environment in East Asia is less predictable and less hospitable to the hegemony of Western-style liberal democracy than it is in Latin America.

In addition, while electoral democracy has become the norm throughout Latin America (although with important exceptions) since the end of the Cold War, East Asia has provided a home for all kinds of political regimes: a military dictatorship in Myanmar; single-party communist rule in China, Vietnam, and Laos; authoritarian rule in Malaysia; a polarized democracy in Thailand; highly populated, multi-insular, fragile democracies in the Philippines and Indonesia; graduated emerging markets with an advanced economic status under electoral democratic rule, like South Korea and Taiwan; and a mature parliamentary democracy in Japan. A wider range in the types of government, coupled with more competitive, conflict-prone geopolitical conditions, means that the impact of harsh financial shocks and economic crises on political regimes could differ significantly and potentially be more subject to instability in East Asia than in Latin America.

A second factor differentiating East Asia from Latin America is religious conflict. In East Asia, the rise of the Jemaah Islamiyah network and other terrorist groups has made religious-based terrorism a significant danger in countries as widely divergent as Indonesia, the Philippines, Singapore, Malaysia, and Thailand.[30] Threats to democracy from religious terrorism are not significant in Latin America. This is not to say that there is no religious conflict in Latin America or in the Western Hemisphere, but the Americas do not have the equivalent of the globally funded, supported, and encouraged form of armed takeover by radical Islamists or jihadists that exists in countries as different as Afghanistan, Somalia, Thailand, Indonesia, and the Philippines. This factor could become a significant central element in some East Asian countries.

The third relevant factor is the politicization of ethnicity. Ethnic cleavages have played a prominent role in some of the major countries in Southeast Asia, such as Indonesia and Malaysia.[31] Often conflicts between indigenous majorities and more prosperous ethnic minorities have increased the risks of political instability and institutional breakdown, including in Latin American nations (Bolivia and Ecuador).

EASTERN EUROPE

The twentieth anniversary of the fall of the Berlin Wall in November 2009 took place amid the worst financial and economic collapses since the fall of communism. No other region of the world has been as negatively affected by the 2008–9 global financial and economic implosion as Central and Eastern Europe. The average fall in annual GDP for these emerging economies in 2009 was –6.2%, although there was substantial intraregional variation: the greatest declines were in the Baltic countries (between –13% and –18%), and the lowest were in the Czech Republic (–4.3%) and Poland (its GDP grew about 1% in 2009).[32] Popular sentiment turned somber throughout the region as real GDP contracted "by more than at any time since the height of the transition [from communism] in 1994."[33] These numbers, and the financial channel responsible for the ferocity of the collapse (local currency devaluation amid extensive indebtedness in foreign-denominated currency) make it seem as if Central and Eastern European countries are going through their own version of Latin America's 1982 external debt crisis.

In terms of my analysis, the main political factor in Eastern Europe is the relative rise in the costs for anti-democracy action that European Union (EU) membership has imposed on its members and would-be members. As of 2011, ten Eastern European countries enjoyed the benefits of membership, which, in the context of the 2008–9 global financial and economic crises, means EU financial support (in conjunction with the IMF, where the governments of Western European countries and the United States control a majority of votes) through credit and guarantees to help save the most vulnerable countries in the region.[34]

Other elements among the prevailing politicoeconomic conditions in Eastern Europe can also be interpreted within my framework, such as the potentially decisive role the military can have in deciding the fate of political regimes. In this respect, North Atlantic Treaty Organization (NATO) membership for a dozen East European countries (including non-EU members like Croatia and Albania) has redirected their national military establishments toward collective security issues and international peacekeeping missions. The reputational and material costs of potential suspension from EU and/or NATO membership if democracy is threatened in any the member countries has raised the relative costs for anti-democracy action.

Interests-based mechanisms also present significant intraregional variation, although a more-or-less general public perception since 1989 and the fall of communism is, as a recent survey has put it, that of "the continuing power and wealth of the old system's elite, who have proved much better at running the capitalism they decried than the socialism they preached."[35] The opening of political and economic spheres after the collapse of communism has also meant that "for the young, flexible, and ambitious, the past 20 years have proved a bonanza. For the losers—the old, the timid, the dim—life has been punishingly difficult."[36] Worsening general conditions and a rapidly widening gap between winners and losers in the wake of the 2008–9 global financial and economic busts could easily become more politicized, leading to polarization.

Ideas-based mechanisms probably present the greatest source of conflict for democracy in Eastern Europe. In terms of political ideologies, an economic crisis and a sense of growing inequality and injustice can give way to the type of right-wing populism that looks for scapegoats (to explain current ills) and promises redress. This process, which was prevalent in many Eastern European countries during the rise of fascism in the 1920s–30s (back then Jews and Communists were targeted), has been most worrisome in Hungary, where ethnonationalism and the persecution of Roma (gypsies) has been both a cause and an effect in raising the stakes for political adversaries, creating risks for and pressures against democratic governance.[37] Still, the costs of jeopardizing EU and NATO membership are so great that it is highly unlikely that long-lasting political conflict could challenge or break democracy, even in a country as apparently polarized as Hungary.[38]

A more general point is the difference between Eastern Europeans' past legacy of living under totalitarian rule during the Cold War years, compared with what most countries in Latin America experienced, where, with the exception of Cuba, the prevailing form of non-democratic rule was authoritarian. In the early twenty-first century, a majority of the populations in both regions could be against non-democratic regimes, but, given the differences in their previous types of political rule, and the fact that Eastern Europe's neighbor, Russia, is still led by authoritarian rule and is the dominant regional power, Eastern Europeans will probably cling to liberal democracy more strongly during periods of crisis than in other emerging economies in other parts of the world.

As for economic policy, Eastern Europe's integration into the EU ensured a rapid extension of credit and guarantees through the EU's European Central Bank (ECB) and the IMF after the 2008 global financial and economic implosions. Today's politicians and policymakers have continued to invoke the Great Depression and the lessons learned from it, so the result of the most recent global crisis was the largest-ever internationally coordinated monetary and fiscal expansion, led by the world's twenty major economies, in the fall–winter of 2008. Preventing another Great Depression became the order of the day, and, in the European Union, this meant first and foremost containing the self-feeding and potentially crippling financial collapse of Eastern European economies,[39] followed by propping up the fiscal position of southern European ones. In Greece, Ireland, and Portugal, sovereign crises have been managed through bailouts by the ECB/EU/IMF troika. Still, even if some of the peripheral EU economies were to default on their debts or, in the extreme, leave the euro currency domain, their EU membership is not in question. Given the democratic clause embedded in the EU membership agreement, democracies in peripheral countries will remain relatively safe, even in the face of harsh economic crisis, due to the high costs of being cast adrift from the European project, with its multiple resources and opportunities. Also, East Europeans' general abhorrence of the command economy systems in place during communist rule means that it is reasonable to expect capitalism, and its Anglo-American free market version, to retain its general appeal in the region. Of course there will be significant intraregional variation, but "the absence of a credible alternative economic model is evident" in Eastern Europe.[40] In short, even though the populations in Eastern European countries continue to have important reservations about their capitalist "post-Communist societies, they are not questioning the fundamental values of democracy and free markets. . . . Few want to turn back the clock to 1989."[41]

In short, despite the worst financial and economic fallout in Eastern Europe since the dual transitions from totalitarian to democratic rule and from command to market economies in the early 1990s, the costs for moving away from democracy are high. As in Latin America, even though Eastern European governments might rise and fall, and political unrest and instability in the face of deep economic crises might be likely in the 2010s, democratic regime rule should survive, particularly in the ten Eastern European member countries of the EU.

FINAL THOUGHTS

Financial markets will always be complex systems and, therefore, inherently unstable. Even though, more often than not, their incremental changes can look like a continuous trend, these are interspersed with wild oscillations, without any apparent regularity.[42] In monetary terms, this means that billions will continue to be made and lost in present and future financial markets, regardless of the extent of domestic, international, or even globally coordinated regulation. In political economic terms (the fight over the allocation of scarce resources and opportunities among competing groups), financial booms and busts will continue to polarize and politicize winners and losers. Hurt individuals and groups will organize and take to the streets in protest. Opposition parties and movements will jump on the bandwagon of discontent and try to replace the incumbents, who, in turn, will have to show that they are effective at crisis management in the relatively short term—particularly if an economic crisis has turned into repeated hyperinflationary episodes, as it did in many major Latin American economies in the 1980s and early 1990s.

Rather than focusing merely on economic policy reasons for why the Great Recession did not become another Great Depression, this work has examined and contrasted the more general issue of the impact of harsh financial shocks and economic crises on political regimes in general, and, in particular, on the chances for democracy's survival in three Southern Cone countries, starting with the late 1920s–early 1930s and culminating with the post–2008–9 global busts.

The main contribution of this exercise has been to highlight a group of mechanisms (institutional, interests-based, and ideas-based) whose structural changes since the Great Depression have raised the likelihood of democratic regime survival in the face of recurrent economic shocks and crises since democracy returned to Argentina (1983), Uruguay (1984–85), and Chile (1989–90). The relevance of these structural changes was shown by contrasting the Great Depression years (part I) with the 1982 debt crisis and the emerging markets crises in the late 1990s–early 2000s (part II). While the two democratic regimes that existed in the late 1920s in Latin America (Argentina and Uruguay) broke down during the early years of the depression (1930–33), democracy returned not only to these two countries, but also to Chile, in the course of the post-1982 debt crises years; it survived in all three countries after the emerging markets crises of 1997–2002; and it weathered the fallout of the 2008–9 global financial and economic busts.

These structural changes have not been general, let alone universal. Snapshots of politicoeconomic conditions in the aftermath of the 2008–9 global financial and economic crises in regions outside of the three Southern Cone countries suggest that in order for my analytical framework to help explain potential political regime outcomes more generally, it would have to open up new avenues of investigation: the prospects for democracy in the face of geopolitics in a region characterized by a plurality of powers increasingly influenced by a rising one, such as the situation in East Asia with China; the challenges to basic order and security for nation-states in East Asia that face growing religious-based conflict by Islamic jihadists; the politicization of ethnicity for some Andean as well as East Asian nations; and, for Eastern European countries, the higher costs that anti-democracy actions face, given the significant penalties that suspension from or delays in accession to European Union membership entail. These are some avenues for further research that might enrich future cross-regional research on the political impacts of harsh financial shocks and economic crises.

This book has emphasized structural changes in institutions, interests, and ideas that, since the 1980s, have allowed electoral democracy to be more resilient in the face of harsh financial shocks and economic crises. Nonetheless, their substantial empirical variations suggest that a wide diversity of conditions arising out of specific contexts will always exist, and that democracy and democratization have been and will continue to be complex social processes that defy easy generalizations, even when we examine a small subset of relatively modern, well-to-do, emerging market countries like Argentina, Chile, and Uruguay.

Notes

INTRODUCTION

1. The concept "creative destruction" is most closely associated with Schumpeter, *Capitalism, Socialism, and Democracy*. The author argued that capitalism is "a form or method of economic change [that] never can be stationary." The essential fact of capitalism is the creative destruction "that incessantly revolutionizes the economic structure from *within* [author's emphasis], incessantly destroying the old one, incessantly creating a new one" (82–3). Before Schumpeter, Karl Marx and Werner Sombart also thought about capitalism as an incessant process of the destruction and creation of wealth. Note that whereas Schumpeter's emphasis was on the economic consequences (innovation and progress) of creative destruction, I focus on some of its political consequences (democratic survival or transition).

2. Financial shocks are only one among many other triggers of harsh economic crises, but they are the common starting point for my analysis of the historical cases compared in this work.

3. The three-type classification of political regimes (democratic, totalitarian, and authoritarian) that has dominated political science since the 1970s was pioneered by Juan J. Linz and his reflections regarding the distinctiveness of Franco's political regime in Spain. The original articles are referenced in Linz and Stepan, *Problems of Democratic Transition*, 38–39.

4. See Gourevitch, *Politics in Hard Times*. An indicator of the major revival of interest in politics in hard times as a general subject of study in mainstream Anglo-American political science was the choice of a title and general themes to explore for the American Political Science Association's (APSA) 2010 annual meeting in Washington, DC, on September 2–5: "The Politics of Hard Times: Citizens, Nations, and the International System under Economic Stress."

5. See the regime-change database in Przeworski et al., *Democracy and Development*, 59–69.

6. On the long-term incidence of international economic shocks and the way they affected Latin American economies, see Elliott, *Empires*, chapters 4–6; Fukuyama, *Falling Behind*, chapters 4–7; Maddison, *Contours*, chapter 2; North, Summerhill, and Weingast, "Order, Disorder."

7. The author is grateful to an anonymous reviewer for highlighting the importance of significant pendulum swings in economic thinking and economic policymaking since the early decades of the twentieth century to Latin American politics and political economy.

8. Przeworski et al., *Democracy and Development*, 40–43.

9. See Hagopian and Mainwaring, introduction to *Third Wave of Democratization*. See also P. H. Smith, *Democracy in Latin America*, part 1, chapters 1–4.

10. See Dahl, *Polyarchy*; Acemoglu and Robinson, *Economic Origins*. I am grateful to Jonathan Hartlyn and Cynthia McClintock for reminding me, during a panel presentation at the APSA's 2010 meeting to emphasize Dahl's thinking in my analysis regarding the relative costs that political adversaries face when fighting over the fundamental rules of the game (types of political regimes).

11. Przeworski et al., *Democracy and Development*.

12. Acemoglu and Robinson, *Economic Origins*.

13. See, for example, Mahoney and Rueschemeyer, *Comparative Historical Analysis*; Pierson, *Politics in Time*; Thelen, "Historical Institutionalism"; King, Lieberman, Ritter, and Whitehead, *Democratization in America*.

14. George and Bennett, *Case Studies*, 206.

15. Rueschemeyer, Huber Stephens, and Stephens, *Capitalist Development and Democracy*, 5.

16. There is a vast amount of literature on the three pillars—interests, institutions, and ideas—in comparative politics and political economy. This covers a wide range of topics, including methodology; changes in economic ideas that help create new, long-term economic policy orientations; transitions from communism and command economies; changes from protectionism to free trade; the creation of foreign policy systems; the construction of welfare states; and the shaping of global institutions and international development policy. For good overviews of this literature, see Lichbach and Zuckerman, *Comparative Politics*; Hay, "Review: Ideas, Interests, and Institutions."

17. North, *Institutions*, 4. North and colleagues continue to highlight this distinction in their most recent work. See North, Wallis, and Weingast, *Violence and Social Orders*, 15–18.

18. See Conniff, foreword to *Populism in Latin America*. I follow this perspective, which emphasizes the mass communications and organizational aspects of populism, alongside the personality and leadership traits of individual populist leaders.

19. The author is grateful to an anonymous reviewer for suggesting that I consider populism not simply as a series of instances of nationalist populist experiments—be they in the 1930s, 1970s, or since the early 2000s—but more fundamentally, as a building block for the ideas component of my analysis.

20. Wikipedia, "Whig History," http://en.wikipedia.org/wiki/Whig_history [accessed July 29, 2010]. The original identification of this type of historiography was the influential text by Butterfield, *Whig Interpretation of History*.

CHAPTER 1: FINANCIAL SHOCKS, ECONOMIC CRISES, AND DEMOCRACY

1. Books whose analyses inspired the building blocks and comparative perspective developed in this work are Gourevitch, *Politics in Hard Times*; Sikkink, *Ideas and Institutions*; Haggard and Kaufman, *Political Economy*; and Linz and Stepan, *Problems of Democratic Transition*.

2. See, for example, Mahoney and Rueschemeyer, *Comparative Historical Analysis*; Pierson, *Politics in Time*; Thelen, "Historical Institutionalism"; King, Lieberman, Ritter, and Whitehead, *Democratization in America*.

3. Eaton, *Politics beyond the Capital*, 5.

4. P. H. Smith, *Democracy in Latin America*, 348, 349, 353; Boix, *Democracy and Redistribution*, 100; R. Collier, *Paths toward Democracy*, 23; Rueschemeyer, Huber Stephens, and Stephens, *Capitalist Development and Democracy*, 160–61.

5. In Argentina the Sáenz Peña law of 1912 extended voting rights to its male population, but with a strong qualification: only Argentine-born or naturalized males were eligible. Given the substantial proportion of recent immigrants from southern Europe in Argentina, whose numbers exploded between the 1880s and the 1920s (40% of the country's male population in 1930 was foreign born), the 1912 electoral reform originally extended voting rights to slightly more than half of the country's adult males.

6. R. Collier, *Paths toward Democracy*, 23; Boix, *Democracy and Redistribution*, 100.

7. Rueschemeyer, Huber Stephens, and Stephens, *Capitalist Development and Democracy*, 162.

8. P. H. Smith, *Democracy in Latin America*, 349.

9. I am grateful to Peter De Shazo for his critical reading of a draft of the manuscript and for the precision and richness of his comments, particularly regarding the Chilean case. See also De Shazo, *Urban Workers*.

10. Therborn, "Travail."

11. I continue to follow Rueschemeyer, Huber Stephens, and Stephens, *Capitalist Development and Democracy*, and P. H. Smith, *Democracy in Latin America*, for the classification and regime trajectories of the Southern Cone countries, and for other Latin American nations when appropriate.

12. P. H. Smith, *Democracy in Latin America*, 348–49, 352–53; Rueschemeyer, Huber Stephens, and Stephens, *Capitalist Development and Democracy*, 160–61.

13. Bulmer-Thomas, *Economic History*, 191.

14. Rueschemeyer, Huber Stephens, and Stephens, *Capitalist Development and Democracy*, 157.

15. O'Rourke and Williamson, *Globalization and History*, 13–14.

16. Ibid., 23.

17. Thorp, *Progress, Poverty, and Exclusion*, 99.

18. The author is grateful to Peter De Shazo for urging me to highlight both key similarities and differences of the three Southern Cone countries' economies during the three decades preceding the Great Depression, which for Chile meant more vulnerability to exogenous shocks, compared with Argentina and Uruguay.

19. Harvey, "Economic Shock."

20. I am grateful to Laurence Whitehead for an excellent discussion we had at Nuffield College in Oxford on economic shocks on July 12, 2008.

21. Minsky, *Stabilizing an Unstable Economy*; Mandelbrot and Hudson, *(Mis)behavior of Markets*, 82–87.

22. Kindleberger, *Manias, Panics, and Crashes*, 89.

23. "Diagnosing Depression."

24. Ibid.

25. See, for example, "Austerity Debate," the weeklong public debate hosted in the Comment pages of the *Financial Times*.

26. Discussions about the battle for the future of macroeconomics and finance economics as disciplines in the light of the 2008 collapse can be found in "Briefing"; Krugman, "How Did Economists?"

27. Reinhart and Rogoff, *This Time Is Different*, 229–30.

28. For a useful review of this literature, see D. Collier and Norden, "Strategic Choice Models."

29. The most important collaborative projects that helped to define this literature were Linz and Stepan, *Breakdown of Democratic Regimes*; O'Donnell, Schmitter, and Whitehead, *Transitions from Authoritarian Rule*; Linz and Stepan, *Problems of Democratic Transition*.

30. Boix, *Democracy and Redistribution*, 18.

31. Acemoglu and Robinson, *Economic Origins*, 19–20. These authors underscore the importance of who gets to define policies, because policies affect the production, allocation, and redistribution of power and resources (material and otherwise). Like Boix, Acemoglu and Robinson see the choice of political regime as basically being the result of redistributive struggles in which individuals try to advance their socioeconomic and political interests and position through group action, which can be at the expense of other groups and individuals, if necessary.

32. Rueschemeyer, Huber Stephens, and Stephens, *Capitalist Development and Democracy*, 5.

33. There is a vast amount of literature on the three pillars of interests, institutions, and ideas that covers a wide range of topics, including methodology; changes in economic ideas that help create new, long-term economic policy orientations; transitions from communism and command economies; changes from protectionism to free trade; the creation of foreign policy systems; the construction of welfare states; and the shaping of global institutions and international development policy. For a cogent overviews of the literature, see Lichbach and Zuckerman, *Comparative Politics*; Hay, "Review: Ideas, Interests, and Institutions."

34. Acemoglu and Robinson, *Economic Origins*, 40. See also Boix, *Democracy and Redistribution*, 14.

35. Acemoglu and Robinson, *Economic Origins*, 40–41. See also Boix, *Democracy and Redistribution*, 14–15.

36. Dahl, *Polyarchy*; Acemoglu and Robinson, *Economic Origins*. I am grateful to Jonathan Hartlyn for reminding me during a panel presentation at the 2010 APSA meeting about the importance of Dahl's thinking regarding the relative costs that political adversaries face when fighting over the fundamental rules of the game.

37. Rueschemeyer, Huber Stephens, and Stephens, *Capitalist Development and Democracy*, 53–63, 69–75.

38. Dahl, *Polyarchy*, 15, quoted in Acemoglu and Robinson, *Economic Origins*, 79.

39. Boix, *Democracy and Redistribution*, 26.

40. Acemoglu and Robinson, *Economic Origins*, 31.

41. Hagopian and Mainwaring, *Third Wave of Democratization*; see also "Latinobarómetro Poll."

42. See F. E. González, *Dual Transitions*, in particular the conclusion where the implications of dual transitions in Latin America are drawn for East Asia and Eastern Europe.

43. North, *Institutions*, 4.

44. Ibid., 5.

45. For recent panoramic views of the drama of democratization in Latin America, see Domínguez and Shifter, *Constructing Democratic Governance*; Peeler, *Building Democracy*; Vanden and Prevost, *Politics of Latin America*.

46. Boix, *Democracy and Redistribution*, 38–44.

47. Acemoglu and Robinson, *Economic Origins*, 32–33.

48. For a recent recount of that history, see Chapman, *Bananas*.

49. Boix, *Democracy and Redistribution*, 47–53; Acemoglu and Robinson, *Economic Origins*, 38–40.

50. Rueschemeyer, Huber Stephens, and Stephens, *Capitalist Development and Democracy*, 7–8.

51. Ibid., 8.

52. Acemoglu and Robinsons, *Economic Origins*, 39.

53. Rueschemeyer, Huber Stephens, and Stephens, *Capitalist Development and Democracy*, 8.

54. Goldstein and Keohane, *Ideas and Foreign Policy*, 4, quoted in Blyth, "Review: 'Any More Bright Ideas?,'" 240.

55. Blyth, "Review: 'Any More Bright Ideas?,'" 246.

56. The author is grateful to a panel participant at the 2010 APSA meeting for highlighting the need to distinguish ideas from ideologies.

57. Blyth, *Great Transformations*.

58. A useful, accurate portrait of Prebisch as an influential shaper of economic ideas and economic policy in international and domestic spheres can be consulted in Wikipedia, http://en.wikipedia.org/wiki/Raúl_Prebisch.

59. The author thanks an anonymous reviewer for reminding me about the paradigm-shifting influence of Raúl Prebisch in Latin America. In light of such an important reminder, the author has included the faces of the principal economists that acted as gurus for the major pendulum swings in economic ideas and economic policy.

60. Wirth, foreword to *Populism in Latin America*, vii–viii.

61. Conniff, *Populism in Latin America*, 4.

62. Laclau, "Towards a Theory," 143.

63. Dornbusch and Edwards, *Macroeconomics of Populism*.

64. Laclau, "Towards a Theory," 174–75.

65. Wirth, foreword to *Populism in Latin America*, vii–viii.

66. The author is grateful to an anonymous reviewer for helping me to highlight such differences.

67. Conniff, *Populism in Latin America*, 5.

CHAPTER 2: ECONOMIC CRISIS AND DEMOCRACY
DURING THE GREAT DEPRESSION

1. Coatsworth and Taylor, *Latin America*.

2. O'Rourke and Williamson, *Globalization and History*, 14.

3. Coatsworth, "Structures, Endowments, and Institutions."

4. Maddison, *World Economy*.

5. Kindleberger, *Manias, Panics, and Crashes*.

6. Thorp, *Progress, Poverty, and Exclusion*, 98; Bulmer-Thomas, *Economic History of Latin America*, 158–60.

7. Bulmer-Thomas, *Economic History*, 156.

8. Marichal, *Century of Debt Crises*.

9. Ibid., 174.

10. Frieden, *Global Capitalism*, 141. I closely follow this author's interpretation of the onset and subsequent development of the Great Depression.

11. Ibid.

12. Thorp, *Progress, Poverty, and Exclusion*, 104.

13. Kindleberger, *Manias, Panics, and Crashes*, 33.

14. Frieden, *Global Capitalism*, 174.

15. Kindleberger, *Manias, Panics, and Crashes*, 120.

16. Ibid., 73.

17. Guha, "Bankers Debate Asset Pools," 3.

18. Eichengreen, *Golden Fetters*; Bernanke, *Essays*.

19. Shlaes, *Forgotten Man*, 7.

20. Frieden, *Global Capitalism*, 181–82.

21. The author thanks an anonymous reviewer for highlighting the trade channel as a factor that allowed Argentina and Uruguay to overcome the perpetuation of falling economic activity in the early 1930s. For example, the highly criticized Roca-Runciman Treaty (1932) and Uruguay's own version of a preferential treaty for British investors in 1935 helped the two countries weather the economic storm better than would have been the case without securing access to Great Britain as a market for their countries' beef exports.

22. Frieden, *Global Capitalism*, 173, 191.

CHAPTER 3: INSTITUTIONS

1. When Ibáñez assumed the presidency in 1927, he was a colonel. He became a general in 1930.

2. The author thanks an anonymous reviewer for this observation.

3. The author thanks an anonymous reviewer for this observation.

4. P. H. Smith, "Breakdown of Democracy," 14–15.

5. Gibson, *Class and Conservative Parties*.

6. The author thanks an anonymous reviewer for this observation.

7. Potash, *Army and Politics*, 76.

8. L. E. González, *Political Structures and Democracy*.

9. Castañeda, *La utopía desarmada*, 32. The author believes that the roots of the Communist Party in Uruguay were so deep and well established that they allowed it to survive the end of the Cold War better than any other of its Latin American counterparts. As a result, the Communists were leading members of the Frente Amplio, the left-wing coalition that elected Tabaré Vázquez to the mayorship of Montevideo in 1990, and to the presidency of Uruguay in 2005.

10. Oddone, "Formation of Modern Uruguay," 464.

11. Lindahl, *Uruguay's New Path*, 185.

12. Oddone, *Uruguay entre la depresión*, 113.

13. Ibid., 17. See also Lindahl, *Uruguay's New Path*, 173.

14. Weinstein, *Uruguay*, 68–73. Entrenched bipartisan competition in Uruguay meant that even though President Terra abolished the *colegiado*, he was forced to share power with a council of ministers whose appointment had to be approved by the legislature, in effect forcing Colorado and Blanco coparticipation.

15. S. Collier and Sater, *History of Chile*, 216.

16. Ibid., 237.

17. Drake, "Chile, 1930–58," 271.

18. See, for example, Garretón, *Chilean Political Process*; S. Collier and Sater, *History of Chile*, 214.

19. The author is grateful to Peter De Shazo for highlighting these differences and encouraging me to explore them further.

20. Conniff, *Populism in Latin America*, 10–11.

21. League of Nations, *World Economic Survey, 1923–1933*, quoted in S. Collier and Sater, *History of Chile*, 223.

22. Romero, *Breve historia contemporánea*, 52.

23. Pigna, *Los mitos*.

24. Potash, *Army and Politics*, 12.

25. Rock, *Authoritarian Argentina*.

26. Drake, "Chile's Populism Reconsidered," 65.

27. Nunn, *Military in Chilean History*, 130. The author thanks an anonymous reviewer for reminding me to emphasize this point.

28. The author is grateful to Peter De Shazo for reminding me about the key institutional watershed created by the 1924 reforms in Chile.

29. S. Collier and Sater, *History of Chile*, 222.

30. Drake, "Chile's Populism Reconsidered," 66.

31. Nunn, *Military in Chilean History*, 194–95.

32. Ibid., 215.

33. Deutsch, *Las Derechas*, 144.

34. Nunn, *Military in Chilean History*, 216.

35. See P. H. Smith, *Democracy in Latin America*, 10. This distinction is based on the fact that although there was a relatively level playing field for all participating parties in Chilean elections (i.e., they were fair), there were literacy requirements that prevented a significant proportion of the adult population from voting (i.e., elections were not free) between 1932 and 1970. In contrast, in Argentina there was full male suffrage (elections were free), but electoral competition was rigged (unfair) between 1930 and 1943.

36. See Oddone, "Formation of Modern Uruguay," 458–59.

37. Jacob, *El Uruguay de Terra*, 58.

38. Ibid, 60.

39. Gillespie, "Uruguay's Transition," 173.

40. A. Edwards, "Latin America," 137.

41. Ibid., 143.

42. "Convention," 163.

43. Ibid.

44. Frieden, *Global Capitalism*, 188.

45. Jacob, *El Uruguay de Terra*, 76–77.

46. Oddone, *Uruguay entre la depresión*, 180–81.

47. Ibid., 176.

CHAPTER 4: INTERESTS

1. Acemoglu and Robinson, *Economic Origins*, 31–32.

2. Marichal, *Century of Debt Crises*, 171–72.

3. Thorp, "Latin America," 63.

4. Oddone, *Uruguay entre la depresión*, 17–18.

5. Goddard, *Getting There*.

6. Flink, *Automobile Age*, chapters 2–5.

7. Thorp, *Progress, Poverty, and Exclusion*, 103.

8. Drake, "Chile, 1930–58," 275.

9. Bulmer-Thomas, *Economic History*, 198.

10. The author is grateful to Peter De Shazo for urging me to emphasize the overdependence of the Chilean economy on the proceeds from nitrate mining and exporting.

11. O'Brien, *Century of U.S. Capitalism*, 89–90.

12. Pike, *Chile and the United States*, 233–34.

13. Thorp, *Progress, Poverty, and Exclusion*, 111.

14. O'Brien, *Century of U.S. Capitalism*, 90.

15. Ibid., 74.

16. S. Collier and Sater, *History of Chile*, 222.

17. O'Brien, *Century of U.S. Capitalism*, 74.

18. The author is grateful to Peter De Shazo for pointing to Rojas Flores's *La dictadura de Ibáñez*, an important source that highlights the growth of working-class organization, mobilization, and protest in Chile after the brutal 1930 economic collapse.

19. Romero, *Breve historia contemporánea*, 104.

20. Aguilar, *Marxism in Latin America*, 9.

21. Pigna, *Los mitos*, 155.

22. P. H. Smith, "Breakdown of Democracy," 15.

23. Pigna, *Los mitos*, 156.

24. Solberg, *Oil and Nationalism*, 154.

25. Romero, *Breve historia contemporánea*, 89–90. See also P. H. Smith, "Breakdown of Democracy," 23.

26. Oddone, *Uruguay entre la depresión*, 47–48.

27. Jacob, *El Uruguay de Terra*, 90–92.

28. Oddone, *Uruguay entre la depresión*, 48–49.

29. Ibid., 49.

30. Jacob, *El Uruguay de Terra*, 92.

31. Bulmer-Thomas, *Economic History*, 217.

32. Thorp, *Progress, Poverty, and Exclusion*, 116.

33. Jacob, *El Uruguay de Terra*, 23–26; Oddone, *Uruguay entre la depresión*, 118–21.

34. P. H. Smith, *Democracy in Latin America*, 348–53.

35. Rueschemeyer, Huber Stephens, and Stephens, *Capitalist Development and Democracy*, 8.

36. Ibid., 183.

37. S. Collier and Sater, *History of Chile*, 222.

38. Rock, "Argentina," 450–51.

39. Romero, *Breve historia contemporánea*, 85–86.

40. Finch, "Uruguay since 1930," 199.

41. Ibid.

42. S. Collier and Sater, *History of Chile*, 224–25.

43. The author is grateful to an anonymous reviewer for highlighting this paradox.

CHAPTER 5: IDEAS

1. Merquior, "The 'Other' West."

2. Hale, "Political and Social Ideas," 396–97.

3. On the radical Left, see Aguilar, *Marxism in Latin America*; on the extreme Right, see Deutsch, *Las Derechas*.

4. Pike, *Chile and the United States*, 235.

5. Ibid., 239.

6. Angell, "Left in Latin America," 93–95.

7. Oddone, *Uruguay entre la depresión*, 153, 154, 160.

8. Romero, *Breve historia contemporánea*, 109–10.

9. This is a concept that scholars of social and political mobilization use to identify some of the ideational bases that facilitate the coordination needed for collective action. See, for example, Tarrow, *Power in Movement*.

10. Frieden, *Global Capitalism*, 176.

11. See, for example, "Austerity Debate," the weeklong public debate hosted in the Comment pages of the *Financial Times*.

12. Thorp, *Progress, Poverty, and Exclusion*, 98.

13. Conniff, *Populism in Latin America*, 8–9.

14. Ibid., 5.

15. Marshall, *Demanding the Impossible*, 504–18.

16. Rocker, *Anarcho-Syndicalism*, 109.

17. Ibid., 115–30.

18. Marshall, *Demanding the Impossible*, 504.

19. Peter De Shazo, pers. comm. with the author, Aug. 27, 2010.

20. Areces, "La revolución de 1930," 32–33; Jacob, *El Uruguay de Terra*, 18.

21. Castañeda, *La utopía desarmada*, 34.

22. The author thanks Peter De Shazo for clarifying the evolution of Socialist and Communist movements in Chile. De Shazo noted that the reason why Chile was the only country in Latin America that had a viable Marxist Socialist Party was the influence of anarchist leaders, who did not go along with communism after 1920, and became top Partido Socialista leaders. See also Drake, *Socialism and Populism*.

23. Castañeda, *La utopía desarmada*, 33.

24. Ching and Pakkasvirta, "Latin American Materials."

25. Michael Lowry, quoted in Castañeda, *La utopia desarmada*, 35.

26. Ciria, "Los partidos políticos," 68–72.

27. Oddone, *Uruguay entre la depresión*, 174.

28. Frieden, *Global Capitalism*, 210.

29. Deutsch, *Las Derechas*, 141.

30. Potash, *Army and Politics*, 12.

31. Ibid.

32. Hale, "Political and Social Ideas," 298.

33. Rock, *Authoritarian Argentina*, chapter 1.

34. Romero, *Breve historia contemporánea*, 61.

35. Oddone, *Uruguay entre la depresión*, 152–53.

36. Martín Echegoyen, key *herrerista*, quoted in Weinstein, *Uruguay*, 71.

37. Luis Alberto de Herrera, quoted in Weinstein, *Uruguay*, 72.

38. Linz, *Breakdown of Democratic Regimes*, 14.

39. Thorp, *Progress, Poverty, and Exclusion*, 120.

40. S. Collier and Sater, *History of Chile*, 226.

41. Romero, *Breve historia contemporánea*, 97–99.

42. Ibid., 65.

43. S. Collier and Sater, *History of Chile*, 229–31.

44. Ibid.

45. Marichal, *Century of Debt Crises*, 203.

46. Oddone, *Uruguay entre la depresión*, 64–65.

47. Ibid., 87–89.

48. Ahamed, *Lords of Finance*, 481.

CHAPTER 6: 1982 DEBT CRISIS AND 1997–2002
EMERGING MARKETS CRISES

1. Kindleberger, *Manias, Panics, and Crashes*, 1.

2. Bulmer-Thomas, *Economic History*, 360.

3. Frieden, *Global Capitalism*, 343.

4. Kindleberger, *Manias, Panics, and Crashes*, 8.

5. Frieden, *Global Capitalism*, 366.

6. Thorp, *Progress, Poverty, and Exclusion*, 208.

7. Ffrench-Davis, *Chile entre el neoliberalismo*, 198–99.

8. Ibid., 210.

9. Bulmer-Thomas, *Economic History*, 359, 363 (table 10.5, col. B).

10. Thorp, *Progress, Poverty, and Exclusion*, 206 (table 7.1, col. 2).

11. Bulmer-Thomas, *Economic History*, 363.

12. Wikipedia, "Paul Volcker," http://en.wikipedia.org/wiki/Paul_Volcker [accessed Sept. 30, 2009].

13. Bulmer-Thomas, *Economic History*, 378 (table 11.1), 363 (table 10.5, col. C), 364.

14. Frieden, *Global Capitalism*, 374.

15. Thorp, *Progress, Poverty, and Exclusion*, 216.

16. Kindleberger, *Manias, Panics, and Crashes*, 28.

17. Frieden, *Global Capitalism*, 374

18. Ibid., 375.

19. Thorp, *Progress, Poverty, and Exclusion*, 220.

20. P. H. Smith, *Democracy in Latin America*, 347–53.

21. Frieden, *Global Capitalism*, 375.

22. See Huntington, *Third Wave*; Przeworski, *Democracy and the Market*; Linz and Stepan, *Problems of Democratic Transition*.

23. See Ramos, *Neoconservative Economics*.

24. Aside from Ramos's work, the author is grateful to an anonymous reviewer for suggesting that I highlight this point in the main text.

25. O'Donnell, *Counterpoints*.

26. International Monetary Fund, "World Economic Outlook Database."

27. Vasquez, "Brady Plan."

28. Unal, Demirguc-Kunt, and Leung, "Brady Plan."

29. International Monetary Fund, "World Economic Outlook Database."

30. Blustein, *Chastening*, 11.

31. Frieden, *Global Capitalism*, 389

32. Ibid., 390.

33. Blustein, *Chastening*, 247.

34. Friedman, *Lexus*, 240.

35. Mussa, *Argentina and the Fund*, 17.

CHAPTER 7: INSTITUTIONS

1. See Peeler, *Latin American Democracies*.

2. Linz and Stepan, *Problems of Democratic Transition*, 205.

3. Haggard and Kaufman, *Political Economy*, 80–81.

4. F. E. González, *Dual Transitions*, 106–12; Linz and Stepan, *Problems of Democratic Transition*, 205–6; Haggard and Kaufman, *Political Economy*, 80.

5. F. E. González, *Dual Transitions*, 42–44.

6. Ibid., 21.

7. For a detailed analysis, see Siavelis, *President and Congress*.

8. Pharr and Putnam, *Disaffected Democracies*.

9. Cavallo et al., *La historia oculta del régimen*, 429.

10. Cavarozzi, "Patterns of Elite Negotiation," 224.

11. Ibid.

12. Atkins, *Latin America*, 246–48.

13. Muñoz, "Chile's External Relations," 308.

14. Ibid., 317–18.

15. F. E. González, *Dual Transitions*, 95.

16. Ffrench-Davis, *Chile entre el neoliberalismo*.

17. The author is grateful to an anonymous reviewer for suggesting this point.

18. F. E. González, *Dual Transitions*, 90–92.

19. I do not equate human rights with the promotion of democracy, but I do signal their intimate connection, in that the basic civil and political individual rights that a liberal democratic regime purports to enforce throughout a given territory are also the basic yardsticks that are used to evaluate the extent to which human rights are protected in that territory at a given point in time. For a discussion of this issue, see Freedom House's approach to and methodology for evaluating democratic governance through the lens of civil and political rights throughout the world (www.freedomhouse.org/template.cfm?page=2).

20. Santa-Cruz, "Election Monitoring," 143.

21. The author is grateful to an anonymous reviewer for this comment, highlighting the Peronist machine as a significant source of pressures from below in the second half of 2001.

22. Veigel, *Dictatorship, Democracy, and Globalization*, 1–3.

23. De Riz, "From Menem to Menem," 150.

24. Ibid., 142, 150. "Between 1989 and 1993, President Menem dictated 308 'need' and 'urgency' decrees, which was unprecedented in the history of constitutional governments in Argentina" (150). See also Ferreira-Rubio and Goretti, "Cuando el presidente gobierna."

25. Running on the right from within the Peronist Party and facing probable defeat in the second round of the 2005 election, ex-president Menem declined to participate, leaving incoming President Kirchner without a general victory at the polls. The author thanks an anonymous reviewer for reminding me to highlight the different ideological background and milieu of Peronist leaders Eduardo Duhalde and Néstor Kirchner.

26. See L. E. González, *Political Structures and Democracy*.

27. Alberts, "Why Play by the Rules?" 857.

28. Costa Bonino, "Uruguay," 90, 76.

29. Cason, "Electoral Reform," 95.

30. Buquet, "Reforma política," 17.

31. See Veigel, *Dictatorship, Democracy, and Globalization*, 10. He concludes that the demise of the armed forces as a government alternative strengthened the PJ and the trade union movement that the military had tried to rend apart.

32. Levitsky, "Argentina," 105, 108.

33. Ibid., 108.

34. Red de Seguridad y Defensa de América Latina (RESDAL), "Comparative Atlas of Defense."

35. Bergara et al., "Political Institutions," 7.

36. Forteza et al., "Understanding Reform."

37. Bergara et al., "Political Institutions," 23, 37.

38. Ibid., 28.

39. "Obedience and Final Stop." These laws "prevented Argentinean nationals from being persecuted and sentenced for certain crimes committed in Argentina during the 'dirty war'" (*Yearbook of International Humanitarian Law*, 450).

40. Ibid.

41. Organization of American States, *Charter*.

42. Amnesty International, *Uruguay Report 2008*, www.amnesty.org/en/region/uruguay/report-2008.

43. Roht-Arraiza, "Pinochet Effect."

44. Organization of American States, *Charter*.

45. Ibid., Article 19.

46. The OAS Inter-American Commission on Human Rights, *Annual Report on Human Rights, 1992–93*.

47. See Canton, "Amnesty Laws."

48. Marcelo Ferreira, "Los limites de la voluntad popular," *Página 12*, May 24, 2011, www.pagina12.com.ar/diario/elmundo/4-168708-2011-05-24.html.

49. Valenzuela, "Paraguay," 45.

50. Brau and McDonald, *Successes*, 125–46.

51. Bluestein, *And the Money*.

52. Rush, "Argentina, Brazil Pay."

53. Paris Club website, http://www.clubdeparis.org/en/.

54. Bergara et al., "Political Institutions," 18.

55. Ibid., 16.

56. Mesa-Lago and Muller, "Politics of Pension Reform," 695–96.

57. Steneri, "Comment," 144.

58. Seelig and Terrier, "Uruguay 2002–3," 127.

59. Ibid., 138.

CHAPTER 8: INTERESTS

1. Bulmer-Thomas, *Economic History*, 316.

2. Thorp, *Progress, Poverty, and Exclusion*, 179–81.

3. Valdés, *Pinochet's Economists*.

4. For an interdisciplinary review of different perspectives on Chile's traditional economic elites, see Drake, "Review: Buoyant Bourgeoisie."

5. For the formation, development, and fall of the *conglomerados*, see Silva, *State and Capital*, chapters 5, 6.

6. Dahse, *El mapa*, 12.

7. Silva, "Capitalist Coalitions."

8. Huneeus, "Technocrats and Politicians."

9. Arriagada, *Por la razón*, 172.

10. Haggard and Kaufman, *Political Economy*, 81.

11. S. Collier and Sater, *History of Chile*, 376.

12. Ibid.

13. F. E. González, *Dual Transitions*, 89.

14. Ffrench-Davis, *Chile entre el neoliberalismo*, 166.

15. Ibid., 210–12.

16. S. Collier and Sater, *History of Chile*, 371–72.

17. The author is grateful to an anonymous reviewer for asking me to highlight the counterintuitive reason why General Pinochet and his free-market-loving Chicago boys did not contemplate denationalizing the state copper monopoly, given their supposed comprehensive market liberalization plan, known popularly as El Ladrillo. See, for example, Valdés, *Pinochet's Economists*; Schamis, *Re-Forming the State*.

18. Marichal, *Century of Debt Crises*.

19. Ffrench-Davis, *Chile entre el neoliberalismo*, 163–64 (figs. IV.1, IV.2).

20. Ibid., 164–65 (figs. IV.2, IV.3).

21. Honohan and Klingebiel, "Controlling the Fiscal Costs," 29–30 (table A1). The only bigger bailout in Latin America was Argentina's, under the *Proceso* military regime in 1980–82, which was equivalent to 55% of annual GDP. The fiscal cost of other state bailouts of the private sector included 31% of annual GDP in Uruguay in 1981–84; 22% in Venezuela in 1994–97; close to 20% in Mexico in 1994–97; 13% in Brazil in 1994–96; around 5% in Colombia in 1982–87; and just over 3% in the United States in 1981–91 (the savings and loan crisis).

22. Thorp, *Progress, Poverty, and Exclusion*, 244.

23. Ibid., 243.

24. Frieden, *Global Capitalism*, 425.

25. For Peronism's change from being dominated by labor to being dominated by clientele networks, see Levitsky, "From Labor Politics." Regarding the *piquetero* movement, see Svampa, *Entre la ruta*. The author thanks Mariano Turzi for references regarding pressures from below in Argentina.

26. Hornbeck, *Argentine Financial Crisis*.

27. Alcañiz and Scheier, "New Social Movements," 273.

28. Ibid.

29. Epstein, "*Piquetero* Movement," 106.

30. Ibid, 104.

31. Alcañiz and Scheier, "New Social Movements," 274–75.

32. Ibid., 110.

33. Levitsky and Murillo, *Argentine Democracy*.

34. "Record Capital Flight from Argentina Last Year: 23 Billion USD," *MercoPress*, Jan. 27, 2009.

35. International Monetary Fund, "International Financial Statistics (IFS)" database, www.imf.org/external/data.htm#data [accessed Dec. 1, 2009].

36. Costa Bonino, "Uruguay," 85.

37. According to data in the "Latinobarómetro Poll."

38. Bergara et al., "Political Institutions," 49.

39. CEPAL, "CEPALSTAT" database [accessed Nov. 16, 2009]. In 2000, 13% of Uruguay's population was over the age of 65, compared with 10% in Argentina, 7% in Chile, and 6% as the average for all of Latin America.

40. Forteza et al., "Understanding Reform," 19.

41. "2002: El colapso del Estado," *El País* (Uruguay), Dec. 31, 2002.

42. "PIT-CNT: 'Cada vez que habla Batlle más gente se adhiere al paro general,'" *La República* (Uruguay), July 23, 2003.

43. "Nuevo caceroleo a las 20.00 en rechazo al 'fiscalazo' del gobierno de coalición," *La República* (Uruguay), May 24, 2002.

44. Nelson Fernández, "Batlle acumula problemas y enfrenta su peor momento," *La Nación* (Argentina), Nov. 2, 2000.

45. "El gobierno dice que los saqueos son organizados," *La Nación* (Argentina), Aug. 2, 2002.

46. Instituto Nacional de Estadísticas (Uruguay), www.ine.gub.uy.

47. Nelson Fernández, "Preocupa en Uruguay la expansión de los grupos piqueteros," *La Nación* (Argentina), Sept. 11, 2004.

48. Forteza et al., "Understanding Reform," 17.

49. Connoly and de Melo, "Political Economy of Protectionism," 10.

50. Forteza et al., "Understanding Reform," 17.

51. Bergara et al., "Political Institutions," 12.

52. World Bank Group, "World Development Indicators" [accessed Dec. 1, 2009].

53. Geithner, "Lesson from Argentina's Crisis," 60.

54. Jude Webber, "Argentina 'Delighted' Over Debt Swap Success," *Financial Times*, June 23, 2010.

55. Seelig and Terrier, "Uruguay 2002–3," 140.

56. De la Plaza and Sirtaine, "Analysis," 4.

57. Press Office, Executive Branch of the Republic of Uruguay, "En Uruguay no habrá corralito," press release, May 24, 2002.

58. Seelig and Terrier, "Uruguay 2002–3," 130.

59. Goodman and Engardio, "Uruguay."

60. Nelson Fernández, "Batlle acumula problemas y enfrenta su peor momento," *La Nación* (Argentina), Nov. 2, 2000.

61. William Rhodes (Citigroup), quoted in Goodman and Engardio, "Uruguay."

62. Lederman and Sanguinetti, "Trade Policy Options," 100–102.

63. World Trade Organization, "Trade Policy Review: Report by the Secretariat, Argentina, 2007," www.wto.org/english/tratop_e/tpr_e/tp277_e.htm.

64. World Trade Organization, "Trade Policy Review: Report by the Secretariat, Uruguay, 2006," www.wto.org/english/tratop_e/tpr_e/tp264_e.htm.

65. Forteza et al., "Understanding Reform," 29.

66. Kossman, "Power Struggles," 12.

67. Ibid., 22.

CHAPTER 9: IDEAS

1. Sikkink, *Mixed Signals*, 152.

2. On the capacity of transnational networks to influence domestic politics and decision making, see J. Smith, *Social Movements*, 158–59. She, in turn, follows the seminal work by Finnemore and Sikkink, "International Norm Dynamics."

3. Sikkink, *Mixed Signals*, 156.

4. President Reagan, quoted in Sigmund, *United States and Democracy*, 149.

5. The author thanks Peter De Shazo for highlighting this important factor.

6. Sikkink, *Mixed Signals*, 175–76.

7. Marcel Niedergang, "Un entretien avec le général Pinochet," *Le Monde*, May 8, 1987.

8. Williamson, *Latin American Adjustment*.

9. S. Edwards, *Crisis and Reform*.

10. Minsky, *Stabilizing an Unstable Economy*; Mandelbrot and Hudson, *(Mis)behavior of Markets*.

11. Ramos, *Neoconservative Economics*.

12. Corvalán, *De lo vivido*, 274–76. Almeyda and his unreformed faction distanced themselves from the insurrectionary path espoused by the communists, while the social democratic faction led by Carlos Briones became the most influential socialist force and was a key political actor during the *proceso de amarre* (negotiated constitutional reforms) between October 1988 and March 1990.

13. Boeninger, *Democracia en Chile*, 302.

14. Meller, *Un siglo*.

15. F. E. González, *Dual Transitions*, 94.

16. Ibid., 99.

17. Silva, *State and Capital*, 203.

18. P. H. Smith, *Democracy in Latin America*, 313.

19. De Ferranti et al., *Inequality in Latin America*, 55–58.

20. See Pagés-Serra, *Good Jobs Wanted*.

21. See, for example, Castañeda, "Latin America's Left Turn"; Weyland, "Rise"; Castañeda and Morales, *Leftovers*.

22. Adrián Venutra, "Fueron anuladas las leyes del perdón," *La Nación* (Argentina), May 6, 2005.

23. The author is grateful to an anonymous reviewer for spelling out this critique.

24. "Latinobarómetro Poll."

25. Costa Bonino, "Uruguay," 78.

26. Gillespie, "Role of Civil-Military Pacts," 203.

27. Bergara et al., "Political Institutions," 7.

28. Gillespie, "Role of Civil-Military Pacts," 205.

29. Jorge Zabalza, quoted in Montero, "Tupamaros."

30. Comisiones Unidas Antiimperialistas (ComUnA), press release, June 12, 2009.

31. Gillespie, "Role of Civil-Military Pacts," 205.

32. Quoted in Costa Bonino, "Uruguay," 80.

33. Levitsky, "Argentina," 113.

34. Forteza et al., "Understanding Reform," 4; "The Next Chile," *Economist*, Feb. 3, 2007.

35. Bergara et al., "Political Institutions," 5.

36. "Batlle: La globalización no existe y los que luchan contra ella están dementes," *La República* (Uruguay), Apr. 2, 2002.

37. "The Next Chile," *Economist*, Feb. 3, 2007.

38. Bergara et al., "Political Institutions," 42.

39. Ibid., 11.

40. Costa Bonino, "Uruguay," 77.

41. Press Office, Presidency of the Republic of Uruguay, "Elogian actitud uruguaya frente a la deuda," press release, Mar. 26, 2003.

42. Daniel Renfrew, "Frente Amplio Wins Elections in Uruguay," *World Socialist Web Site*, Nov. 4, 2004, www.wsws.org.

43. "Uruguay Politics: Labor Relations Grow Tense," *Economist Intelligence Unit*, Sept. 12, 2008.

44. Nelson Fernández, "Primer paro general contra Tabaré," *La Nación* (Argentina), Aug. 19, 2008.

CONCLUSION

Epigraphs. "Citigroup Chief Stays Bullish on Buy-Outs," *Financial Times*, July 9, 2007; "Greenspan Concedes Error in Regulation," *New York Times*, Oct. 23, 2008.

1. Reinhart and Rogoff, *This Time Is Different*, 20.

2. Ibid., 233.

3. Ahamed, *Lords of Finance*. This volume became a standard reference among policymakers, bankers, financial journalists, and think-tank analysts in the wake of the post–Lehman Brothers global credit bust.

4. Eichengreen, *Golden Fetters*, xi.

5. Bernanke, "Nonmonetary Effects."

6. For the debate about the extent to which economics and economists should be exonerated or convicted—given the 2007–9 global bust of financial markets and the global financial system, built around the "perfect market hypothesis," which was then followed by the "return of the master" after the massive, internationally coordinated, Keynesian response by the governments of the world's largest economies in their attempt to put a floor on the spiral of price declines from autumn 2008 to 2009—see Arvind Subramanian, "How Disgraced Economists Managed to Make Amends," Comment, *Financial Times*, Dec. 28, 2009; Martin Wolf, "The Challenges of Managing Our Post-Crisis World," Comment, *Financial Times*, Dec. 30, 2009; Skidelsky, *Keynes*.

7. Shlaes, *Forgotten Man*, 173; Frieden, *Global Capitalism*, 178.

8. Bureau of Labor Statistics, U.S. Department of Labor, www.bls.gov; Mortgage Bankers Association, "Delinquencies Continue to Climb in Latest MBA National Delinquency Survey," Mar. 5, 2009, http://www.mbaa.org/NewsandMedia/PressCenter/68008.htm.

9. Reinhart and Rogoff, *This Time Is Different*, 230.

10. Ibid., 234.

11. The author thanks Cynthia McClintock for reminding me during a panel presentation at the 2010 APSA meeting that the "depth and breadth" of the Great Depression is potentially the most relevant factor in explaining the collapse of a majority of both democratic and nondemocratic political regimes in Latin America during the early 1930s. The author also thanks Peter De Shazo for pointing out that cautious macroeconomic management in a majority of Latin American countries since the 1990s has meant that their macroeconomic fundamentals were stronger and on a more solid footing in the aftermath of the 2008–9 global busts.

12. See, for example, Alan Beattie, "Promoting Exports Full of Risk for World Economy," *Financial Times*, Aug. 10, 2010.

13. "Finding a Bolthole in a Risky World," editorial, *Financial Times*, June 5, 2010.

14. Roett, "How Reform Has Powered," 51.

15. González, "Mexico's Drug Wars."

16. "Uneven Economies," editorial, *Financial Times*, July 19, 2010.

17. Departamento Administrativo Nacional de Estadísticas (Colombia), www.dane.gov .co/daneweb_V09/#twoj_fragment1-4/; Banco Central de Ecuador, www.bce.fin.ec/con tenido.php?CNT=ARB0000003; Instituto Nacional de Estadística (Bolivia), www.ine.gob. bo; Superintendencia Nacional de Administración Tributaria (Peru), www.sunat.gob.pe; Servicio Nacional Integrado de Administración Aduanera y Tributaria (Venezuela), www .seniat.gob.ve/portal/page/portal/PORTAL_SENIAT/.

18. Weyland, "Rise."

19. Rouquié, *Military and the State*, chapter 10.

20. Weyland, "Rise."

21. Evidence of US government involvement was published in Eva Golinger, "The Proof Is in the Documents: The CIA Was Involved in the Coup against Venezuelan President Hugo Chávez," venezuelafoia.info, http://www.vcrisis.com/index-USAID2.html. A report that denied such involvement was produced by the Office of the Inspector General, US State Department, "A Review of U.S. Policy toward Venezuela, November 2001–April 2002," oig.state.gov/documents/organization/13682.pdf.

22. See Jeremy Bigwood, "New Discoveries Reveal US Intervention in Bolivia," https:// nacla.org/node/5094/.

23. See Rochelle Gollust, "US Says Ecuadoran Expulsions Threaten Relationship," Feb. 19, 2009, Voice of America News, www.voanews.com/english/news/a-13-2009-02-19-voa74 -68712847.html; "Ecuador Expels World Bank Envoy," BBC News, Apr. 27, 2007, http://news .bbc.co.uk/2/hi/americas/6598027.stm.

24. Mainwaring, Bejarano, and Leongómez, *Crisis of Democratic Representation*. For a critique, see Weyland, "Rise."

25. Madrid, "Rise of Ethnopopulism"; Van Cott, *From Movements to Parties*.

26. "Ecuador Defaults on Foreign Debt," BBC News, Dec. 18, 2008, http://news.bbc.co .uk/2/hi/7780984.stm.

27. "Peru's García Unpopular Despite Boom," *Christian Science Monitor*, July 24, 2008.

28. See, for example, Roett and Paz, *China's Expansion*.

29. "Finding a Bolthole in a Risky World," editorial, *Financial Times*, June 5, 2010.

30. Vaughn et al., *Terrorism in Southeast Asia*.

31. See, for example, Chua, *World on Fire*.

32. European Bank for Reconstruction and Development (EBRD), *Transition Report 2009: Transition in Crisis?*, as commented on by Martin Wolf, "Victory in the Cold War Was a Start as well as an Ending," *Financial Times*, Nov. 11, 2009.

33. "Economies in Transition: Eastern Europe and the Former Soviet Union Overview," *Economist Intelligence Unit*, 2009, 1.

34. Martin Wolf, "Past Imperfect, Future Tense," *Financial Times*, Dec. 13, 2009.

35. "Walls in the Mind," *Economist*, Nov. 7, 2009, 25.

36. Ibid., 24.

37. "Downturn Stirs Ethnic Tensions in Hungary," *Financial Times*, Dec. 13, 2009.

38. Martin Wolf, "Past Imperfect, Future Tense," *Financial Times*, Dec. 13, 2009.

39. "Victory in the Cold War Was a Start as well as an Ending," *Financial Times*, Nov. 11, 2009.

40. Ibid.

41. Martin Wolf, "Past Imperfect, Future Tense," *Financial Times*, Dec. 13, 2009.

42. Mandelbrot and Hudson, *(Mis)behavior of Markets*, 111–22.

Bibliography

Institutional Sources

Amnesty International, www.amnesty.org.

Argentina, Ministerio de Economía y Finanzas Públicas, http://noticias.mecon.gob.ar.

Banco Central de Chile, www.bcentral.cl/index.asp.

Banco Central de la República Argentina, www.bcra.gov.ar.

Banco Central del Uruguay, www.bcu.gub.uy/Paginas/Default.aspx.

CEPAL [Comisión Económica para América Latina y el Caribe], "CEPALSTAT: Databases and Statistical Publications," http://websie.eclac.cl/infest/ajax/cepalstat.asp ?carpeta=estadisticas&idioma=i.

Chile, Ministerio de Hacienda, www.hacienda.gov.cl.

International Monetary Fund (IMF), "World Economic Outlook Database," various years, www.imf.org/external/pubs/ft/weo/2011/01/weodata/index.aspx.

Organization of American States (OAS), *Charter of the Organization of American States*, www .oas.org/dil/treaties_A-41_Charter_of_the_Organization_of_American_States.htm.

OAS Inter-American Commission on Human Rights, *Annual Report on Human Rights, 1992–1993: Uruguay*, www.cidh.oas.org/annualrep/92eng/Uruguay10.029.htm.

Uruguay, Ministerio de Economía y Finanzas, www.mef.gub.uy/portada.php.

World Bank (WB), "World Development Indicators," http://data.worldbank.org/data-cata log/world-development-indicators/.

World Trade Organization (WTO), "Trade Policy Reviews," www.wto.org/english/tratop_e /tpr_e/tpr_e.htm.

Newspapers and Periodicals

Business Week

Clarín (Argentina)

Economist

El Mercurio (Chile)

El País (Uruguay)

Financial Times

La Nación (Argentina)

La República (Uruguay)

La Segunda (Chile)

La Tercera (Chile)

MercoPress

New York Times

Wall Street Journal

Washington Post

SECONDARY SOURCES

Acemoglu, Daron and James A. Robinson. *Economic Origins of Dictatorship and Democracy.* Cambridge: Cambridge University Press, 2006.

Aguilar, Luis E. *Marxism in Latin America.* New York: Knopf, 1968.

Angell, Alan. "The Left in Latin America since c. 1920." In *The Cambridge History of Latin America, Volume VI, 1930 to the Present,* part 2, edited by Leslie Bethell. Cambridge: Cambridge University Press, 1995.

Ahamed, Liaquat. *Lords of Finance: The Bankers Who Broke the World.* New York: Penguin, 2009.

Alberts, Susan. "Why Play by the Rules? Constitutionalism and Democratic Institutionalism in Ecuador and Uruguay." *Democratization* 15, no. 5 (2008), 849–69.

Alcañiz, Isabella and Melissa Scheier. "New Social Movements with New Party Politics: The MTL *Piqueteros* and the Communist Party in Argentina," In *Latin American Social Movements in the Twenty-First Century: Resistance, Power, and Democracy,* edited by Richard Stahler-Sholk, Harry E. Vanden, and Glen David Kuecker. Lanham, MD: Rowman & Littlefield, 2008.

Areces, Nidia R. "La revolución de 1930." In *La década infame,* edited by Alberto Ciria et al. Buenos Aires: Carlos Pérez, 1969.

Arriagada, Genaro. *Por la razón o la fuerza: Chile bajo Pinochet.* Santiago: Editorial Sudamericana, 1998.

Atkins, G. Pope. *Latin America and the Caribbean in the International System,* 4th ed. Boulder, CO: Westview Press, 1999.

"The Austerity Debate: FT Series on the Fierce Argument between Deficit-Cutting and Stimulus." *Financial Times,* July 19–23, 2010.

Bergara, Mario et al., "Political Institutions, Policymaking Processes, and Policy Outcomes: The Case of Uruguay." Report to the Inter-American Development Bank, 2006.

Bernanke, Ben S. "Nonmonetary Effects of the Financial Crisis in the Propagation of the Great Depression." *American Economic Review* 73 (1983), 257–76.

Bernanke, Ben S. *Essays on the Great Depression.* Princeton, NJ: Princeton University Press, 2004.

Blustein, Paul. *The Chastening: Inside the Crisis That Rocked the Global Financial System and Humbled the IMF,* revised and updated. New York: Public Affairs, 2003.

Blustein, Paul. *And the Money Kept Rolling In (and Out): The World Bank, Wall Street, the IMF, and the Bankrupting of Argentina.* New York: Public Affairs, 2005.

Blyth, Mark M. "Review: 'Any More Bright Ideas?' The Ideational Change of Comparative Political Economy." *Comparative Politics* 29 (Jan. 1997), 229–50.

Blyth, Mark. M. *Great Transformations: Economic Ideas and Institutional Change in the Twentieth Century.* Cambridge: Cambridge University Press, 2002.

Boeninger, Edgardo. *Democracia en Chile: Lecciones para la gobernabilidad.* Santiago: Andrés Bello, 1997.

Boix, Carles. *Democracy and Redistribution.* Cambridge: Cambridge University Press, 2003.

Brau, Eduard and Ian McDonald, eds. *Successes of the International Monetary Fund: Untold Stories of Cooperation at Work.* New York: Palgrave Macmillan, 2009.

"Briefing: The State of Economics." *Economist*, July 18, 2009, 65–69.

Bueno de Mesquita, Bruce and Hilton L. Root, eds. *Governing for Prosperity*. New Haven, CT: Yale University Press, 2000.

Bulmer-Thomas, Victor. *The Economic History of Latin America since Independence*. Cambridge: Cambridge University Press, 1994.

Buquet, Daniel. "Reforma política y gobernabilidad democrática en Uruguay: La reforma constitucional de 1996." *Revista Uruguaya de Ciencia Política* 10 (1998), 9–24.

Butterfield, Herbert. *The Whig Interpretation of History*. New York: Norton, 1965 (first published in 1931).

Canton, Santiago A. "Amnesty Laws." In *Victims Unsilenced: The Inter-American Human Rights System and Transitional Justice in Latin America*, edited by Katya Salazar and Thomas Antkowiak. Washington, DC: Due Process of Law Foundation, 2007.

Cason, Jeffrey. "Electoral Reform, Institutional Change, and Party Adaptation in Uruguay." *Latin American Politics and Society* 44, no. 3 (2002), 89–109.

Castañeda, Jorge G. *La utopía desarmada*. México: Joaquín Mortíz, 1993.

Castañeda, Jorge G. "Latin America's Left Turn." *Foreign Affairs* (May/June 2006), 28–43.

Castañeda, Jorge G. and Marco A. Morales, eds. *Leftovers: Tales of the Latin American Left*. New York: Routledge, 2008.

Cavallo, Ascanio. *La historia oculta de la transición*. Santiago: Grijalbo, 1998.

Cavallo, Ascanio et al. *La historia oculta del régimen militar*. Santiago: La Época, 1988.

Cavarozzi, Marcelo. "Patterns of Elite Negotiation and Confrontation in Argentina and Chile." In *Elites and Democratic Consolidation in Latin America and Southern Europe*, edited by John Higley and Richard Gunther. Cambridge: Cambridge University Press, 1992.

Chapman, Peter. *Bananas: How the United Fruit Company Shaped the World*. New York: Canongate, 2007.

Ching, Erik and Jussi Pakkasvirta. "Latin American Materials in the Comintern Archive." *Latin American Research Review*, 35, no. 1 (2000), 138–49.

Chua, Amy, *World on Fire*. New York: Doubleday, 2002.

Ciria, Alberto. "Los partidos politicos." In *La década infame*, edited by Alberto Ciria et al. Buenos Aires: Carlos Pérez, 1969.

Coatsworth, John H. "Structures, Endowments, and Institutions in the Economic History of Latin America." *Latin American Research Review* 40, no. 3 (2005), 126–44.

Coatsworth, John H. and Alan M. Taylor, eds. *Latin America and the World Economy since 1800*. Cambridge, MA: Harvard University Press, 1999.

Collier, David and Deborah L. Norden. "Strategic Choice Models of Political Change in Latin America." *Comparative Politics* 24, no. 2 (1992), 229–43.

Collier, Ruth Berins. *Paths toward Democracy: The Working Class and Elites in Western Europe and South America*. Cambridge: Cambridge University Press, 1999.

Collier, Simon and William F. Sater. *A History of Chile, 1808–1994*. Cambridge: Cambridge University Press, 1996.

Connoly, Michael and Jaime de Melo. "The Political Economy of Protectionism in Uruguay." In *The Effects of Protectionism on a Small Country*, edited by Michael Connoly and Jaime de Melo. Washington, DC: World Bank, 1994.

Conniff, Michael L., ed. *Populism in Latin America*. Tuscaloosa: University of Alabama Press, 1999.

"Convention on the Pan American Union." *American Journal of International Law* 22, no. 3 (Suppl.: Official Documents, July 1928), 161–66.

Córdova, Abby and Mitchell A. Seligson. "Economic Shocks and Democratic Vulnerabilities in Latin America and the Caribbean." *Latin American Politics and Society* 52, no. 2 (Summer 2010), 1–35.

Cortés Conde, Roberto. *The Political Economy of Argentina in the Twentieth Century*. New York: Cambridge University Press, 2009.

Corvalán, Luis. *De lo vivido y lo peleado*. Santiago: LOM, 1997.

Costa Bonino, Luis. "Uruguay: Democratic Learning and Its Limits." In *Political Learning and Redemocratization in Latin America*, edited by Jennifer L. McCoy. Miami: North-South Center Press at the University of Miami, 2000.

Dahl, Robert A. *Polyarchy: Participation and Opposition*. New Haven, CT: Yale University Press, 1971.

Dahse, Fernando. *El mapa de la extrema riqueza*. Santiago: Aconcagua, 1978.

De Ferranti, David et al. *Inequality in Latin America and the Caribbean: Breaking with History?* Washington, DC: World Bank, 2003.

De la Plaza, Luis and Sophie Sirtaine. "An Analysis of the 2002 Uruguayan Banking Crisis." Policy Research Working Paper 3780.4, World Bank, 2005.

De Riz, Liliana. "From Menem to Menem: Elections and Political Parties in Argentina." In *Argentina: The Challenges of Modernization*, edited by Joseph S. Tulchin, with Allison M. Garland. Wilmington, DE: Scholarly Resources, 1998.

De Shazo, Peter. *Urban Workers and Labor Unions in Chile, 1902–1927*. Madison: University of Wisconsin Press, 1983.

Deutsch, Sandra McGee. *Las Derechas: The Extreme Right in Argentina, Brazil, and Chile, 1890–1939*. Stanford, CA: Stanford University Press, 1999.

"Diagnosing Depression." *Economist*, Dec. 30, 2008, www.economist.com/node/12852043 ?story_id=12852043 [accessed June 11, 2009].

Domínguez, Jorge I. and Michael Shifter, eds. *Constructing Democratic Governance in Latin America*, 3rd ed. Baltimore: Johns Hopkins University Press, 2008.

Dornbusch, Rudiger and Sebastian Edwards, eds. *The Macroeconomics of Populism in Latin America*. Chicago: University of Chicago Press, 1991.

Drake, Paul W. *Socialism and Populism in Chile, 1932–52*. Urbana: University of Illinois Press, 1978.

Drake, Paul W. "Review: The Buoyant Bourgeoisie of Chile." *Latin American Research Review* 21 (1986), 166–77.

Drake, Paul W. "Chile, 1930–58." In *The Cambridge History of Latin America, Volume VIII, Latin America since 1930: Spanish South America*, edited by Leslie Bethell. Cambridge: Cambridge University Press, 1991.

Drake, Paul W. *Labor Movements and Dictatorships: The Southern Cone in Comparative Perspective*. Baltimore: Johns Hopkins University Press, 1996.

Drake, Paul W. "Chile's Populism Reconsidered, 1920s–1990s." In *Populism in Latin America*, edited by Michael L. Conniff. Tuscaloosa: University of Alabama Press, 1999.

Eaton, Kent. *Politics beyond the Capital: The Design of Subnational Institutions in South America*. Stanford, CA: Stanford University Press, 2004.

Edwards, Agustín. "Latin America and the League of Nations." *Journal of the Royal Institute of International Affairs* 8, no. 2 (Mar. 1929), 134–53.

Edwards, Sebastian. *Crisis and Reform in Latin America: From Despair to Hope*. Oxford: World Bank / Oxford University Press, 1995.

Eichengreen, Barry. *Golden Fetters: The Gold Standard and the Great Depression, 1919–1939*. New York: Oxford University Press, 1995.

———. *Globalizing Capital: A History of the International Monetary System*, 2nd ed. Princeton, NJ: Princeton University Press, 2008.

Elliott, John H. *Empires of the Atlantic World: Britain and Spain in America, 1492–1830*. New Haven, CT: Yale University Press, 2006.

Epstein, Edward. "The *Piquetero* Movement in Greater Buenos Aires: Political Protests by the Unemployed Poor during the Crisis." In *Broken Promises: The Argentine Crisis and Argentine Democracy*, edited by Edward Epstein and David Pion-Berlin. Lanham, MD: Lexington Books, 2006.

Ferreira-Rubio, Delia and Mateo Goretti. "Cuando el presidente gobierna solo: Menem y los decretos de necesidad y urgencia hasta la reforma constitucional (1989–1994)." *Desarrollo Económico* 36, no. 141 (1996), 443–74.

Ffrench-Davis, Ricardo. *Chile entre el neoliberalismo y el crecimiento con equidad: Reformas y políticas económicas desde 1973*. Santiago: J. C. Sáez, 2009.

Finch, Henry. "Uruguay since 1930." In *The Cambridge History of Latin America, Volume VIII, Latin America since 1930: Spanish South America*, edited by Leslie Bethell. Cambridge: Cambridge University Press, 1991.

Finnemore, Martha and Kathryn Sikkink. "International Norm Dynamics and Political Change." *International Organization* 52 (1998), 887–917.

Flink, James J. *The Automobile Age*. Cambridge, MA: MIT Press, 1990.

Forteza, Álvaro et al. "Understanding Reform: The Uruguayan Case." Working paper, Universidad de la República, Departamento de Economia (Montevideo), 2003.

Frieden, Jeffry A. *Global Capitalism: Its Fall and Rise in the Twentieth Century*. New York: Norton, 2006.

Friedman, Thomas. *The Lexus and the Olive Tree*. New York: Farrar, Straus, and Giroux, 2000.

Fukuyama, Francis, ed. *Falling Behind: Explaining the Development Gap between Latin America and the United States*. Oxford: Oxford University Press, 2008.

Garretón, Manuel Antonio. *The Chilean Political Process*. Boston: Unwin Hyman, 1989.

Geithner, Timothy. "Lesson from Argentina's Crisis." Working paper, International Monetary Fund, Oct. 8, 2003.

George, Alexander L. and Andrew Bennett. *Case Studies and Theory Development in the Social Sciences*. Cambridge, MA: MIT Press, 2005.

Gibson, Edward. *Class and Conservative Parties: Argentina in Comparative Perspective*. Baltimore: Johns Hopkins University Press, 1996.

Gillespie, Charles G. "Uruguay's Transition from Collegial Military-Technocratic Rule." In *Transitions from Authoritarian Rule: Latin America*, edited by Guillermo O'Donnell,

Philippe C. Schmitter, and Laurence Whitehead. Baltimore: Johns Hopkins University Press, 1986.

Gillespie, Charles G. "The Role of Civil-Military Pacts in Elite Settlements and Elite Convergence: Democratic Consolidation in Uruguay." In *Elite and Democratic Consolidation in Latin America and Southern Europe*, edited by John Higley and Richard Gunther. Cambridge: Cambridge University Press, 1992.

Goddard, Stephen B. *Getting There: The Epic Struggle between Road and Rail in the American Century.* Chicago: University of Chicago Press, 1996.

Goldstein, Judith and Robert Keohane, eds. *Ideas and Foreign Policy: Beliefs, Institutions, and Political Change.* Ithaca, NY: Cornell University Press, 1993.

González, Francisco E. *Dual Transitions from Authoritarian Rule: Institutionalized Regimes in Chile and Mexico, 1970–2000.* Baltimore: Johns Hopkins University Press, 2008.

González, Francisco E. "Mexico's Drug Wars Get Brutal." *Current History* 108 (2009), 72–76.

González, Luis E. *Political Structures and Democracy in Uruguay.* Notre Dame, IN: Notre Dame University Press, 1992.

Goodman, Joshua and Pete Engardio, "Uruguay: A Well-Executed Model for Debt Workouts." *Business Week*, Sept. 29, 2003.

Gourevitch, Peter. *Politics in Hard Times: Comparative Responses to International Economic Crises.* Ithaca, NY: Cornell University Press, 1986.

Guha, Krishna. "Bankers Debate Asset Pools and Arbitrage." *Financial Times*, Aug. 25, 2008.

Haggard, Stephan and Robert R. Kaufman, *The Political Economy of Democratic Transitions.* Princeton, NJ: Princeton University Press, 1995.

Hagopian, Frances and Scott Mainwaring, eds. *The Third Wave of Democratization in Latin America: Advances and Setbacks.* Cambridge: Cambridge University Press, 2005.

Hale, Charles A. "Political and Social Ideas in Latin America, 1870–1930." In *The Cambridge History of Latin America, Volume IV, c. 1870 to 1930*, edited by Leslie Bethell. Cambridge: Cambridge University Press, 1986.

Harvey, Campbell R. "Economic Shock." *Free Dictionary*, http://financial-dictionary.thefreedictionary.com/Economic+shock [accessed June 11, 2009].

Hay, Colin. "Review: Ideas, Interests, and Institutions in the Comparative Political Economy of Great Transformations." *Review of International Political Economy* 11, no. 1 (Feb. 2004), 204–26.

Honohan, Patrick and Daniela Klingebiel. "Controlling the Fiscal Costs of Banking Crises." Policy Research Working Paper 2441, World Bank, 2000.

Hornbeck, J. F. *The Argentine Financial Crisis: A Chronology of Events.* CRS Report for Congress RS21130, Jan. 31. Washington, DC: Congressional Research Service, 2002.

Huneeus, Carlos. "Technocrats and Politicians in an Authoritarian Regime: The 'ODEPLAN' Boys and the '*Gremialistas*' in Pinochet's Chile." *Journal of Latin American Studies* 32 (2000), 461–501.

Huntington, Samuel P. *The Third Wave: Democratization in the Late Twentieth Century.* Norman: University of Oklahoma Press, 1991.

Jacob, Raúl. *El Uruguay de Terra, 1931–1938.* Montevideo: Ediciones de la Banda Oriental, 1983.

Kindleberger, Charles P. *Manias, Panics, and Crashes: A History of Financial Crises*, 5th ed. Hoboken, NJ: Wiley and Sons, 2005.

King, Desmond, Robert C. Lieberman, Gretchen Ritter, and Laurence Whitehead, eds. *Democratization in America: A Comparative-Historical Analysis*. Baltimore: Johns Hopkins University Press, 2009.

Kossman, Jasmin. "Power Struggles in the Uruguayan Policy-Making Process: A Study of the Power Relations Revealed by the Debate Surrounding a Potential Free Trade Agreement with the United States." Working paper, Kings College, University of Cambridge, 2007.

Krugman, Paul. "How Did Economists Get It So Wrong?" *New York Times Magazine*, Sept. 6, 2009, 36–43.

Laclau, Ernesto. "Towards a Theory of Populism." In *Politics and Ideology in Marxist Theory: Capitalism, Fascism, Populism*. London: NLB, 1977.

"The Latinobarómetro Poll: A Slow Maturing of Democracy." *Economist*, Dec. 10, 2009, www .economist.com/node/15080535?story_id=15080535 [accessed Jan. 21, 2010].

Lederman, Daniel and Pablo Sanguinetti, "Trade Policy Options for Argentina in the Short and Long Run," *Integration and Trade* 7 (July–Dec. 2003), 99–133.

Levitsky, Steven. "From Labor Politics to Machine Politics: The Transformation of Party-Union Linkages in Argentine Peronism, 1983–1999." *Latin American Research Review* 38 (2003), 3–36.

Levitsky, Steven. "Argentina: Democracy and Institutional Weakness." In *Constructing Democratic Governance in Latin America*, 3rd ed., edited by Jorge Domínguez and Michael Shifter. Baltimore: Johns Hopkins University Press, 2008.

Levitsky, Steven and Maria Victoria Murillo, eds. *Argentine Democracy: The Politics of Institutional Weakness*. University Park: Pennsylvania State University Press, 2005.

Lichbach, Mark and Alan S. Zuckerman, eds. *Comparative Politics: Rationality, Culture, and Structure*, 2nd ed. Cambridge: Cambridge University Press, 2009.

Lindahl, Göran G. *Uruguay's New Path: A Study in Politics during the First Colegiado, 1919–1933*. Stockholm: Library and Institute of Ibero-American Studies, 1962.

Linz, Juan J. *The Breakdown of Democratic Regimes: Crisis, Breakdown, and Reequilibration*. Baltimore: Johns Hopkins University Press, 1978.

Linz, Juan J. and Alfred Stepan, eds. *The Breakdown of Democratic Regimes*, 4 vols. Baltimore: Johns Hopkins University Press, 1978.

Linz, Juan J. and Alfred Stepan. *Problems of Democratic Transition and Consolidation: Southern Europe, South America, and Post-Communist Europe*. Baltimore: Johns Hopkins University Press, 1996.

Maddison, Angus. *The World Economy: Historical Statistics*. Paris: OECD [Organisation for Economic Co-Operation and Development], 2003.

Maddison, Angus. *Contours of the World Economy, 1-2030 AD*. Oxford: Oxford University Press, 2007.

Madrid, Raúl L. "The Rise of Ethnopopulism in Latin America." *World Politics* 60 (2008), 475–508.

Mahoney, James and Dietrich Rueschemeyer, eds. *Comparative Historical Analysis in the Social Sciences*. Cambridge: Cambridge University Press, 2003.

Mainwaring, Scott, Ana María Bejarano, and Eduardo Pizarro Leongómez, eds. *The Crisis of Democratic Representation in the Andes*. Stanford, CA: Stanford University Press, 2006.

Mandelbrot, Benoit and Richard L. Hudson. *The (Mis)behavior of Markets: A Fractal View of Risk, Ruin, and Reward*. New York, Basic Books, 2004.

Marichal, Carlos. *A Century of Debt Crises in Latin America*. Princeton, NJ: Princeton University Press, 1989.

Marshall, Peter. *Demanding the Impossible: A History of Anarchism*. London: HarperCollins, 1992.

Meller, Patricio. *Un siglo de economía política chilena, 1890–1990*. Santiago: Andrés Bello, 1996.

Merquior, José Guilherme. "The 'Other' West: On the Historical Position of Latin America." *International Sociology* 6, no. 2 (1991), 149–63.

Mesa-Lago, Carmelo and Katherine Muller. "The Politics of Pension Reform in Latin America." *Journal of Latin American Studies* 34 (2002), 687–715.

Minsky, Hyman P. *Stabilizing an Unstable Economy*. New York: McGraw-Hill, 1986.

Montero, Hugo. "Tupamaros: De las armas a las urnas." *Revista Sudestada* 67 (2008), www.revistasudestada.com.ar/web06/article.php3?id_article=477.

Muñoz, Heraldo. "Chile's External Relations under the Military Government." In *Military Rule in Chile: Dictatorship and Opposition*, edited by J. Samuel Valenzuela and Arturo Valenzuela. Baltimore: Johns Hopkins University Press, 1986.

Mussa, Michael. *Argentina and the Fund: From Triumph to Tragedy*. Washington, DC: Institute for International Economics, 2002.

North, Douglass C. *Institutions, Institutional Change, and Economic Performance*. Cambridge: Cambridge University Press, 1990.

North, Douglass C., William Summerhill, and Barry R. Weingast. "Order, Disorder, and Economic Change." In *Governing for Prosperity*, edited by Bruce Bueno de Mesquita and Hilton L. Root. New Haven, CT: Yale University Press, 2000.

North, Douglass C., John Joseph Wallis, and Barry R. Weingast. *Violence and Social Orders: A Conceptual Framework for Interpreting Recorded Human History*. Cambridge: Cambridge University Press, 2009.

Nunn, Frederic M. *The Military in Chilean History: Essays on Civil-Military Relations, 1810–1973*. Albuquerque: University of New Mexico Press, 1976.

"Obedience [Obediencia Debida] and Final Stop [Punto Final] Acts." *Yearbook of International Humanitarian Law* 6 (2003), 627–633.

O'Brien, Thomas. *The Century of U.S. Capitalism in Latin America*. Albuquerque: University of New Mexico Press, 1999.

Oddone, Juan. "The Formation of Modern Uruguay, c. 1870–1930." In *The Cambridge History of Latin America, Volume V, c. 1870 to 1930*, edited by Leslie Bethell. Cambridge: Cambridge University Press, 1986.

Oddone, Juan. *Uruguay entre la depresión y la guerra, 1929–1945*. Montevideo: Fundación de Cultura Universitaria, 1990.

O'Donnell, Guillermo. *Counterpoints: Selected Essays on Authoritarianism and Democratization*. Notre Dame, IN: University of Notre Dame Press, 1999.

O'Donnell, Guillermo, Philippe Schmitter, and Laurence Whitehead, eds. *Transitions from Authoritarian Rule*, 4 vols. Baltimore: Johns Hopkins University Press, 1986.

O'Rourke, Kevin H. and Jeffrey G. Williamson. *Globalization and History: The Evolution of a Nineteenth-Century Atlantic Economy.* Cambridge, MA: MIT Press, 1999.

Pagés-Serra, Carmen. *Good Jobs Wanted: Labor Markets in Latin America.* Economic and Social Progress in Latin America 2004 Report. Washington, DC: Inter-American Development Bank, 2003.

Peeler, John A. *Latin American Democracies: Colombia, Costa Rica, and Venezuela.* Chapel Hill: University of North Carolina Press, 1985.

Peeler, John A. *Building Democracy in Latin America*, 3rd ed. Boulder, CO: Lynne Rienner, 2009.

Pharr, Susan J. and Robert Putnam, eds. *Disaffected Democracies: What's Troubling the Trilateral Countries?* Princeton, NJ: Princeton University Press, 2000.

Pierson, Paul. *Politics in Time: History, Institutions, and Social Analysis.* Princeton, NJ: Princeton University Press, 2004.

Pigna, Felipe. *Los mitos de la historia argentina, 3: De la ley Sáenz Peña a los albores del peronismo.* Buenos Aires: Planeta, 2006.

Pike, Frederick B. *Chile and the United States, 1880–1962.* Notre Dame, IN: University of Notre Dame Press, 1963.

Potash, Robert A. *The Army and Politics in Argentina, 1928–1945: Yrigoyén to Perón.* Stanford, CA: Stanford University Press, 1969.

Przeworski, Adam. *Democracy and the Market: Political and Economic Reforms in Eastern Europe and Latin America.* Cambridge: Cambridge University Press, 1991.

Przeworski, Adam et al. *Sustainable Democracy.* Cambridge: Cambridge University Press, 1995.

Przeworski, Adam et al. *Democracy and Development: Political Institutions and Well-Being in the World, 1950–1990.* Cambridge: Cambridge University Press, 2000.

Ramos, Joseph. *Neoconservative Economics in the Southern Cone of Latin America, 1974–83.* Baltimore: Johns Hopkins University Press, 1986.

Red de Seguridad y Defensa de América Latina (RESDAL). *A Comparative Atlas of Defense in Latin America, 2008 edition.* Buenos Aires: RESDAL y SER en el 2000, 2008, www.resdal.org/atlas/atlas-libro08-ingles.html.

Reinhart, Carmen M. and Kenneth S. Rogoff. *This Time Is Different: Eight Centuries of Financial Folly.* Princeton, NJ: Princeton University Press, 2009.

Rock, David. "Argentina from the First World War to the Revolution of 1930." In *The Cambridge History of Latin America, Volume V, c. 1870 to 1930*, edited by Leslie Bethell. Cambridge: Cambridge University Press, 1986.

Rock, David. *Authoritarian Argentina: The Nationalist Movement, Its History, and Its Impact.* Berkeley: University of California Press, 1993.

Rocker, Rudolf. *Anarcho-Syndicalism.* London: Secker and Warburg, 1938.

Roett, Riordan. "How Reform Has Powered Brazil's Rise." *Current History* 109 (Feb. 2010), 47–52.

Roett, Riordan and Guadalupe Paz, eds. *China's Expansion into the Western Hemisphere: Implications for Latin America and the United States.* Washington, DC: Brookings Institution Press, 2008.

Roht-Arraiza, Naomi. "The Pinochet Effect and the Spanish Contribution to Universal Jurisdiction." In *International Prosecution of Human Rights Crimes*, ed. Wolfgang Kaleck,
Michael Ratner, Tobias Singelnstein, and Peter Weiss. New York: Springer, 2007.

Rojas Flores, Jorge. *La dictadura de Ibáñez y los sindicatos, 1927–1931*. Santiago: Centro de
Investigaciones Diego Barros Arana, 1993.

Romero, Luis Alberto. *Breve historia contemporánea de la Argentina*. México: Fondo de Cultura Económica, 1994.

Romero, Luis Alberto. *A History of Argentina in the Twentieth Century*, trans. James P. Bren-
nan. University Park: Pennsylvania State University Press, 2002.

Rouquié, Alain. *The Military and the State in Latin America*. Berkeley: University of California
Press, 1987.

Rueschemeyer, Dietrich, Evelyne Huber Stephens, and John D. Stephens. *Capitalist Development and Democracy*. Cambridge: Polity Press, 1992.

Rush, Cynthia R. "Argentina, Brazil Pay Off Debt to IMF: Bankers Nervous." *Executive Intelligence Review* 32 (Dec. 30, 2005), www.larouchepub.com/other/2005/3250arg_brazil
_imf.html.

Salazar, Katya and Thomas Antkowiak, eds. *Victims Unsilenced: The Inter-American Human
Rights System and Transitional Justice in Latin America*. Washington, DC: Due Process of
Law Foundation, 2007.

Santa-Cruz, Arturo. "Election Monitoring and the Western Hemisphere Idea." In *Promoting
Democracy in the Americas*, edited by Thomas Legler, Sharon F. Lean, and Dexter S. Boni-
face. Baltimore: Johns Hopkins University Press, 2007.

Schamis, Hector. *Re-Forming the State: The Politics of Privatization in Latin America and
Europe*. Ann Arbor: University of Michigan Press, 2002.

Schumpeter, Joseph A. *Capitalism, Socialism, and Democracy*. New York: Routledge, 1996
[originally published 1943].

Seelig, Steven and Gilbert Terrier. "Uruguay 2002–3: Recovery from Economic Contagion."
In *Successes of the International Monetary Fund: Untold Stories of Cooperation at Work*,
edited by Eduard Brau and Ian McDonald. New York: Palgrave Macmillan, 2009.

Shlaes, Amity. *The Forgotten Man: A New History of the Great Depression*. New York: Harper
Perennial, 2008.

Siavelis, Peter M. *The President and Congress in Postauthoritanian Chile: Institutional Constraints to Democratic Consolidation*. University Park: Pennsylvania State University
Press, 2000.

Sigmund, Paul E. *The United States and Democracy in Chile*. Baltimore: Johns Hopkins University Press, 1993.

Sikkink, Kathryn. *Ideas and Institutions: Developmentalism in Brazil and Argentina*. Ithaca,
NY: Cornell University Press, 1991.

Sikkink, Kathryn. *Mixed Signals: U.S. Human Rights Policy and Latin America*. Ithaca, NY:
Cornell University Press, 2004.

Silva, Eduardo. "Capitalist Coalitions, the State, and Neoliberal Economic Restructuring in
Chile, 1973–1988." *World Politics* 45 (1993), 541–42.

Silva, Eduardo. *The State and Capital in Chile: Business Elites, Technocrats, and Market Economics*. Boulder, CO: Westview Press, 1996.

Skidelsky, Robert. *Keynes: The Return of the Master.* London: Allen Lane, 2009.

Smith, Jackie. *Social Movements for Global Democracy.* Baltimore: Johns Hopkins University Press, 2008.

Smith, Peter H. "The Breakdown of Democracy in Argentina, 1916–30." In *The Breakdown of Democratic Regimes: Latin America,* edited by Juan J. Linz and Alfred Stepan. Baltimore: Johns Hopkins University Press, 1978.

Smith, Peter H. *Democracy in Latin America: Political Change in Comparative Perspective.* Oxford: Oxford University Press, 2005.

Steneri, Carlos. "Comment on 'Uruguay 2002–3: Recovery from Economic Contagion.' " In *Successes of the International Monetary Fund: Untold Stories of Cooperation at Work,* edited by Eduard Brau and Ian McDonald. New York: Palgrave Macmillan, 2009.

Solberg, Carl E. *Oil and Nationalism in Argentina.* Stanford, CA: Stanford University Press, 1979.

Svampa, Maristella. *Entre la ruta y el barrio: La experiencia de las organizaciones piqueteras.* Buenos Aires: Biblos, 2004.

Tarrow, Sidney. *Power in Movement: Social Movements and Contentious Politics.* Cambridge: Cambridge University Press, 1992.

Thelen, Kathleen. "Historical Institutionalism in Comparative Politics." *Annual Review of Political Science* 2 (1999), 369–404.

Therborn, Göran. "The Travail of Latin American Democracy." *New Left Review* 113–14 (Jan.–Apr. 1979), 71–109.

Thorp, Rosemary. "Latin America and the International Economy from the First World War to the World Depression." In *The Cambridge History of Latin America, Volume IV, c. 1870 to 1930,* edited by Leslie Bethell. Cambridge: Cambridge University Press, 1986.

Thorp, Rosemary. *Progress, Poverty, and Exclusion: An Economic History of Latin America in the 20th Century.* Washington, DC: Inter-American Development Bank, 1998.

Trigo, Abril. *Caudillo, estado, nación, literatura, historia e ideología en el Uruguay.* Gaithersburg, MD: Ediciones Hispamérica, 1990.

Unal, Haluk, Asli Demirguc-Kunt, and Kwok-Wai Leung. "The Brady Plan, the 1989 Mexican Debt Reduction Agreement, and Bank Stock Returns in the United States and Japan." Policy Research Working Paper 1020, World Bank, 1992.

Valdés, Juan Gabriel. *Pinochet's Economists: The Chicago School in Chile.* Cambridge: Cambridge University Press, 1995.

Valenzuela, Arturo. "Paraguay: The Coup That Didn't Happen." *Journal of Democracy* 8, no. 1 (1997), 43–55.

Van Cott, Donna Lee. *From Movements to Parties in Latin America: The Evolution of Ethnic Politics.* Cambridge: Cambridge University Press, 2005.

Vanden, Harry E. and Gary Prevost. *Politics of Latin America: The Power Game,* 3rd ed. New York: Oxford University Press, 2008.

Vasquez, Ian. "The Brady Plan and Market-Based Solutions to Debt Crises." *Cato Journal* 16, no. 2 (2004), 233–43.

Vaughn, Bruce et al. *Terrorism in Southeast Asia.* CRS Report for Congress RL34194, Oct. 16. Washington, DC: Congressional Research Service, 2009.

Veigel, Klaus Friedrich. *Dictatorship, Democracy, and Globalization: Argentina and the Cost of Paralysis, 1973–2001.* University Park: Pennsylvania State University Press, 2009.

Weinstein, Martin. *Uruguay: The Politics of Failure.* Westport, CT: Greenwood Press, 1975.

Weyland, Kurt. "The Rise of Latin America's Two Lefts? Insights from Rentier State Theory." *Comparative Politics* 41 (2009), 145–64.

Williamson, John, ed. *Latin American Adjustment: How Much Has Happened?* Washington, DC: Institute for International Economics, 1990.

Wirth, John D. Foreword to *Populism in Latin America*, edited by Michael L. Conniff. Tuscaloosa: University of Alabama Press, 1999.

Index

Page numbers in *italics* indicate figures and tables